THE BAD OL' BOYS CLUB

B. B. ROSE

Published by ngpress
4787 Riverview Road # 10
Atlanta, Georgia 30327

Publisher's note: This book is a work of fiction. Names, characters, places and incidents are either a product of the author's imagination or are used fictitiously, and any resemblance to actual persons, living or dead, events or locales are entirely coincidental. The use of real locales and similar situations are intended only to give the fiction a sense of reality and authenticity.

ISBN: 978-0-9724727-2-X

First Edition

Printed in the United States of America

3

THIS BOOK IS DEDICATED TO

The young victims of the sexual exploitation industry who have started their lives with a Past that has been thrust upon them, but who now find so many working for them to provide them with a Future

and

Judge Sanford "Sammy" Jones,
Fulton County Juvenile Court, Atlanta Georgia,
who was always there to support children and be an inspiration to all who will continue his work.
1952-2009

ACKNOWLEDGMENTS

With grateful appreciation, The Harold and Kayrita Anderson Family Foundation is acknowledged for its passionate and dedicated commitment to eradicating the prostitution of children in Georgia, its sponsorship of the campaign, A Future. Not a Past., and for ongoing encouragement and support given to all in the field.

This story began simply as the second novel in a series of adventures of Detective Wes T. Wesley, Atlanta Police Department. It became a cause!

The writing of this novel involved cooperation and participation from many people. No matter what their role was in creating this work, all of them became good or better friends. They are now a part of the creativity and the future.

To my...

Editor, Frank Bostwick, who was the catalyst who took this book from a story to a cause.
Writing partner, James Sellers, Major (ret.) Atlanta Police Department, who advised me throughout all phases of developing the plot and the details of being a detective.
New partner - already dedicated to the cause - Kaffie McCullough, Campaign Director of A Future. Not a Past., a program of the Juvenile Justice Fund, who had a vision and never gave up.
Book cover and web site designer, Cheryl Rose, President of Cheryl Rose Web Design and my daughter, who was willing to try a new media to create the emotion for the book's cover.
Manuscript readers who took their time and effort to read for

both content and mechanics with the hope that they found all the slip-ups.

Husband and constant support of my interests and passions, Richard J. L. Martin, who not only encouraged me to keep moving ahead but became a good researcher for additional information to expand the knowledge on the topic of commercial sexual exploitation of children.

...I give my most deep, sincere appreciation.

In addition, I express a hearty thanks to you the readers for being a part of an awakening to a horrifying crime that needs to have everyone's awareness and attention to finding the way to end this assault on our children and the world's humanity.

Chapter 1

Honeybun

Honeybun, woke up with a start, She was sure she had heard something. She opened one eye. She peeped out from her safe, blanket cocoon. Did she see something, or was she just imagining that someone was in her room? She cringed back from the edge of her bed. She was afraid of the dark. She was more afraid of what can happen in the night.

She heard a rustling of cloth and was certain that she could hear breathing. Did one of her sisters sneak into the room? Why would they give up their TV to be in the dark with her? Tears rushed up. Honeybun shivered. She froze as the edge of her bed lowered.

"Hi, little lady. Don't make a sound or I'll hurt you real bad, because I'm tough," a man's voice whispered in her ear.

Honeybun squeezed her eyes tight and tried to push away. A big, scratchy hand covered her mouth. He pulled her away from the wall. Even though her eyes were closed and she could not see him, she knew she couldn't move away.

"You're quite the young lady, alright. Just my kind of sweetie. I like girls a lot. Don't forget. If you make one sound, I'll hurt you so bad that you'll wish you were dead. I don't want anyone to interrupt us. We're gonna have a little fun and then I'm gonna leave and you're not gonna tell anyone about this. That's the game we're playing. I get what I want and you don't get your face all beat up. My fist has your name on it if you ever say a word to anyone."

The scared seventh grader felt the pressure of hard knuckles pushing against her face. She was sure he was going to hurt her.

A thought screamed in her head, 'This is why I hate the dark.' At the same time she felt the pressure on her cheek, she heard a zipper being opened, more rustling of material and a gentle thud as something was dropped to the floor. Honeybun could feel her tears rolling down her usually rosy cheeks toward his big hand.

She felt her favorite, extra large, Georgia State University T-shirt being raised by its hem. "Oh, yes, there's a lovely, sweet body. Just for me. This's gonna be very special. You'll never forget me, little cunt. You'll always keep me in your mind the rest of your life. But, you're never gonna tell anyone or I'll come again. You'll never forget that visit either. I can be really mean if you don't play my game by my rules."

Honeybun knew he was telling the truth. This horrible man knew where she lived so he could always come back. He knew what she looked like. He could recognize her brown hair and fair complexion that was now pale with fear. She couldn't escape. She was a prisoner of the dark. Her life was happy during the day. She even liked going to Middle School where she could learn math and play basketball, but she was terrified of the night

The man roughly spread her legs and rubbed his hands over every bit of her shivering body lingering between her legs and pushing inside of her. Then something much larger was entering her 'down there' and he began pushing up and down faster and faster. 'He's hurting me,' she screamed in her mind, 'but he's not beating my face.' She kept her eyes closed, and did not cry out. How long would he stay?

Almost as fast as he appeared, his body relaxed. He rolled off the girl's body that was still stiff with fright. He reached back and touched her face again with his knobby knuckles. "No words, ever. Our game is just ours." She thought she heard him chuckle. Then he was silent.

Honeybun wondered if he'd gone to sleep. The man hadn't moved for several minutes. She slid sideways again backing up to the wall, and slowly reached for the blanket to cover herself. She was shocked when he clamped his hand between her legs, squeezed tightly and whispered in that awful voice, "Don't try anything tricky, you little slut. Just 'cause I'm finished with you, doesn't mean that you can just up and leave."

She gasped but made no sound. She was still as she could be. She tried not to breathe. She wished that she could simply melt away or somehow pass through the wall like ghosts do in movies. She didn't want to feel that hand again. She prayed that he'd go away.

As if in answer to that prayer, the man sat up on the edge of the bed and put his trousers back on. Honeybun heard the zipper again. She somehow felt safer when she heard that sound. She could hear him moving around the room. Then he was gone. She still didn't look, but wondered if he'd gone out the window. That would be easy since her room was on the ground floor. She didn't move. She tried not to think. Her eyes were still squeezed shut. She waited and waited. She listened for anything that would've been a clue that he was still there or might be returning. She heard nothing.

Finally, Honeybun opened her eyes and looked around the room. It was empty. It looked just the same as it always did. She was alone as she had been only a short time ago. Was she still Honeybun? Other mornings she had found that her life was still the same. She hoped she would tomorrow. She wanted to be the same person who had a mom and two older sisters and who smiled during the day. She began to cry again.

Honeybun tried to reach a tissue to wipe her face. She moved over to the edge of the bed to get the box. She could smell the man's body on that side of the bed. It created a moment of nausea. She wanted to forget him but she couldn't.

She felt the tissue box and started to slide off the bed when she stretched to retrieve the paper handkerchief. She looked down on the floor and there was a wallet. She picked it up, then tiptoed toward the window for better light from the street light nearby. Still feeling afraid and vulnerable, she slowly opened the wallet. She took out a driver's license that was just like what her mother showed at stores for identification and said, "When you're grown up, you'll have a driver's license and your own car."

Honeybun took the card out and put it into her plastic Barbie doll suitcase that she had always kept trinkets in. She felt warm wetness running down her thigh. Absently, she took one of the tissues and wiped away the mess and pushed the tissue into the suitcase to cover up the driver's license. Knowing that it was something that she shouldn't have seen, she put the wallet back on the floor. Feeling very sad and tired, the pretty, curly-headed, young girl climbed back into bed, covered herself completely with the blanket and fell asleep.

The next morning the wallet was gone.

Chapter 2

Wes T. Wesley

Twelve Years Later

Atlanta Homicide Detective Wes T. Wesley was getting into his old, dented Taurus. It was good that he had long legs to reach the accelerator and brakes, because a scuffle with a vicious DUI had broken the seat adjustment more than two years ago. The seat had been locked in one setting ever since. His plan was to head to Krispy Kreme to pick up his usual weekday breakfast of three doughnuts and a large, industrial strength coffee. Even to him, it didn't sound like a great way to start the day, but it was how he'd been doing it for almost all of the twenty years that he'd been on the force.

As he stretched to push the accelerator, his pager sounded. He glared at it. He felt that the time before his calorie-rich morning meal should be his. The least his paging public could do was to give him that time to himself.

"One of these times, I'm going to ignore that damn thing. Take on a life of my own. I'll find something to do where I'm in control rather than every lowlife character in this city." His thoughts were strong enough that he simply looked at that hated, small, black box and let it do its own thing. He backed out of his short driveway, and hissed at his pager. "See, you stupid, dwarf monster, I don't have to let you rule my life. I can pretend you don't even exist."

Wes pulled up to the stop at 10th Street. He watched fourteen cars pass and finally saw a space large enough for him to gun the motor and get into the constant but slow traffic flow. He immediately was stopped at the first traffic light. He drummed his fingers on the steering wheel in time with the rap music blaring from the car stopped directly in front of his. He noticed that the car was loaded with five passengers, all bobbing up and down in time with the music. They were the only action on the street because a line of cars waiting to turn left had clogged the intersection.

Without giving his vow to not touch the pager another thought, Wes picked it up and checked the number. "Holy shit! Why am I such a friggin' jerk? The one person in the whole city who I want to talk to is calling me, and I'm sitting here listening to the sicko words of some rap song."

Automatically, he reached up and smoothed his thick brown hair that complimented his well-tanned complexion. He looked in his rearview mirror, smiled showing straight, white teeth and noted that he thought he looked quite fashionable with a gray and red stripe tie and fresh, gray shirt. He snickered, "as if it matters how I look to return a page."

Keeping his eye on the stalled line of cars, he punched the number that was beckoning him from the dull, digital monitor. Two rings before they were interrupted by what he believed was the sweetest voice in the whole U S of A.

"Detective Wesley, I presume," Janeen Carson answered without identifying herself.

"You got that right, baby. What gets you up and bright eyed so early this morning?"

"Not so early. I'm already in the office and making fresh coffee for the boss and the dean. I'm calling you about something I found on my desk when I got here."

Janeen Carson was the executive assistant to the interim president of Georgia Institute of Technology, located just a few blocks from where Wes now sat. She often said that she was practically born on the campus, because she had taken a job there while she was still in college and had stayed through three presidents. She had matured there, gotten married, and had become a widow all within those few acres that made up the college. It had been her security and her extended family for half of her thirty-something years.

Others, who knew Janeen, agreed that she was a big asset to the campus and the president's office. Yes, she did the job. Her beautifully groomed appearance, trim, athletic figure, gray eyes and clean, shiny brown hair made the perfect image to greet all guests, faculty and students. She made everyone feel that their time was valuable. Their mission with the president was of utmost importance. It was not surprising that several alumni had tried to lure her away with offers of higher salary. She never made the leap. She loved what she did.

Janeen thought she had everything she wanted at Georgia Tech until she met Detective Wes Wesley because of a murder that happened on campus. Actually, she had found a student shot in the president's office, and was the one to notify the police. Hearing Wes' voice now, reminded her that the campus was no longer all that she wanted.

"I'm nervous about asking what you've found. Your track record for finding surprises in your office isn't the best. Do I need to make a detour? I'm only a few blocks away."

"No, no, no. This is not a problem. This is something that might be fun. Well, at least interesting. One of the student groups is having the tele-evangelist, Reverend Temple Carrollton, on campus tonight and I'm inviting you to go with me." Janeen waited to hear Wes's response. She had been attracted to his rich baritone voice when she first met him. She loved that voice.

"I'm not sure he's my style, but if it means I can sit in the audience with you and make out, I'm for it. I'll even pretend to look forward to going."

"I don't know about the making out with one of God's 'lieutenants' looking us over, but the rest of your answer is great. Starts at seven in the Cremins Basketball Coliseum. I'll pick you up at 6:30. Gotta run, Here comes Mr. Landman. See you tonight."

Janeen had hung up in time to greet the president with a hot cup of coffee as he made his way from desk to desk. She was so impressed with this man who never seemed too busy to talk to those who were part of his campus team. He even had time for students and never forgot a name.

Although Kurt Landman had been a businessman all his life, with his casual-style clothes and manner, he looked like his career had always been academia. His gray hair, which he wore short, was beginning to thin. She knew he was at least sixty-five years old but everything about him was youthful. Because of his caring nature, he was the best of all the presidents that she had worked for at Georgia Tech.

. . . .

Wes had made his way almost to Krispy Kreme as he talked to Janeen. He saw the HOT NOW sign was lit up and was convinced that this was his lucky day: an early call from "his girl" (Was he acting like some juvenile? If he were still living at home, his son, Jason, would give him grief about his immature behavior.), sugary, fried doughnuts and an invitation to hear Reverend What's-his-name. Hmm, maybe it wasn't all so lucky, but, as Janeen said, "Well, at least interesting."

Wes was in and out of the doughnut shop in minutes carrying with him a greasy bag holding his breakfast. Several people called to him by name and Billy Joe LaCrosse waved as he got back into his car and shouted out, "See you in the office. We need to talk about the report you haven't filed. The major left you three messages yesterday afternoon."

Wes began reevaluating his impression of his lucky day and decided to postpone the final judgment. When Billy Joe, his Homicide partner, started the day talking about Major Dagmar Dilbert, he knew he was starting his shift at the bottom. She was only interested in Mickey Mouse, bullshit procedures. She had never seen a murder victim at the scene of the crime; never had blood spattered across her face during a shooting or faced a crazy, wild, drugged-up teenager who was trying to prove he could fly off a high rise building.

Dagmar was always pristine clean in a tailored uniform,

standing at their office doors with her department rulebook open in her hand. Wes was sure that she knew it all by heart. Something like a late report could send her into a frenzy that possibly could make the crazy, wild teenager look docile. He hoped he could eat his doughnuts and drink his coffee before DDD, Death by Dagmar Dilbert, descended upon him. Oh, yes, and maybe he could finish the delinquent report.

Detective LaCrosse and Wes had just closed a case that involved the shooting of a young male who had been scalping tickets at the Georgia Dome, the home field for the Atlanta Falcons football team. It had looked like a killing that happened during a holdup, but turned out to be a shooting done by two women, one the man's wife and the other his mistress. Quite by accident, they had ridden a bus together one day as they went to work, discovered that they were both being played by the same man. They decided to pay him back for his lies, the three kids he had fathered with each of them, and all the money he had taken from them to run around with still another woman. Oh, yes, it was the way of the city.

The detective parked his car in the unkempt parking garage that was provided for all vehicles assigned to Homicide and was at his desk in less than three minutes. He opened the bag and enjoyed the aroma of the still warm doughnuts mixed with the smell of strong coffee. Wes took a quick look at his computer, clicked the mouse and watched the half-finished report materialize on the screen. Just a few more details, summarize the extenuating "family" circumstances, and he would have it in the major's manicured hands. What was all the fuss about? They had closed the case only three days ago. Did she think they were a pool of secretaries?

His mouth was full. He had just taken a big gulp of the coffee when the telephone rang. Too bad his gourmet breakfast was being interrupted. Wes thought just before he said, "Homicide-Fugitive. Wesley speaking."

"Oh, how comforting to know you're on the job, Detective.

I wasn't sure that you were still with us since I have nothing on my desk to demonstrate that you are. Has your report on the Georgia Dome murder gotten lost?"

Wes groaned and mouthed Oh, shit! He wanted to tell Dilbert to fuck off, but that would really put her on a rampage. He had seen her when she was really ticked off. Her actions would make a cornered snake look like a simple coil of rope.

"Major Dilbert, how thoughtful of you to check on that. We all know that our internal mail system sometimes doesn't quite equal the U S Postal System. Actually, the report is just about ready to be printed. I'll have it delivered to you as fast as drugs disappear when the flashing blue lights appear. Actually, I had a little trouble with my computer program. Yes, ma'm, you'll have the document within the hour."

"I would have expected a more original excuse. Within the hour, you say? I bet you tell your bill collectors that the check is in the mail, right?"

"You got that right. I've used that reason a few times. Sure enough the check was in the mail just like you will have your report within the hour. I wouldn't disappoint you, Major Dilbert. As soon as it's out of here, I'll have time to start the investigation on the shooting of that man who was found outside the Union Mission. The neighbors in that new residential area adjacent to the Mission are asking who, what and why. I'll just ask them to stay cool until I get my paperwork done."

"Don't get smart with me, Wesley. You know what your job is and if you want to keep it, do it! I'll look for the report in 55 minutes. Guess you better quit dreaming up excuses, and get to your keyboard. I'll let you know when we're going to have our next secretarial training session." Wes winced as she hung up with a bang.

Chapter 3

Eve Zachary

Using his left hand as he completed the report with his right, Wes ate his doughnuts and drank his coffee When he reread the motive and how these two women got together, he thought, "No one's going to believe this. When the major reads this, she's going to be convinced that I made it up simply to finish now. Well, so be it. That's what happened. Some attorneys are going to have a good time when they take this to court."

He was hoping to find Eve Zachary, their Homicide Unit intern, to ask her to take the report to Dilbert's office immediately. Of course the interns were there to learn about their operation, but everyone used them as reliable "gofers." Eve was the best young trainee that they had ever had. When she went out on a case with one of the detectives, she was really a productive member of the team. He and Billy Joe LaCrosse had both been excited when they found out that along with being young and pretty, she had a mind and used it. Her well-rounded body and perky attitude seemed to never run out of energy even on the days when she spent her lunch break running instead of eating. When any detective needed help with research or some other mundane task, Eve would always be available. She never had to be reminded to finish the assignment.

Eve Zachary was in the criminology program at Georgia State University and had been in the top ten in her class every year. The detectives used to joke that if she became a permanent member of the Homicide Unit that there would be a flood of transfer requests to this unit. The young woman never seemed to be aware of her pixie-like face, framed by a fringe of brown bangs that topped her casual gamin haircut. She once thought she looked like Peter Pan. Her smile would captivate both police officer and criminal. Hopefully, if she continued to follow this career, she would be a tough witness for the prosecution in any courtroom.

With a flourish, Wes pushed the print key and stretched before rising from his chair. He would check on Eve while the pages were being printed in duplicate. Knowing that her schedule was normally to come by Homicide each morning before going to her classes, he felt confident that he would have the best delivery service in the city.

Eve poked her head in the door and said to Wes' back, "Hi, it's me, Detective Wesley. Your desk looks like you have been here for hours."

Wes was startled. Eve Zachary had appeared so quickly that he wondered if she was reading his mind.

"No, not that long. I just look all worn out because the Major has already been chewing out my butt."

"She's good at it. Do you think there is any police officer that she has missed?"

"None who I know. We have all learned to stay out of her crosshairs. That's why what I'm going to ask you to do is a huge favor. Maybe one that will let me keep my job."

"Hey, if it's that serious, just ask. I have about an hour before I need to be in class," Eve smiled.

"All you need to do is drop off my Georgia Dome murder report in Dilbert's office within 40 minutes. That will save me, make her as happy as any hooker on the streets on Saturday night and get you to class on time."

"It's done. I'm ready when you are. I'll just stop in Detective LaCrosse's office to tell him I'll be back about two o'clock. I'm working with him on that drug dealer's shooting. You know the body that was found in the middle of Centennial Park. I bet when they built that park for the Olympics, they never planned for it to be a location for drug deals gone sour."

Wes headed to the printer. Then he caught up with Eve in

Billy Joe's office. They had their heads close as they looked at the Centennial Park crime scene photographs. Eve was pointing to one of the photos.

"Detective LaCrosse, did you notice this little pile of dirt here in the corner of the picture? It looks like red clay. Where could that have come from when most of the park is paved?"

"Hmmm, can't say I gave it any thought until right now. Just looked like dirt to me, but you do have a point. Maybe it'll mean something as we put together what evidence we have. Obviously it would appear someone – killer or victim – had been somewhere not paved. That wouldn't be downtown since everything open is covered with asphalt or concrete. Let's not forget about this."

Detective LaCrosse looked up as Wes came into the room. "Hey, Wes, did ya' hear me at Krispy Kreme? I wanted to be sure you got that report done."

"Yeah, it's done. Eve's going to drop it off on her way to class."

"You coward! Won't take a chance of runnin' into the dragon face to face, but you don't mind makin' po' little Eve do it."

Wes looked at the chocolate brown face that now featured a huge, toothy smile. Wes often wondered why he had to spend a fortune to get his son's teeth all in place, but Billy Joe's parents just put together the right genes. With that smile, Billy Joe could look pleasant even when he was handcuffing a resisting hoodlum.

It always amused Wes that his partner still wore a modified Afro rather than the current style of shaving one's head. His wiry, black hair was beginning to be invaded by some shiny gray strands that announced that he had been in the business for a lot of years. Many times, Wes was thankful to have his backup a man with experience and good sense. Billy Joe had both.

The three colleagues said good-bye quickly, because each had something else waiting for attention. There was never a down time in Atlanta Homicide. The numbers of violent crimes were down over the last three years but the city still had numbers too high. Even though crimes against people were reported daily, Atlanta government believed that this city could get along with fewer detectives. It was an unending problem that the chief had to face, but it certainly kept them from being bored on the job.

Wes headed for the door to visit the Atlanta Union Mission, a shelter for the homeless, where several youngsters chasing a basketball had discovered a man's body. The Atlanta detective had begun his interviews the day before. He was hoping that today someone will have important information to add. It was surprising that no one seemed to have heard anything. It was especially surprising since three bullets had ripped through the body that lay only a few yards from the building. It was leaning against the fence that ran the length of the property on Mills Street. Wes was hoping for greatly improved memories today. He knew that clear heads were hard to find right after a body has been discovered.

Chapter 4

Ramblin' Randy

Wes Wesley squeezed his Taurus into the space left in the parking area behind the mission building. He was only a short distance from the door. There was a small sign announcing The Shepherd's Inn, but he could barely see the short walkway. Obviously, the word was out. Maybe 50 people were standing around in small groups. Some were talking loudly; some appeared to be quietly passing on secrets and a few looked like they were praying. There was a nervous energy in the air and Wes hoped that this collection of spectators wasn't going to add difficulties to his job of finding a murderer as soon as possible.

"Detective Wesley. Hey, Detective Wesley. Over here. It's me. Walter." A voice was heard over the buzzing din.

Wes looked toward the edge of the crowd and saw his friend and former "house-mate" who now had a small efficiency apartment in the Midtown area of Atlanta. Walter looked a lot different than the first time Wes had met him here at the Union Mission after Walter had called him to say that he might have some information about one of Detective Wesley's cases. Wes had assumed it was just another crank call, but soon found that it was Walter who could steer him to the murderer.

Walter had been given the reward money that had been offered for information and had taken some of it to pay for computer school. He had stayed with Wes for a couple of months while he recovered from an attack by the killer who had shot the student in the office of the president of Georgia Tech. During the time he had shared his home, Wesley was proud of Walter and what he had accomplished. Today he no longer looked like a down-and-out homeless man. He stood with a pride that had not been there before. His wave toward his friend was energetic and confident.

"Walter, what're you doing here?"

"I was goin' home from work and heard about the shootin'. I still have several friends who often stay at this shelter, so I came to see if I could help. It's payback time, Detective. You helped me when I had nowhere to go. I want to be around if someone needs me."

Wes was touched by the sincerity in Walter's voice. He had always felt there was a strong, moral man under the hand-me-down clothes and behind eyes that reflected a weariness of the street life. He had taken Walter into his home. He had never regretted it. Even Wes' son, Jason, had liked Walter. He met him when he was home for a break from college and later told his father, "Gee, Dad, you're one cool, crazy guy. You can send a man to death row in a blink of your eye, but you keep finding other men you want to save. Are you an avenger or a guardian angel?"

Wes put his memories aside. "How're things going, Walter? Are you still operating a smokin' keyboard? I used to watch you practicing on the computer when your fingers were flying."

"Yes, sir, I love this job. I get to do my favorite thing in life, and someone pays me for it. I work at night, eleven to seven, catch some sleep, then have the rest of the day for myself. It's awesome!"

"I'm really proud of you, Walter. But let's talk about the shooting here yesterday. What do you know?"

"Hey, man, you want me to be your dep-u-ty again? I can do it. I always got the time for you."

"Well, let's start with if you knew the dead man."

"Yeah, I knew who he was. Din't know him too good. He was one of those guys who's always lovin' or fightin' his booze and drugs. One day he's sane and the next he be crazy. Even when he seemed OK, sometimes he'd talk about what a big shot he was. Din't look like no big shot to me, but then we have had all kinds here," Walter nodded his head several times as if agreeing with his own assessment of the residents of the Union Mission.

"The drugs and stuff will show up in the autopsy, which might be the motive for shooting him. Just a plain-old-vanilla drug killing. If that's the story, Walter, I'll be out of here so fast you'll think you dreamed seeing me. Then we can get together just for fun over a couple beers at Manuel's."

"Manuel's sounds good to me. I like the bar of choice of the Atlanta Police Department. That plus havin' the best fries in town. Must be a good copy of heaven."

"We'll do it this weekend, if you have time. Now what else do you know about this case today?"

"Well, most of the time he called himself Ramblin' Randy like he thought he was a cowboy or somethin'. Then when he was all greased up, he'd almost cry, call himself Randall Lee and babble about how he used to have a house almost as big as the Union Mission. We all have our dreams, right?" Walter looked wistful as if seeing both Ramblin' Randy's dreams and his own. Walter's dreams had come true because of another murder. He never wanted to forget the huge gift he had been given because of that tragedy.

Wes had taken out his small notepad and was jotting down a few words. As he gathered more facts, he'd review everything he'd learned. The story would appear just like magic. It happened every time. The stories didn't always lead to the killer, but they had their own drama; they held the secrets of many lives.

"I don't know much more. He'd been around, in and out, for a long time. I guess you'll get a lot more information from the director, Mr. Oni. He knows us all."

"OK. I do have to go see him. I told him I'd be here early and already I'm pushing that. If you think of anything else, we can talk about it on Saturday. Is six o'clock at Manuel's OK for you?"

"You got yourself a date. I'm not as pretty as that little Georgia Tech lady, but I'm right up there. If she's a ten, I'm a nine." Walter laughed so hard at his own joke that Wes had to join in.

Walter's brown skin still had the smoothness of youth, but the gray in his hair and his wary, dark eyes immediately delivered the message that this man had seen hard, aging times. He was tall, lanky. He wore a simple sport shirt, clean jeans and fairly new Nike' sneakers. He had a thin gold chain at his neck that had been the memento he had bought when he first received the reward money. "I'll wear this to my grave to always honor a wonderful man who believed in me." This was his vow to Andy Dren, the Georgia Tech student who had been his friend and was murdered on the campus the year before.

Wes entered the building and was immediately in a narrow landing with a stairway dominating the one wall. There was a desk crowded into a corner straight ahead where several men stood doing nothing. They were laughing and talking, but he was sure that they were watching him as if they were expecting him to arrive. He asked a man for the location of the director's office. He soon found that he had a talkative escort as he was directed to the elevator.

"Hey, man, do I know ya? Ya' look like someone I seen 'round. I'm here lots, ya' know. Always doin' what I can, ya' know. Always things to do here. I knows why you're here. You need some help? I can do it guar-an-damn-teed. Try me, man."

"I don't need anything right now but maybe later after I speak with the director."

"Yeah, man. Ya' jus' talk to da boss. I'll wait right here for ya'. Ya' don' even have ta look fo' me, ya' know. I'll watch fo' ya'."

"That's great. I'll see you when I leave," Wes said realizing that no matter what he was planning to do, this man would be right here when he completed his meeting. "Thank you for getting me here. See you later."

"Ya' jus' git on dis here elevator and yo' man will be at de next stop. And den I'll see ya'. Yeah, yep, I'll be here, man. Don' ya' worry 'bout ole Jasper. He's a man of his word, ya' know. See ya'."

Wes shook hands with "Ole Jasper," looked him in the eye and wondered what he knew. Might he have a clue about the shooting of Randall Lee aka Ramblin' Randy?

True to Ole Jasper's word, a man was waiting for him when the elevator door opened. The huge man extended a hand and said, "Good to see you again." The black executive director had a shiny bald head and large brown eyes. Wes had not remembered from yesterday what an imposing figure Kunle Oni presented. He emanated a vitality that seemed to fill the entire room.

"Detective Wesley, thank you for being here. Even before our tragedy yesterday, I'd heard much about you. We need you desperately. Not only are our men concerned about what happened here in our yard, but the neighbors are already verging on hysteria. Whenever anything goes wrong around here, the first blame is on our men. It's not fair, but it's the fact."

"Mr. Oni, believe me, you're not the only ones who usually are in the middle of negative controversy. Hardly anyone stays friends with Homicide for very long. Unfortunately, we make them think about things they don't want to face. And, maybe that's what you and I are going to do here. Can we go somewhere quiet and talk?"

"Let's go to my office. That's one spot at the Mission where I have some control over my time. When I'm in the hallways, I must be a magnet. Everyone draws close with something to say, and I like to be available to listen." The director motioned for Wes to follow him to his office. Wes was intrigued how light Oni's step was and how gently he closed the door. He offered him a seat. "Do you mind if I tape our conversation, Mr. Oni?"

"I don't mind at all, but I do mind you calling me 'Mr.' I think we're going to go through some hard stuff. Call me by my given name, Kunle. I hope I may call you 'Wes.' Now let's get to work."

Wes liked the man immediately. He also appreciated that he

was a man of action and didn't intend to waste time with small talk. Social niceties could be saved for later; now they needed to work at finding a killer.

Detective Wesley placed his tape recorder on the desk between them. "May 4, Detective Wes Wesley interviewing Mr. Kunle Oni, Director of the Atlanta Union Mission." He placed the recorder halfway between them and said, "OK, Kunle, I'm ready if you are. My first question is: Where were you the night of May third?"

Kunle Oni, chuckled, "It's amazing, detective, you sound exactly like the guys on NYPD or CSI."

"Actually, those programs are as close to what we do as what we do. The big difference is our pay scale. So where were you last night?"

"Out raising money, my after hours job. You can imagine living in Atlanta, we never have enough. I was at the downtown Ritz Carlton talking with four business leaders about putting up a matching gift to build our endowment. I must boast that I went home with a commitment of $50,000 each so I have $200,000 to start a small campaign. I can give you each man's name and telephone number so you can check out my story – or do you call it an alibi? Believe me, Wes, working in a shelter, you're very aware of alibis, lies, white lies, excuses, fabrications and mis-speaks. It wouldn't be surprising if one of our men would come forward and say he killed Randy. Sometimes they get reality all mixed up."

"Do you think one of your men did kill him? Did he have any obvious enemies?"

"I guess all the guys have enemies, but I really don't believe Randy had anyone here who hated him. Sometimes I would have said that he hated himself. When he would go back on the sauce, he wasn't always the most loveable person. But he wasn't vicious nor did he take out his misery on others. No, rather than be nasty, there was a better chance that he would become maudlin. He regretted all that he had lost because of his addictions. He once was quite successful."

"Tell me what you know about the victim. How did he get his nickname, 'Ramblin' Randy?'"

Kunle sat quietly for a moment, gathering his thoughts. He obviously knew the history of Ramblin' Randy. He was wondering where to begin.

"Randy has been around here for about three years. Sometimes we'd see a lot of him. Other times he'd disappear for weeks or months at a time. It was quite certain that he was back to drinking or doping again. We never knew where he went, but he always came back. Unfortunately, he came back again and someone killed him. He'd been back for almost two weeks and was really low-profiling it. Had hardly spoken to anyone. He just seemed content to be back 'home.' His name Ramblin' didn't come from his meandering. Randy, believe it or not, was an alumnus of Georgia Tech. You know: the Ramblin' Wreck of Georgia Tech."

"Georgia Tech! Then I guess the real story is how he worked his way from the campus just a few blocks down Techwood Drive to the Union Mission."

"Not really a very unusual story. He started out in all the right directions. Built a business, had a family and lived in prestigious Buckhead. Then started drinking. Threw it all away. All the experts say: Stress. Too much, too fast. I guess those are as good reasons as any. The truth is simply that Randall Robert E. Lee, a community leader and highly respected man, lost his way. He couldn't face Randall Lee anymore and became Ramblin' Randy, street person and drunk."

"Robert E. Lee? Are you kidding?"

Kunle Oni laughed and pointed directly at Wes. "How can a man who has the name of a street in Atlanta be surprised at someone named after his great, great, maybe another great uncle? How about that Wes T. Wesley?" He had pronounced it West Wesley.

"You got a point there. I'd probably rather be named for

a general than a street." The two men were interrupted by the buzzing of the telephone. Oni raised his unruly eyebrows and picked up the receiver. "Oni." He listened for a minute, then said, "I think we'll come down now so you can get on to your meeting. Just wait there." He turned to Wes. "I asked one of our resident managers to put together Randy's possessions. He's done that so if it doesn't mess up your routine, let's go take a look. You may find something that will help you, detective."

Chapter 5

Wes T. Wesley

As they worked their way back to the first floor and walked down a long, narrow hall, Wes was surprised to find the areas as neat and clean as any hotel he had ever seen. Except for a small group of men watching television, the entire floor seemed to be unoccupied. He was jolted when Kunle Oni appeared to know his thoughts, "Most of the men in this area are here only at night. These are our dormitory rooms for the homeless. They begin to gather in the late afternoon, have a hot dinner, spend the night and are out of here by dawn. That's our night shelter. We also have day shelter for those men who work at night. Keeps everyone busy, but the men themselves do a lot of the work."

"I guess I never gave your operation much of a thought, I knew the 'mission' of the Union Mission, but knew nothing about how you make it work."

"Well, Wes, you may come back anytime. We always have a place for good volunteers. Actually, we have some great volunteers who have been with us longer than some of our clients."

Wes looked ahead. He saw a man dressed in a dark suit and a bright green T-shirt waiting for them at one of the doorways. He smiled as they approached, "Good morning, Kunle. Good morning, Detective Wesley. I'm Pritchett Price, one of the managers on this floor. I've gathered Randy's treasures for you. Unfortunately, it won't take you long to go through them."

He motioned toward a box that was on a small, dented metal desk. The carton looked forlorn, unrelated to the room. Wes thought that it was appropriate for it to look forlorn. It represented an entire life. One full life of loss. If the stories

r's Head

EverRoast® Chicken was voted
Best New Deli Meat in the 2010
Better Homes and Gardens Best New Product Awards

Bo

were true, Randall Robert E. Lee had a history of many losses.

"Thank you, Mr. Price. I hope that what you have collected can give us a clue to who would kill Randy Lee."

Wes looked into the box that originally held copy paper. Printed on the sides was 'Kinko's,' a 24-hour copy and business center in Atlanta. The cardboard container's first use was for the benefit of persons who were living busy, productive lives. Its current use was to finalize a life that had become a waste of productivity.

"Randy had only been back with us for ten days this time. He was here earlier in the spring and then took one of his leaves of absences. I would guess by the way he looked, he had spent most of his time away from here dead drunk or stoned. Who knows, maybe he made someone mad, and they followed him here," Pritchett Price theorized. Wes lifted several items out of the box.

Randy's things. Clothing that was so faded and worn that he was sure that they were items that had been gotten right here at the Union Mission, a pair of drugstore reading glasses, an empty pack of cigarettes, a tattered photo of several children in front of a big house, a Bible with the first page completely covered with the words I'm sorry, I'm sorry, I'm sorry, I'm sorry. Obviously Randall Lee was a man who understood how much he had lost. Price was probably correct; there was nothing that gave a clue to why someone had decided to end a life that probably had actually ended years ago.

"I'd like to take this with me, Kunle. I'll spend more time on it when I can thoroughly examine each item," Wes said.

"No problem. We want you to find whoever is responsible ASAP. Besides his few possessions are worth practically nothing."

Wes turned to Pritchett Price. "How well did you know Randy?"

"Maybe as well as anyone here but, let me tell you, that wasn't very well. He was not a social animal. One thing I'm sure of is that he was filled with demons. He didn't sleep well. He often referred to regrets about his life, cried a lot. I think he wanted to go back to Buckhead and ask to start over, but it never happened. He was filled with guilt that ate away at him like acid."

Wes asked more questions of Price who then left to go to his meeting. Oni had set aside an area for the detective to meet with other residents and staff. He spent more than an hour asking and answering questions. He was beat. He felt he had learned very little. Actually, he was getting nowhere. A man was dead and no one had a clue as to why. He was ready to head back to his office.

Kunle Oni walked him to the door, gave him his work and home telephone numbers, and invited him to call any time. Wes left the building again passing the Shepherd's Inn sign. Now he understood its meaning: it was the overnight place that was named in honor of the most well known shepherd, Jesus. He hoped that it was both a shelter and a comfort to those who needed a bed.

"Hey, hey, Mr. Detective, here's Ole Jasper. Jus' like I said. Tole ya' I'd be here. Kin I do somethin' to help? Carry messages, watch for traffic while you pull out, get ya' a cuppa java?" The wiry, little man was almost dancing a jig. He had enough energy stored up to light up the whole block.

'I wonder if the man ever just sits down.' Wes thought, but said, "Thanks for waiting to say good bye."

"Well, we don' get lots of big fuckin' VIPers here. And I knows ya' is one. Walter tole me all 'bout ya'. I'm proud to say hi-bye to Atlanta's finest. The guys in Precinct 5 next door are OK, but Detective Wesley is the number one su-preeem-o."

"Thank you, and Walter too, for all the votes. If I run for office, I'll come find you."

"Ya' do it, man. For a coupla bucks, I can get ya' all the damn votes ya' need," Jasper said proudly while giving Wes a salute.

Wes laughed as he unlocked his car door. Jasper was so quick that he had the door open before the detective touched the handle. He clapped the older man on the shoulder, said thank you and told him he would see him the next time he came to the Union Mission.

"Jus' let me know, ya' know. I'll have java ready and be at the door. Now I'm gonna go tell Walter that everthin' he said was true, ya' know. Ya' is as tall as a basketball player and as strong as a wrestler and as fast as a football player. Yeah, man, ya' got it all."

Wesley was still laughing as he drove out of the parking lot, down Mills Street passing the police precinct just a few feet from where Randy had been shot. How come no one saw anything? Where were the police when a murder was occurring in their backyard? Where was Ole Jasper when somebody really needed him?

Chapter 6

Eve Zachary

Wes checked in with the medical examiner, Glenda Rather, to follow up on some points related to the shooting of Ramblin' Randy. Then he had picked up take-out pizza and ate it at his desk. He spent the afternoon on a domestic homicide. He had taken several calls from the couple's children who wanted to tell him that their dad was a good guy and shouldn't be charged with murder just for 'offing' their old lady. It was a routine day in Atlanta. He was thinking about his evening with Janeen and the evangelist, Temple Carrollton, when Eve Zachary popped into his office.

"Hey, boss, it's me. Your day's over. It's after six o'clock. I know what time you started."

"I appreciate your concern, but I happen to know that you were here before I was."

Eve leaned against the doorframe. "You know how it is when you're working with Billy Joe. Not only does he get lots done, he has to tell you every story that might relate to the case. He sure is a talker!"

"Not news, Little Eve. It's one of the crosses we must bear to have a good partner."

The two of them laughed together about Detective Billy Joe LaCrosse before Eve asked, "How did your investigation go at the Union Mission?"

"Not a clue. People were available and helpful. If they know anything, I'm missing the signs. The case has some interesting background. It's a surprise but the victim was once a successful, rich, community leader."

"Really? I guess all kinds can lose it."

"You got that right, Eve. Keep that in mind when you're dealing with all these characters on both sides of a Homicide. Most people aren't what they appear on the surface," Wes hesitated, winked at the young intern and added, "Except thee and me and maybe we can include Billy Joe. We're the models for 'What you see is what you get.'"

"Wow, on that great testimonial, I think I'll go back to Billy Joe's office and work on my thesis or study that little pile of red clay in Centennial Park. Have a nice evening. See you tomorrow."

"Eve, do you want to examine the remaining possessions of Ramblin' Randy Lee? I plan to do that first thing in the morning. Maybe you'll see something that I don't. At first glance, it's a zero."

"Sure, look for me when you're ready. I'll be here, sir."

Wes laughed at the 'sir.' Made him feel like a dinosaur. He guessed that maybe he was to someone still in college. Certainly his son, Jason, would agree if he and Eve compared notes.

Wes gave her a high five and closed up the work he had spread out on his desk. Even though he was late, he still had time for a quick shower, a bite to eat and to be on time to go with Janeen to get "saved" by Temple Carrollton.

• • • •

Eve had chosen technology in criminology for her research and paper. She had begun clipping newspaper stories and matching them with the files kept by the Atlanta Police Department. The power of the topic was still a mystery in itself. She wasn't sure exactly where she was going with the information when she started, but she was excited at the potential that technology had in solving crimes. Some of Eve's prized news clippings were the ones that related the story of the class at John Marshall Law School in Chicago that had researched several life convictions, added DNA information and found those men were not guilty. She saw the futility and frustration of the accused when he repeated, "I'm innocent. I didn't do it," only to be ignored and slammed into a life so painful that death might be a prayer.

Already her file was getting fat with open cases, some more than twenty years old. She had many to choose and would have to decide which ones had the most impact. She thought about having to live in a prison knowing that you had never done anything worse than get some speeding tickets. She shuddered. It was frightening to her. She shuddered again. Her thoughts turned 180 degrees. She wondered about living with the knowledge that another person was locked up or executed for a crime that was done by you. Was the reaction simply, 'too bad' or 'dumb bastard, you're locked up? I'm free.'

Eve jotted some notes following her train of thought. They might be used in her interviews with prisoners. She stopped and followed a new direction, What about the victims. What prison do they live in within themselves? How do they escape? DNA and other technology won't do a thing for their incarceration.

"Eve, honey, why are you still here?" Billy Joe LaCrosse was standing at the doorway.

Eve jumped. "Oh, damn, you scared me. I guess I was lost in my mountain of paper."

"You sure were lost. I spoke several times before scarin' you to death. What's in your mind that's so important?"

"I was just putting together some notes for my thesis. You know it's on using technology to solve old cases, but my mind had taken a real turn to the south. Maybe I won't be able to separate technology from human emotions."

"Well, baby, that's why you're here with us: to learn the truth about bein' a Homicide detective. Our work isn't just to find a body, catch a killer, put the killer away. There are lots of things happenin' in between. Some of it's very sad. Some of it's pointless. Some of it's…"

"…Very ugly. Most of it's ugly. So many people have no respect for others. Makes me think of Wes' new case. He said this Ramblin' Randy guy had been a respected, big deal in town. How did he get where he got? Did people stop respecting him or did he not respect people? Did anyone really know him? Billy Joe, do you think anyone will ever know those answers?" Eve was asking important questions that usually never make a police report.

"I don't know the answers about that Randy joker, Eve, but I guarantee that knowin' them would help Wes find the perp. The hidden stories are what we're always tryin' to discover. They can break a deadlocked case almost as fast as a snitch. For me, baby, I like a snitch. If I ran Homicide, I'd provide a cell phone for every known snitch in town."

"See, there's another vote for technology. You're great. I'll definitely add your name to my research resources." Eve laughed while making a note about cell phones. She saw that Detective LaCrosse was getting ready to leave. She could get back to her work, but she would miss his conversation that always included a spin on something that might have seemed unimportant. She looked at her notes: Cell phones – help solve crimes? What if the victims had cell phones? Would they call for help? Could they call for help?

Chapter 7

Temple Carrollton

"I never drove to anything on the Georgia Tech campus before I met you Parking was a real pain. But, hanging out with the president's beautiful assistant, who always has a parking pass, ends that problem. I knew there was a reason I wanted you to be my girl. It's free parking!" Wes said as they arrived at the Robbie Cremins Basketball Coliseum.

"Free parking. Hmm, I'll keep that in mind when you're telling me about the rain and how it would be the humane thing for me to let you stay for the night. I'll just send you to campus with a parking pass. Call it a rain check."

Janeen's eyes sparkled as if reflecting the tiny drops of rain on her cheeks and eyelashes. The evening's mistiness formed soft, cloudy circles around each light that surrounded the sports facility. To Wes, the glistening sidewalks and trees that appeared to be sprinkled with tiny, liquid diamonds created the perfect scene for Janeen. She always shimmered and shone.

Wes guided the car into a space that was a short distance from an entrance already filled with students. They locked the doors and quickly followed the crowd into the building. There was a strange subdued din in the hallway, and they were both struck by the different aura than was always present during a basketball game.

"What a strange feeling. No matter what we might think about Temple Carrollton, obviously the students have a respect for his ravings."

"Wes, what a terrible thing to say! I should have locked you in the car."

"Ah, makes me wonder, was I just the driver for you on a

rainy night?"

"If you're fishing for a compliment, you're not going to get it from me. You're the one who made the nasty remark about Rev. Carrollton, Mr. Cynical."

Wes took Janeen's hand, gave her a quick smile. He didn't care if the Boston Strangler was the speaker. He was there because he wanted to be with Janeen Carson. Actually what he had heard about this charismatic man had all been wildly positive. Almost like the man had hypnotized his many devotees. Wes just wasn't into the dedication that so many people give to television celebrities who made their fame and fortune by trading on spiritual proclamations and people's own self doubts.

"Look at the turnout! The place is full. I guess at least three thousand people are more enthusiastic than you are about Temple Carrollton." Janeen's comment made Wes smile. From the first day Janeen saw him after Andy Dren's murder, she believed he had the most sensual smile in Georgia.

Their aisle seats were on the court, so they had an unobstructed view of the temporary stage. In just minutes, the lights were dimmed and the crowd immediately became still. Wes felt like they were collectively holding their breath with anticipation. What was going to happen? He waited along with the three thousand plus people.

Nothing happened.

Just when he felt that a glitch had occurred, soft music floated lightly from the perimeter of the entire coliseum. It slowly grew in volume until there seemed to be more sound than people. At first he was reminded of a rock concert he attended with his son, but realized that this was not simply uncontrolled noise. Although it was loud, the music made him feel safe, protected. After a few minutes, he was ready to acknowledge that there was a power in the performance of Temple Carrollton. He laughed to himself and thought, "He hasn't even made an appearance, and I feel I've been hooked."

Wes and Janeen concentrated on the stage. They saw nothing.

They looked around the arena. They saw nothing. They waited.

A light appeared in an area that Janeen knew was the location of skyboxes built for alumni who were willing to pay in five figures to watch the basketball team win or lose. They paid either way, but they complained loudly if the team was having a run of bad luck. She answered many of those calls the day after a game.

As the light brightened. It focused on a single man. The music lowered and receded back into the walls. Another minute of silence. The tall, husky man raised his arms above his carefully styled, tawny-colored hair. He spoke in a mellow voice with just a touch of a carefully cultured Southern accent, "Each of you will be blessed because you are here. Your Lord and I both know who is here and will reward you quickly and richly. This is a promise. Remember as good things happen to you during the next week, it is because you were here. It is because you made the sacrifice to give your money and your time to be here tonight for an experience far beyond what has ever entered your life before.

"I am a direct link to a better life that will enrich you and all people you touch. Do not hold back. Give your talents. Give your emotions. Give your body and your soul. Tell others that you now have seen the way. Your future can be whatever you envision. Your key to your desires is acceptance of my ministry that has been dedicated to you through our Lord. You all are my treasured sons and daughters."

A burst of applause began from the back of the arena and spread throughout the crowd. The noise was tremendous but as the audience reacted, the music rose again to an even higher crescendo. The light went out. The music stopped and everyone waited in darkened silence.

In what seemed too little time to move from the sky box to the stage, the evangelist was standing in front of them, wearing a sparkling silver robe with shiny gold trim and a headset microphone. Temple Carrollton was ready to entice and recruit his newest followers. He understood his power. He reveled in the effect that he had on his recruits when he rested his eyes for just a few seconds on a face that radiated self-doubt and longing for what he promised. He had been using his crafty charisma to convince more than a million young people that he should be their first and most important charitable institution for the rest of their lives. After all, it was because of him that they got anything they wanted. And it was because of them, that he got the things he wanted. He was constantly and happily amazed how much disposable money the younger generation had available.

"Innocents and sinners, listen! Take into your hearts the message that comes from a higher being. I am only the lowly messenger. My devotion to each and every one of you is to be your constant advisor and caretaker. If something negative happens in your life, it is because you have turned away your own devotion to my complete concern for you and your future. Do not take that chance! Do not become a victim of your own lack of commitment. Keep me and my devoted lieutenents nestled in your protective breast, internalize your dreams so we can feel those reflections. By having you support my ministry, I will continue to help you actualize your vision. If I am healthy, you will flourish. Your future lies in your strength of commitment to me and to the direct line I have to your Lord. Let me hear now the power of your convictions."

The audience burst into applause, shouts and stamping feet. Over the human response, Wes could actually feel the crushing volume of the music. He wondered if the huge windows along the promenade were still intact. He had attended many basketball games in this building, but he had never heard such a spontaneous reaction that actually seemed to have a power of its own. He wondered about the needs of the people in the audience that they could become so engulfed in the environment that Temple Carrollton had created in only a few minutes.

The charismatic preacher raised both his arms and his head. He then gave a delicate signal, like a symphony director ending the concert, for the people to be silent. The music simply disappeared. The spotlight on Temple Carrollton became brighter. In a very short time, the arena was devoid of even the smallest sound. The audience of several thousand had followed a slight motion of one man   Temple Carrollton began speaking in a low tone. Everyone leaned forward to pay closer attention to his words. It was difficult to hear exactly what was being said but soon the voice rose to its former volume. The people relaxed knowing they were not missing something that was being said to them. The minister continued to reel them in, to convince them that they were his only interest. They obviously came to receive comfort and hope. Temple Carrollton gave them both.

Wes looked at his watch and was surprised that about an hour had passed since the first lowering of the lights. He had let his mind wander briefly from time to time, but he had not been bored. He could still feel the intensity of the audience as the preacher closed his eyes and hesitated, producing another moment of complete stillness. Wes waited in anticipation. The others waited too.

"I can feel your needs and your hopes. They are like burdens on my soul. I take up those burdens with joy because they are yours. Through your appearance here tonight and the opening of your mind as I speak, you have shared your most cherished thoughts. I want to keep them within my heart and work on them for you. I can do that only if I stay strong and healthy and able to inspire and encourage you through my mediation and ministry. It is time for you to show your Lord and Temple Carrollton that you want us to surround you in all you do. Give generously of your material capabilities and of a memento of your true self. Place your money and a personal token in the blessed containers. The token is for me to always remember you so I can use it for your benefit.

Keep in mind that every time your plans go according to your desires, every time you get what you have asked for, it is through your gifts to me that I can support you. When your life seems at a low point or your vision is no longer clear and positive, consider the extent of your financial sacrifice tonight and consider renewing your commitment. I can serve you as long as I stay healthy and not burdened by everyday worry. Because of you, hopefully, when you need me, I will be strong enough to inspire you to do your best.

"My lieutenants will pass through the audience ready to receive your monetary and material gifts to your own future. These outstanding young men have been blessed because of our ministry to so many successful people. They are willing to take the time to transfer their power to you by looking you straight in the eye. Welcome this blessing as you share your abundance with them."

Temple Carrollton fell gracefully to the floor. There was a startled exclamation from the assembled group. Spontaneously some people rose from their seats. Before a rush of bodies bore down on the stage, an army of about twenty men all dressed alike in dove gray jackets with silvery lapels appeared. They encircled the artistically arranged body. One man from the phalanx bent over his leader, gently removed the headset and spoke quietly into the microphone, "Do not fear. Dr. Carrollton is fine. He has simply expended every ounce of his energy for you and your problems. Now is the time to help make him vigorous for your future." He laid the headset next to the prostrate body and led the dove gray, uniformed army from the stage.

Wes looked at Janeen and smiled. She returned his smile and took his hand, pulling him closer so she could whisper in his ear. "It cost $50 to come here tonight and I bet he'll get almost that much again from each person. That could be a $300,000 appearance. No wonder the marketers all target their advertising at the younger generation."

Wes added, "When you are 'investing' in your own bright future and all the things you ever wanted, one hundred bucks isn't a bad deal. I think I should add something to those silver lined buckets, because I kept thinking about what we might do with the rest of the evening. You know, just hedge my bets on one of my desires."

Janeen was ready with a quick response, but saw that one of the Carrollton men had arrived at their row. He touched Wes lightly on his shoulder and waited for him to turn around. Wes moved his head slightly. He was looking directly into the blue eyes of an attractive blond man about twenty years old. He looked like he had just been scrubbed by his mother to go to the first day of school. His features were so perfectly chiseled that he could have been a movie star.

As Wes reached into his pocket for his wallet, the man continued to look directly into Wes' eyes as if compelling a response from him. Wes said nothing. The man waited while Wes took a bill and placed it in the shiny bucket that was already half full with bills and personal tokens. The young man's face seemed to glow as he smiled, "Thank you for giving to your future." He took a step to proceed down the aisle and then said, "Temple Carrollton is in your life."

Chapter 8

Janeen Newman Carson

A half-hour later Wes and Janeen were back in the car, heading toward her townhouse just a mile away. She had chosen this location because she never had to face the horrendous Atlanta commuter traffic. Since she had become a young widow just a few years after her marriage, her personal life had been drawn closer and closer to her professional life at the Georgia Institute of Technology. The campus and its 'family' had provided a refuge for her when she felt so alone. It helped her to grow beyond the young, inexperienced woman who first responded to a job opening in the alumni department.

Having met Wes had expanded her social life and greatly improved her daily routine. Going home and eating her dinner while watching CNN news was no longer the highlight of her day. She had liked Detective Wes T. Wesley from the day he was assigned to investigate the murder that had occurred on campus. It amazed her that with all he had experienced as an FBI agent followed by his years investigating homicides in Atlanta, this detective had managed to keep a gentleness to his demeanor. It was especially evident when he spoke of his son. Wes' features softened, his mouth relaxed, his eyes glowed with pride. Father and son not only shared a family but also shared a career since Jason was now pursuing the criminal justice curriculum at the University of Virginia.

"A very interesting evening. Thanks for asking me to go…I think."

"I know what you mean. The dynamics and the power that Temple Carrollton demonstrates can feel good. It's also frightening. It points out how so many young people today need a strong mentor. The comfort and direction that they should be getting in their families and extended families are just not there. They come to Temple Carrollton for what used to be right in our homes," Janeen mused.

"Yep, you got that right. I vacillate from being impressed with his style to being turned off by his blatant commercialism. If those kids are as gullible as they appear to be, they will truly believe when something good happens to them, it was because of Carrollton. When something isn't working, they better send him some more money. I wonder how many continue to support his 'health.'"

Janeen nodded her head. She had the same questions that Wes had expressed. She did not believe that Temple Carrollton was dedicated to all the young people who followed him like puppies. "Did you notice that he never aligned himself with any religion? He always referred to 'your' Lord or 'the' greater being, etc. He wiggled out of being responsible for having to conform to anything. Each person does that for him or herself. Very clever. Also I think it makes it easier to get onto campuses. He can say that he is not pushing a religion. He is giving opportunity and support to the students' plans for success. Everyone on a campus is dedicated to that."

"Very interesting point. A point that was pounded, gently of course, into every head that was there tonight," Wes was remembering all the dramatic theatrics that were the heart of the Carrollton appearance, "I wonder if we could send old Temple to our prisons to help the inmates embrace a more high-principled life."

"Won't work. Where would the inmates get the $100 and up to guarantee a healthy life for the man? Speaking of a healthy life, how about some tofu and green tea before you go home?"

"Yuk! Come on, Janeen, you know that isn't even human, let alone healthy. How about a handful of your chocolate chip cookies and coffee? I'll need a little caffeine to stay awake for some 'healthy' relationship with my favorite person."

Janeen laughed as she got out of the car. Wes followed her to the small porch. He put his arm around her waist as she unlocked the door. He kissed her on the cheek. She moved her head and tracked his kiss that ended lightly on her nose. He kissed the tip of her nose again and then lifted her face so he could kiss her lips. A warmth surged through his body, and he was sure that Janeen felt the same joy. From the very first time he had visited her home, they both sensed similar needs and reactions in each other. After twenty years as a single father, Wes had given up the hope of finding someone who could understand his feelings. Someone who would accept him as he was. It was too late to try to change. Then Andy Dren was shot at Georgia Tech and meeting Janeen had given him new hope.

"Actually, you're more powerful than the performance we just saw. You can make me believe in Santa Claus, the Easter Bunny and angels in one kiss. Now, Wes Wesley, that's some big time power."

"I love you," Wes whispered, nuzzling his face into the silkiness of her hair.

"Love you too. Now let's get out of this damp air and hang out in my warm kitchen with cookies and coffee while you tell me about your day"

. . . .

Wes held the hot mug in his one hand and half a cookie in the other. He was thinking that this was a perfect way to end his day. When you faced death, violence and misery for a living; a normal small event like enjoying a bite to eat with your best friend was highly cherished.

Janeen's days were usually filled with the intellectual pursuit of young students that prevails on a respected campus. He liked to hear about these normal and happy things. Even when she faced the everyday challenges of keeping diverse groups and people fairly happy, there was still an overlay of the excitement of new beginnings and future expectations. Because her career was so different than his, he always was surprised that she was still intrigued by his work.

"Well, we got an interesting shooting today. In fact, you may even know the victim."

"Oh, no, Wes. I don't want to know about any more of your homicides. Once in a lifetime is enough," she said and then added curiously, "Why do you think I would know the person?"

"I just thought you might know his name. He was a graduate of Georgia Tech. Although from what little I know, that relationship was many lifetimes ago."

"OK. What does all of that mean? 'Many lifetimes ago'?" Janeen's interest had been piqued.

"This victim had been a successful businessman, had owned a home in Buckhead, had a family and was exactly the type of graduate Tech liked to brag about. Then he went sour. Got into booze, drugs and who knows what else. He lost all of the above. He ended up a transient guest at the Union Mission and was shot outside that facility last night. His name was Randall Lee. Known more recently as Ramblin' Randy."

"Wes, I do know that name! He has been the subject of conversation of several people because of what happened to his life. Everyone says: what a waste. He at one time was highly respected. I can't believe that he has been murdered. Who did it?"

"No idea at this point. Haven't been able to find a motive yet so we don't even have a direction to follow. We just need some more time and we'll catch the perp. You'll be interested that I ran into Walter when I was at the Union Mission. He looks good and says he loves the computer work that he's doing."

"Isn't it strange? Andy Dren is killed, which is a tragedy. Then something good, I mean Walter being able to learn computer technology because of the reward money, results."

"It gives hope to the homicide business. Maybe I could apply for a do-gooder grant saying that our murders can have positive results for the homeless. They get jobs and find a comfortable place to live." Wes winked at Janeen letting her know that he surely was not serious.

"Sounds rather strange but that's what happened to Walter. Let's hope that a wasted life like Randall Lee's might also have a positive side. What I hear though, sounds rather bleak. I wonder what Temple Carrollton would say about Randall's life?"

"Probably: You shouldn't have stopped sending me money." Wes finished his coffee as if putting an end to the conversation, went to Janeen and pulled her to her feet. "Let's not think about what I did today. How about some words that have a more personal touch. Like maybe I missed you, I'm glad we're here. Hey, come closer so I can appreciate every little bit of you."

"Nice words, sir. Could I entice you into a few actions that support those thoughts?"

"Not here in the kitchen, but I think moving to the sofa in front of the fireplace would be a perfect beginning."

"We don't need a fire but it's great for creating a mood," Wes said brushing his lips against Janeen's cheek.

"I'm for that. At this point in my life, I go for soft, warm light. Small candles are even better."

"Wonderful lady, you're adorable in any light. You would be gorgeous if you had all the theatrical lighting that Temple Carrollton used tonight. Damn, you are a real star. Not just a fake, manufactured person to scam others."

"There you go again trying to discredit our ticket to success and happiness. Better be careful or you'll find yourself back walking a beat in a stiffly starched uniform." Janeen poked Wes on the side of his chest and added, "You'll have to wear that shiny, gold badge right here."

"No way, that's where I wear my big, red, heart that says 'I love Janeen, even if she is hoodwinked by Temple Carrollton.'" Wes laughed and held her hand over his heart as he whispered, "I'm going to get you to forget the Preacher of the Day. Come closer....closer....closer."

Chapter 9

Ramblin' Randy

Eve was already communing with her computer when Wes called out a cheerful good morning. He leaned into the office where the intern was inputting information and asked, "Are you ready for the Randall Lee treasure hunt?"

"You bet. I was beginning to think I was going to have to take my break before you even got here. Good afternoon, Detective."

Wes glanced at his watch. It was exactly six minutes before eight. He thought he was early and this youngster was chiding him about his tardiness.

Wes smiled, accepting her little joke, "Better watch your smart mouth, missy. Remember you want to stay on the good side of us experienced officers so you have the best thesis in history. Surely you wouldn't want us to send you to traffic instead of homicide."

"Please, please, not that! I promise to respect both your expertise and your age."

"Oh, oh. You are looking for trouble, Little Miss Eve. Enough of all this small talk. Let's get to the big Kinko box. I brought you a doughnut. Still hot." Wes enjoyed kidding around with Eve just as he did with his son. Since they were both about the same age, he often thought of them together as 'the kids.' It was fun having Eve in Homicide almost daily since Jason did not often get home.

Eve followed Wes into his office. He put the bag of doughnuts and two containers of coffee on the filing cabinet. Then placed the box on his cluttered desk. When he looked inside, he was again reminded how little some people ever had in life. Of course in this case it was more a contrast, what little this man had after he had so much.

As he turned to get his first doughnut, Wes said, "OK. It's your case. Start looking at the contents and tell me what you conclude about the victim or even about why he might have been killed."

Eve gingerly reached into the items that had been dropped into the box. She wondered if Randy had placed them there before he was shot or if one of the staff at the Union Mission loaded the box after the news of his murder. She did not know if it made a difference to looking for clues, but she just would have liked to know. She began looking at each thing trying to figure out what Detective Wesley might see. She wanted to appear that she knew about investigation. She wanted to know if there were clues to finding the murderer. Each goal was important to her.

She left the few pieces of clothing in the box and put the smaller items on the desk: reading glasses, photo of a family, a thin, worn wallet with $32 in it, several paperback books, half full bottle of aspirin, a hair brush, an empty pack of cigarettes, a brittle paper folded into a small square that appeared to be a bookmark for the Bible with many loose pages.

"There we are, Wes. The remains of an entire life. Don't you wonder what remains he left with other people too? Those remains might not even fit into a box."

"What do you mean?"

"Oh, like what his actions did to the lives of other people. How about these kids in this photograph? How about other people's lives that he entered and exited? Those kinds of remains," Eve responded thoughtfully.

"Those are interesting thoughts. Sometimes they can be clues to why a murder occurs. Probably if we knew all those answers, we would be much closer to arresting someone. Now, what do you see in these possessions?"

The room was silent. The lack of conversation seemed to create a cold atmosphere. There was nothing about the Homicide offices that ever seemed warm and friendly. From the peeling paint to the broken blinds, the message was one of indifference.

Wes watched Eve as she carefully examined one piece of evidence after another. He was pleased to note that she took her time, appeared to be giving each article serious consideration. Neither felt a need to fill in the silence with unnecessary chatter. He truly believed that Eve could be a good detective. She was methodical and paid attention to details.

Eve felt inside the cigarette pack and extracted a hundred dollar bill that was wedged between the layers of the wrapping. She raised her eyebrows and looked at Wes. "A little rainy day money? Since he was an alcoholic and probably a drug addict, I wonder how he was able to keep that. I wonder how long he had it there. Everything here looks like it's been with him for many years."

"Often, Eve, people who have had wealth feel they must always have cash to touch. If they have to spend it, they will find another way, usually steal it or hit up someone he knows who can give him money. As for this hundred dollars, obviously no one looked closely enough at the cigarettes."

The detective nodded his head for her to continue. He hoped his remarks did not detour her thought processes. He waited. Eve opened the Bible, took out the small square of folded paper and gently opened it. There was one fold that was almost worn through on the crease and two severed folds that had not held up over time. She laid the four separate parts on the desk. Some words on them were completely worn off, a few letters were readable. The paper probably had been soaked from time to time so there were traces of the damage of mildew. Under any other circumstances, a person finding this bit of old paper would have thrown it away. Wes and Eve looked at it more closely.

"Whatever this was a part of, it must have been important to him. It looks like it is very old. I'm not sure, but I think it's that parchment style paper. From the tear lines, it was probably once a part of something larger. Just fell to pieces over the years.

It would be interesting to know what was this important to a man who couldn't even do the right thing for his own family. Wes, would you hand me your magnifying glass? We can look at what's left of the printing."

She bent over the four small pieces and said slowly, "I think this was his name. I can see a small l and a capital L Hmm, this looks like an e. Could be the end of Randall and then Lee. On this other piece, I can see ix, maybe lu and a then all blank. Here's oys and nothing. Everything else is rubbed off through what looks like years of handling and folding." Eve turned each square over to look closely, "This side looks like it has nothing on it. Maybe it never did. Whatever it is, it was only used on one side. We need Vanna White and the contestants of the "Wheel of Fortune" to help fill in the blanks."

Wes had just taken the magnifying glass in his hand when the telephone rang. Not wanting to be interrupted. He frowned but reached for the intruder.

"Wesley."

He waited and listened. Eve saw his eyes widen and then narrow. He nodded his head and continued to listen. Finally after what seemed forever to Eve, Wes said, "Yes, I'll be right on it. Detective LaCrosse and I will come immediately."

He replaced the receiver and looked at Eve, "Damn, this is hard to believe."

"Wes, what is it? What's happened?"

"Temple Carrollton has been found shot. The body was discovered a few minutes ago in his hotel room."

"Temple Carrollton? Isn't that the guy who's the preacher? Wasn't he at Georgia Tech last night?"

"Not only was he at Tech last night, but I was there to hear him. When I think of his following with the 3,000-strong audience, we will be lucky to not have some kind of demonstration by all those students. Son-of-a-bitch, I thought everyone loved him."

"Obviously somebody didn't love him," Eve added philosophically.

"Come on. Let's get Billy Joe and go down to the Marriott. They're trying to keep it quiet, but that isn't going to happen. Once the word gets out, this will make national news. Ramblin' Randy will have to wait."

Eve turned back to the box, replaced each of the items on top of the worn and faded clothing. She held the small paper square for a few seconds before folding it carefully and replacing it in the open page of the Bible. No time now to review the words but the intern noted to do that later. Might give some insight into the real Randall Robert E. Lee.

Chapter 10

Temple Carrollton

Wes parked his unmarked Taurus in the portico of the hotel located in the downtown area of Atlanta. The Marriott Marquis had been called the corporation's flagship. It was designed with the open atrium style that made many guests who entered take a moment to look up. They would wonder just how many floors were there. Glass elevators outlined in tiny lights were a focal point near the center of the atrium.

There was an odd mixture of urban modernism and suburban mall. Glass railings surrounded the mezzanine and escalators lead from the foyer to the open balcony area. Touches of the 1996 Olympics were still in place as a reminder of Atlanta's biggest and most televised sporting event. In contrast were many fresh, green trees covered with the tiny white lights that have become so popular during the holiday season. A selection of muted paintings of gardens, flowers and trees were hung on the few solid walls. The attempt had been made to bring the outdoors into this huge, cavernous opening that had become a signature of John Portman-designed buildings.

Billy Joe went over to the doorman. He quietly told him that they were Atlanta police investigating a call from the hotel. He wanted to be sure that the car was not disturbed, but also that no one overheard his message. He knew the image problem businesses had when Homicide detectives appeared on the scene. Both fact and fiction could fly through a facility in less time than a Georgia tornado. Until they knew the whole situation, they did not want the responsibility of a panicked public.

Wes and Eve joined Billy Joe LaCrosse as they entered the hotel. Surrounded by tourists, conventioneers and family groups;

the three of them easily blended in with the guests milling around the portico and the lobby. Wes had on a dark gray blazer with a lighter shade of gray slacks. Billy Joe was dressed much like Wes except he was all in conservative blue, while Eve wore a lightweight, beige sweater and a pair of tailored, forest green slacks. The threesome walked directly to the concierge desk. Wes asked to see the manager.

The woman behind the desk asked, "May I help you? It may be faster than waiting for Mr. Roswell."

"No, we will see Mr. Roswell. Tell him Wes Wesley and Billy Joe LaCrosse from the city of Atlanta are here in response to his call. Eve Zachary is our assistant."

The concierge hesitated long enough that Wes looked her directly in the eye, nodded his head and said, "Now."

Torn between her general instruction to bother the manager only as a last resort and this authoritative man, who was pushing her to break the rule, she hesitantly reached for the telephone. Wes took a step closer and said quietly, "Don't worry. You're not going to get into trouble. He knows we're coming."

It was only a minute until Canton Roswell joined them. He nervously shepherded them from the concierge station. He said nothing until they were away from everyone in the lobby, "Thank you for coming so quickly. I have several hysterical staff in my office and a few other people who want to know what happened on the 50th floor. That is our penthouse location. I guess we are in for a hard time, but I want to keep this as confidential as possible."

Wes felt a moment of sympathy for the manager. He just wanted to run a first rate hotel not be mixed up in a celebrity murder. "We understand your concern but once this becomes known, the hotel is going to be overrun by media. Temple Carrollton is a big name. Don't be surprised to find yourself on everybody's six o'clock news. Better get ready to handle the media and your guests at the same time. Now can we go to the crime site? Tell us what you know."

"Oh, no. Damn. I don't want to hear those words. I guess I'm still kidding myself that we can get through all of this without having to disrupt the hotel operations."

Billy Joe touched the man on the shoulder and said, "Sir, you might have another five minutes to enjoy fairy tales, because it's definite that the media already has the news by now. Sometimes we barely get to a murder scene before they do."

They had reached a service elevator and the door opened upon their arrival. A slight, dark complexioned woman in a maid's uniform with an identification pin that displayed the name Sarita exited the elevator. "Oh, Señor Roswell. It is awful. That wonderful man is dead. How could anyone shoot the messenger of God? They will go to hell. A terrible mistake has been made." She crossed herself and burst into tears.

"Sarita!" Canton Roswell said sharply, "This is a terrible thing, but I don't want any of you talking about this to anyone. We must protect our guests. Now get hold of yourself and see Mrs. Ching about a temporary assignment on another floor."

Sarita burst into tears again and scurried down the hallway away from the main lobby. Wes knew from experience that the story about Temple Carrollton was about to move from staff person to staff person like a wild fire jumping from tree to tree. The media folks would be looking for their 'experts on the scene' and Sarita would be ready with her tearful opinions. It happens every time.

The service elevator did not seem to rise with the same speed or grace that the spectacular lobby elevators did. Nothing behind the scenes of this flashy hotel appeared to have a similar façade. This was the everyday working area that kept the shiny public areas compelling and enticed visitors to come back again and again. Looking good was not the point in the operating arena. Efficiency and economy were the objectives.

Canton Roswell held the door for the others to follow. He walked directly toward a door halfway down the hallway. A police officer in a city uniform was standing with a paunchy man who easily could be identified as a hotel security man by his walked-over heels and cheap suit. They had been talking quietly until they saw the four people approaching. They waited for the foursome to reach them. The short, round man with a shiny forehead - matching the shine on his pants - that extended to the middle of his head, stepped forward.

"Billy Joe, son-of-a-bitch. It's good to see you."

"Dino, how did you get so lucky to pull this cushy job?" Billy Joe asked the security man, "I thought you'd retired to Florida."

"I did. Took a part time job with Marriott security in Miami and was promptly transferred to Atlanta. What's wrong with this picture? My wife was so pissed that she wouldn't even come back. She said, 'come visit now and then.' So I do." Dino laughed and then added, "Maybe this isn't going to be so cushy for a while. Are you ready to go see the preacher? I hear he was awesome last evening at Tech but that was his last show."

"Who told you that?" Wes asked.

"Temple Carrollton, himself."

"You actually talked to him last night?"

"Sure did. When he returned from the campus about eleven o'clock, I rode up in the elevator with him. Then walked him right here to this door. I guess I was almost the last person to see him alive."

"What do you mean 'almost'?"

"Shit, he gave me the impression that he was expecting someone later. You know he had a reputation of being a ladies man."

"Hmm, the messenger of God also fooled around with mortal women. Isn't that an interestin' combination," Billy Joe smiled broadly like he had learned about a serious flaw in the character of the good Reverend. "Do you know if that person ever appeared?"

Before Dino could respond, Wes asked, "Did he say he was expecting a woman? That might be very important to the investigation."

"No. I have to admit that I put his reputation together with the gleam in his eye when he said he was expecting a visitor. I'm glad you asked that. I wouldn't want to give you the wrong impression before we even begin our investigation."

"No harm done, Dino. We would've heard the rumors soon enough. It doesn't hurt to have a little extra information as we begin. It would be friggin' great to find a person of interest quickly before the whole damn country is lookin' at the Atlanta police and rememberin' how stupid we looked after the Olympic Park bombin'." Billy Joe clapped Dino on the shoulder to assure him that adding his opinion was OK.

"Let's take a look. Eve, if you want to stay out here, that's fine." Wes offered.

"No, I'll be all right, Detective Wesley. It's not my first murder scene."

The suite of rooms was plush. The sitting room did not seem to be disturbed. All the high quality furniture and well-chosen accessories were pristine. No sign of a struggle. No indication that anyone had been there at all. The room probably held important clues, but the lab techs at least wouldn't have to sift through piles of trash to get started.

Wes turned to the Atlanta officer, "Giles, better put up the yellow tape before the media arrives. I don't want those jokers making a mess for us. Dino, keep your attention everywhere. If Giles needs help, be sure you're right at his side. Mr. Roswell, don't touch anything. You don't want your fingerprints on the list of possible killers."

"I'll be careful. Might keep my hands in my pockets."

Wes and Billy Joe were the first to enter the huge bedroom. The bed was slightly rumpled as if someone had sat on it. There were a few pieces of clothing scattered on the bed and a damask covered chair. The room was decorated in cream and shades of taupe. Cream-colored walls and heavy draperies surrounded rich fabrics and ornately painted furniture. The view from the window wall was one of the highlights of staying in this expensive suite.

Atlanta sparkled in the sunlight. Buildings of glass clustered like Disney's Magic Kingdom surrounded by thousands of acres of trees not yet touched by greedy developers.

After the cursory glance out the wide expanse of windows, everyone's attention returned to the room. No furniture out of place, no papers on the night stands. A suitcase closed on the ivory-painted luggage rack. Not one spot noticeable on the thick carpet except where the body of Carrollton lay.

Wes was reminded of the graceful swoon that was part of the evangelist's act last evening. Temple Carrollton looked as carefully arranged in death as he did on stage. The detective had the strange thought that in the coliseum Carrollton was practicing for his final act; his violent death just a few hours later.

"Wes, it doesn't look like Reverend Carrollton struggled or was afraid of his killer. Nothin's out of place. The body looks like he was doin' nothin' unusual before bein' shot. The way this room appears at this point may support Dino's idea that there was a woman here and that she killed him. He was in the bedroom. He was gettin' undressed. His position looks like he wasn't even surprised. Maybe he knew her."

"You may be right, Billy Joe. If it was a woman. Could have been one of his dozens of pretty boy lieutenants. We'll look at all the evidence. We don't want to jump to conclusions. Then perhaps miss something. He could've been with one of his money and token collectors or even an overly impressed student who was at the coliseum. Let's…" Wes hesitated because there were voices speaking loudly from the doorway. "It sounds like our media buddies have arrived. Mr. Roswell said that he wouldn't want them lurking around the entrance. I guess it's best that they're up here. We can handle them, and they are out of sight.

"I hope that Officer Giles and Dino have kept them out of the suite. Eve, will you check it out. Remind them that we don't want anyone traipsing through these rooms?"

Eve nodded her head and was gone. She wondered if Wes sent her on this errand because he thought she was upset. She hadn't been disturbed seeing the body. Temple Carrollton may have been a deity to many people, but he was just the result of another shooting at this point. When you spend time in Homicide, it doesn't take long to become used to the results of the dark side of people.

Chapter 11

Danielle Jarvis Swain

Carefully retracing the track that they had made when they entered the room, Eve returned to the doorway of the hotel suite. She saw the security guard, Dino, and Jeffrey Giles on the other side of the crime scene tape. They were both talking and motioning to a group of people, some who carried cameras. Without even looking, Wes had been right that the media had arrived.

The only face that Eve recognized was Dani Swain, the very attractive anchorwoman for Channel 22. Billy Joe had told Eve that Dani often worked closely with Homicide on high profile cases. She liked to get live interviews and provocative background shots. It was no wonder that she was a favorite with the viewers. The combination of intelligence, sincerity, a beautiful copper-toned face, large, almost black, expressive eyes and a wardrobe that every woman coveted had moved Dani quickly from staff at a small California channel to being an acclaimed Cleveland anchor person. Then she took a huge leap toward success directly to Atlanta.

"Officer Giles, Detective Wesley wanted me to check out if everything is under control out here."

"Yes, ma'm. We're just fine. Tol' all of these guys that no one enters the suite. That means no one." He hardly got the last word out of his mouth before the assembled folks were all talking at once, each trying to be heard over the others.

"Will you confirm that Temple Carrollton has been murdered?"

"Is it true that he was brutally beaten and his screams were heard by many guests on this floor?"

Eve looked at Giles in amazement. Their eyes met and seemed to say, "Where do people get their information?" She thought, 'Thanks to the media, not only is there no privacy anymore, but there are wild and ridiculous stories reported as fact.'

Giles broke his stare and winked at Eve. Then he turned toward the questioners, "Detective Wesley is in charge here. When he's ready and has something to tell you, he will. Most of you know him to be fair with media so calm down, or I'll have the hallway cleared."

Dino Santos took a stance as if he were supporting everything Officer Giles was saying, but he stayed out of the confrontation. He knew, after more than 25 years on the force, that it was the Atlanta police who were heading up this case, not a hotel security guard. He would be available to help. He would only take action if he were told to do so. He realized he might be kept busy just trying to convince the other guests that he and his team could protect them. That was not an easy task when no one knew who had done this, how close they still they might be or what would be their next move. He made a note to talk to Canton Roswell about extra security until the killer was arrested.

Dino watched as Danielle Swain left the group and headed toward Eve. He knew that the anchorwoman had been popular in Atlanta since her first appearance on Channel WPTR. Her dusky complexion was an asset under the harsh lights that made her jet, black hair gleam and her face glow. He never noticed, but he had heard that she was never seen wearing black or white. Her multi-hued wardrobe had been called a trademark for Dani Swain.

Dino was aware that Dani and Eve were more than just pretty. They had an aura of confidence and professionalism that was part of their attractiveness. He liked women who were smart enough to be independent. He smiled to himself as he thought about his cute, little wife who said, "Don't forget to come back to visit. I'll keep your retirement home warm for your return." She was a great gal. He wouldn't want her to be clinging.

"Hi, I'm Dani Swain with Channel WPTR. I don't think we have met, but I assume you are new in Homicide."

"It's so nice to meet you, Ms. Swain. I'm Eve Zachary. Of course I know who you are. I'm in Homicide now. I'm a student intern. I'll be there only while I work on my thesis."

"Then I know who you are, too. Wes Wesley has mentioned you and the excellent research you are doing on technology in police work."

"That's what I'm doing, OK. Technology is going to make a big difference in investigations and evidence for court trials. If we had DNA before, many incarcerated people would not be in prison. Or visa-versa, of course." Eve hesitated and then put her hand to her face, "I'm sorry, I get excited over what I've already learned. I know it's just beginning. I didn't mean to bore you with my favorite subject."

"It isn't boring. Maybe we can talk about it some time, but right now I'm a bit preoccupied with this Temple Carrollton thing. He was so impressive and had such a huge following of students at his event last night. On the eleven o'clock news, we ran the story of that appearance. What a reception he got!"

"I think Detective Wesley was there. Don't you wonder why someone so popular and followed by legions would be shot? That's a real mystery."

Dani quickly saw a new angle to the Temple Carrollton murder, "That would probably make the best story of all. We might get that information after Wes arrests the killer. Maybe it was a fanatic. Maybe it was a mistake. You know, maybe the killer won't even know who he killed until he sees it on TV."

Eve's eyes twinkled, "Or reads it in the newspaper."

"Oh, don't wound me, Eve. We in television like to think that everyone gets their daily news-fix on television, preferably Channel 22."

The two young women laughed together and then noticed that Wes and Billy Joe had appeared at the door. They were talking to two men who were carrying the unmistakable crime scene kits. Spontaneously, the newsmen and women crowded into the hallway and started calling out questions, using Wes' name with hopes of getting his attention.

"Wes, over here. Gerard from the Journal."

"Detective Wesley," a female voice called, trying to sound breathless to get him to look her way.

Obviously it was not working. He did not even hesitate. He walked directly to Eve and said, "I want you to work closely with Billy Joe to look for anything that seems unusual or looks like a clue to what happened here and who might have been here. Billy Joe will call the shots, but I want you to be attentive about everything you see."

Eve was pleased that she was being recruited as a member of the team rather than just an observer. Not only was this an important case, but working for Homicide was like being an historian. Always looking for the reason of life and death. This was why she had chosen the study of technology as her thesis topic. It was new enough to allow for speculation and possibilities that had never before been available. Technology was already rewriting some historical scenarios.

"Yes, sir," she said to Wes, and added in Billy Joe's direction, "I'm ready when you are."

"Let's go. The scene looks so clean that I think it'll be hard to find many bits of information."

Eve smiled and nodded her head toward Dani signaling the end of their conversation.

Dani smiled and said to Eve, "See you again." She then turned to Wes, smiled broadly and asked, "What should I know about the background of Rev. Carrollton that I won't find on Google?"

"I'm sure you can get on your computer what we have now. We're going to need a lot more than what we have, which is mostly his own hype. Let me know if you find anything that would be helpful, Dani. I'll do the same. You've always been a good team member for us." Wes was speaking over his shoulder to his pretty friend. He threw her a wave of his hand and disappeared back into the hotel suite.

． ． ． ．

"While the tech guys are in the bedroom, let's start in the sittin' room. You've been at a murder scene before so just do your job. Talk to me whenever you want. Yell, if you can't get my attention," Billy Joe told Eve.

Both became involved in the concentration that it takes to ferret out the most minuscule clues. They were both quiet; absorbed in their own observations and notes. Wes' notes began to fill the pages of his small notebook. Billy Joe looked at his notes and realized most of them were comments about what was not there: Carpet appears to have very few footprints. No clothing or other personal items found beyond the victim's. No glasses or dishes; clean or dirty. Eve had found one cigarette butt in an otherwise clean ashtray.

"Billy Joe, do we know if Carrollton was a smoker?"

"Not now, but we will soon. We'll bag that butt and the ashtray that it's in. Sure are slim pickins' here."

They continued to search for items that just did not fit or could "talk" to them. About the time they felt they had seen everything there was to see, the other officers entered the room.

"If we didn't have a body, I'd say that nothing happened here. This appears to be the cleanest murder site I've ever seen," Clancy Jones, Crime Scene Technician, said looking at Billy Joe, "I think you and Wes are really gonna earn your big salaries on this one."

"Yeah, right. We get $4.35 more a month than you do, but we're always on 24/7. You sure have the easy life. Bet you haven't even been shot at this year."

"Billy Joe, you never are stumped for words or a quick reply. I don't know why I even think I can catch you unprepared."

"I just talk the truth. You know that. And, Clancy, are you talkin' the truth? This whole place is clean? Just like here in the sittin' room?"

"Looks like no one was ever here except the good reverend himself. But, we'll take a look at what little we have. We might find a clue to get you and Wes off your fancy asses. Give us a call. We'll be in touch if we find anything."

Jones and his silent partner opened the door to the hallway. It was as if they flipped the audio button. Voices of all kinds sprang up with questions and other words to get attention. The media was predictable. Police often wondered why they hadn't figured out that the police were predictable too. They were not giving away any information that might hamper their investigation and that was the kind of information that the media wanted.

"Sounds like we hit the jackpot with one lowly cigarette butt." Eve said hopefully to Billy Joe. "I'd like to see if we could check out the DNA on this. Maybe we'd find someone who we're never going to find otherwise."

"You might be right, suga', but I think you're really bonkers on technology. We have a lot of good investigative work that is successful. We can't shove it all aside to let your new fangled ideas take over."

"Oh, Detective LaCrosse, I didn't mean to imply that at all. It's just knowing that if this is Carrollton's or somebody else's might be helpful. I guess the first thing to determine is if he smoked."

"Sure, but right now, let's go see what Wes is findin' in the bedroom." Billy Joe had closed the discussion and immediately returned his attention to his job.

Wes was hunkered down beside the body. The medical folks had not yet arrived so he was careful not to touch Temple Carrollton. The small gun shot wound in the chest hardly looked like enough to kill a man, especially a man who announced he could control other people's lives.

He looked up when Billy Joe entered the room. "Not much here. How about the sitting room?"

"Negative. One cigarette butt that Eve wants to do a DNA test on. I think then we'll see it all recorded in her thesis. Surely she'll get an A+ if she can include the Case of the Mysterious Reverend."

"Ha! If I'm going to do that, you two better get moving very fast to solve the case. Who did kill the Mysterious Reverend?" Eve had just followed Detective LaCrosse into the room.

"Who knows? Not us. Actually we're lookin' to you, Eve. You must have a suspect by now that technology is gonna prove your point," Billy Joe kidded their intern.

"No problem, guys. I'm just going to keep it to myself so you aren't out of a job. Or maybe I'll leak my ideas to Dani Swain and become a star of her next news show."

Eve liked the banter that was always circulating among the Homicide detectives. Even though this was a career that always was focused on the low side of life, the group often used biting humor to get them through the rough times. Sometimes the kidding turned out to be close to the truth.

"Wes, I think we have an ungrateful little pain in the ass here. Maybe we should cast her out. Let's get ourselves a new intern who understands the word "appreciation.""

Wes started to laugh and looked at Eve expecting to see a look of astonishment. Maybe even a little fear that Billy Joe was serious. Instead he found an expression of amusement and even confidence. She wasn't at all upset by his partner's bluster.

"I don't think Eve is the least bit intimidated so let's just keep her. It's easier than teaching a new intern," Wes hesitated a moment and then added, "Eve, are you willing to put up with Billy Joe's warped sense of humor to have the opportunity to work with the best Homicide detectives in the history of Atlanta?"

"Wow, that sounds like a great trade off, Detective Wesley. I'll be really looking forward to meeting the detectives you're talking about."

"Uh, oh. Billy Joe, you're right. We've gotten ourselves a pain in the ass. But, OK. You're our pain in the ass, and we'll keep you. Now why don't you two check out the closet and the bathroom? We have a hell-uv-a lot to do. We want to be ready for the big media push. They're going to love this one."

Chapter 12

Matthew Christian

Loud voices erupted in the hallway just as Wes, Billy Joe and Eve were about to leave the sitting room. Wes responded immediately, "If that noise is coming from those media animals, I'm having the whole damn crew thrown out. That'll give them something to put in their news. Let's go out there and do it ourselves."

Wes strode to the door just as Jeffrey Giles was propelled backwards into the room. A young man followed him. From the body language of the two men, it was easy to see that the policeman had been pushed. In one fluid movement, Giles turned around and reached for his baton as he called out loudly and with authority, "As a police officer, I'm telling you again to stop where you are!"

"Get out of my fucking way. I want to know what has happened here! Where is Temple?" The man raised his hands again. He started toward Giles who struck out with his baton and hit the man's wrists. There was a crack that sang out the sound of bone breaking. The man screamed and grabbed his one wrist. He stopped and Giles said quietly, "That's the way. Just stop."

If everything hadn't happened so fast, Billy Joe and Wes would have laughed. Jeffrey Giles had followed the rules of the Police Escalation Ladder perfectly: announce who you are, handle the problem without putting yourself in danger, keep control of the situation, and stay cool. Too bad the perpetrator now had a broken wrist, but that's the chance you take when you attack an officer.

"You bastard! I think you broke my wrist. I'm going to sue the city. Don't you know who you're dealing with? I'm one of

Temple Carrollton's closest associates. He'll never let this action go unpunished. Now get the hell out of here."

"Temple Carrollton isn't going to do anything for you. Now who are you? What're you doing here?" Wes took the command of the situation.

"If that's what you think, bozo, you'll find out how much power he has. Wait till he calls your mayor. Maybe even your governor."

"Calm down. This is going to hit you hard. Carrollton is dead."

The young man forgot his damaged wrist. He looked stricken. His eyes widened. He made no sound, but his mouth moved as if he were saying, "dead?" He looked directly at Wes with an expression of horror and disbelief. The detective took him by the arm, guided him to a chair and said very quietly, "I'm sorry, but it's true."

"But, b-b-but I just saw him here last night. We talked about how well the show went at Georgia Tech. He was flying high from his success. No way could he have had a heart attack or something." The clear, blue eyes filled with tears that began to slide down his cheeks, "He was always so careful about what he ate, what he drank. How can this be? He was supposed to live forever."

"Well, even the good reverend wasn't gonna to do that," Billy Joe interjected.

Wes was watching the young man intently. He realized that this was the person who passed the basket to him last night in the coliseum and had said, "See you around." He had looked so polished then and so broken now. Where did he fit into the life and death of his employer?

"What do you mean? You saw him here last night?"

"As we often did, I stopped by after the show and talked a little while. Not long, because he said he had a visitor coming. Probably a woman. He always had young women captivated. He called them his li'l darlins. He had everything: looks, money, personality, fame, a following that surpassed any man of God. Billy Graham would have been thrilled to have so many worshipers." He put his head down and covered his face with his hands. He began to sob as if his world was gone.

When the young man moved his hands to his face, he winced. He looked at his wrist as if the pain was a surprise. He touched the place that was already swollen and had a very red mark. He gulped several times, and looked at Officer Giles, "I never attacked anyone before."

"Don't worry. I forgot already. We'll get you to a doc as soon as Detective Wesley says it's OK."

"Detective? What do you mean, detective?"

"Son, Temple Carrollton didn't have a heart attack. He was shot."

"Shot? This is all wrong. Are you sure you know who Temple is? Are you sure this is the right person?"

"There is no confusion who was killed. Now, who are you?"

The lieutenant of the Reverend Carrollton looked blankly at Wes. It seemed that he was trying to decide who he was. Wes wondered if the kid was really losing it. Everyone waited patiently. Not a sound was heard. Even the media folks in the hallway were quiet. Wes took a step closer to the man and repeated, "Who are you, son?"

"Oh, yes, I'm sorry. I'm Matthew Christian. I am, was, one of the servants of the great Temple Carrollton, the most perfect man since Jesus. Reverend Carrollton has saved thousands of people by shepherding their lives on the right path, giving them the wisdom to be successful in everything they do, and turning their misdirected lives to the golden reward. This is not only the end of the earthly life of our true leader; this will be a loss for multitudes he will never touch."

Billy Joe looked over Matthew's head at Wes and rolled his big eyes. Wes raised his eyebrows. He knew Billy Joe was thinking the same thoughts as he was: Matthew Christian was not yet thinking clearly. He seemed to be reciting the party line that he obviously had offered many times. He would have liked to send him off to Grady Hospital Emergency, but he first wanted to get some more answers from him.

"Matthew, who might have wanted to kill Reverend Carrollton? Who were his enemies? Was he ever threatened by anyone at his shows?"

Matthew looked through Wes as if he wasn't there. His eyes were riveted on the door into the bedroom. He must have been trying to reach the person from whom he was obviously directed.

"Matthew, do you hear me? Was Carrollton ever threatened?"

"Of course not! He was a saint. He was the salvation of all who followed him. He gave his life...he gave his life today...for them. He had...he had no enemies. The question is preposterous!"

"Matthew, let's get real here," Billy Joe said loudly, "No one goes through life without pissin' off some folks. Even bad drivin' creates ragin' lunatics these days. Your boss was in the limelight constantly. He musta got to a few loony tunes from time to time. What about the ones who heard the promise of success and then didn't get it? Wouldn't they feel like he jerked their chain?"

"No! They all knew that as long as they helped to keep Temple healthy and happy with their gifts, the good in their lives was because of his protection. They knew. They believed. They believed because it's true. The bad came from another aura. Never from Temple!

Wes decided that he would try another tactic, "Matthew, was the reverend married? Have a family?"

If Wes hadn't been looking closely at the handsome young man, he might have missed the narrowing of his eyes. As he waited for the response, he wondered what had caused the hesitation.

"No, Temple wasn't married. He said that his life was dedicated to everyone. He didn't have time just for his own gratification. His marriage was to his followers."

"How did that relate to what you refer to as his li'l darlins?" Billy Joe asked; heavy sarcasm in his voice.

Eve wondered if Wes and Billy Joe were playing the good cop bad cop game. She had a few questions of her own but was not going to break up the rhythm that her colleagues had begun. She was feeling some of the same reactions as Billy Joe, but she would wait to see if he continued on this line of questioning.

For the first time since entering the room, Matthew's face softened and a small smile grew, "Well, he was a vital, attractive, youthful man. He had his needs, which he took care of, shall we say, after hours? None of these ladies stayed in his life for long. They learned that his dedication was to the Lord."

"Now, that could be interestin'. What about one of them takin' revenge for bein' left behind? Did he have a girl in every city?" Billy Joe asked.

"Well, the answer to the first part of that question is, no. They worship their leader. They know being close to Temple is being as close to God as they may ever be. Being one of his 'friends' may give them the successes they want. They give to his well being."

Wes was getting tired of this chapter and verse about the pay-as-you-go success concept. He felt there was something to be learned, but he decided that questioning Matthew Christian down at the Homicide offices might be more effective. The half man-half boy may become more realistic in that atmosphere.

"Matthew, I'm going to have Officer Giles take you over to the hospital. It's only a few blocks from here. Let him know where we can contact you and also give him the names of some people we should speak with. Include Carrollton's manager and administrative staff. We need to get a picture of what has happened here. We need to find a killer...for you, your organization and for the city of Atlanta. I don't think I need to say this, but don't leave town and don't disappear. That is the message we'll be giving to the others from your group who are here in the hotel."

"When can we have the, the, the…When can we have Temple to make arrangements?"

"Not till after the medical examiner releases the body."

"Detective, Temple should not have to be subjected to the scrutiny of a medical examiner. He must be treated with dignity and respect as he always has been. I want to ask you to let us have him now. Surely if you know he was shot, you know how he died."

Wes looked at Matthew Christian with both pity and amazement. He had observed the reactions of many people under these circumstances. He thought he could predict how most would respond, but this young man was quite different. One moment he was lost in grief, the next he seemed to be programmed and following a script. He certainly was not in touch with reality.

"Matthew, this is not your choice. A person has been murdered. There is the law. That's how we do the job whether we're dealing with a preacher or a homeless person. You go with Officer Giles. We'll talk later. As soon as we can release the body, you'll be informed."

Giles reached out to provide a steadying hand to Carrollton's follower. He expected a rebuff, but it did not happen. Matthew accepted the gesture of comfort and easily stood up. His head was bowed. His thick, blond hair glimmered in the overhead light. Jeffrey Giles looked back at Wes, nodded his head as if to say, "I have it under control," and went out to maneuver through the crowd in the hallway. Just as they reached the door, Wes said, "Matthew, did Temple Carrollton smoke?"

"No. I don't think he ever smoked."

Chapter 13

Billy Joe LaCrosse

Wes and Billy Joe were ready to call it a day. They had both pursued telephone tips from people who were sure they had seen Temple Carrollton's murderer. None of them proved to be of much help. Between those calls, Wes had called Matthew Christian at his hotel room and made an appointment with him for the next morning. The young man seemed much calmer than when he last saw him. Wes wondered if they gave him a stiff pain killer at Grady Hospital Emergency.

Billy Joe stretched his long arms out making an arc from above his head back down to the desk. It felt good. "Well, Wes, what's your take on this killin'? Every track I go down, nothin' makes sense. Why can't it just be a simple bang, bang you're dead and who the fuck cares? You know, like the homeless guy at the Union Mission. In some ways, he was already gone before he was shot."

"Right. We have no serious clues yet on Carrollton. Actually, even though maybe no one cares, there are no clues on the Ramblin' Randy killing either. It's funny but both of these murderers seem to live charmed lives. Although the setting was different, the area around the body at the Union Mission was as clean of clues as the hotel suite," Wes hesitated and then added, "Billy Joe, I think we need to get some other guys working on our team on this Carrollton case. There's going to be too much media interest. It will create political interest. The mayor's not going to want to look like he doesn't have the safest and sanest city in the U S of A."

"Yeah, you're right about that, buddy, but we ain't goin' to be able to give him a sane city. Be real! This is Atlanta. Hmmm, did you purposely forget to mention that our Dilbert bitch would love to have a reason to skewer our heads on the most visible flagpole in town? And, too much negative screechin' from the media always makes her go ballistic. They might catch her with her uniform unpressed. Not to worry, I can e-mail her before I leave. What're a couple minutes when it's our heads that could be sittin' above Old Glory?"

Wes could always count on Billy Joe doing his share on any case and keeping up his part of the word 'partner.' He once said to Wes, "Hey, man, if I hadn't met Cleo first and you looked just like Halle Berry, this would have been a match made in heaven. As it is, you're one damn fine detective and that's enough for me."

"Good timing. It's late enough now that we won't have to worry about the major seeing the request until tomorrow. Ole Dagmar won't have a chance to spoil our evening with a tirade on departmental costs.

"In addition, we need to split up tomorrow. You do some serious, as they say 'in depth,' interviewing of family and former associates of Ramblin' and I'll hit the Carrollton entourage. Eve's doing some background on the good reverend. I think I can get her to do some on Lee. After tomorrow we'll have a few other guys for our A Number One Team," Wes was organizing the day for both of them

"OK we'll meet with them later, but first the schedule for tomorrow is doughnuts, coffee and then I'll head to Buckhead, the former home of one fuckin' dead drunk. What a damn waste. Have everythin' and throw it away for booze. He was smart enough to get through Georgia Tech. Then he goes dumb? What's wrong with this picture?"

"We need to find out what's wrong with that picture. Then we might know who popped him. Right now I'm going to forget about this for a couple of hours and see if I can find someone who wants to have dinner with me."

"You got yourself a date. In fact, two. Eve was askin' whether

I wanted to go to the Roman Lily for a bite. We'll all go. She's a friend of the main cook and says the food's great. Let's do it. We never socialize. Work, work work. That's us," Billy Joe liked the idea of spending some casual time with two of his favorite people. His pleasant thought was interrupted.

"Wesley! Telephone." Two words shouted from another office. He knew they probably weren't ending their workday quite yet.

The detective retraced his steps with Billy Joe right behind him. As partners, they didn't leave the other one stuck and just walk away. They had been together too long for that.

"Shit! Why now? Call me on Atlanta time not my time."

Wes took the call back in his office. Billy Joe sat down on the extra chair and watched.

"Wesley."

"Hey, it's Dani. I just hung up from a strange call. Might just be a crank, but I wanted you to know. I don't know why they picked me."

"Why not pick you, sweetheart? You're the eyes and ears of the world. Everyone knows it. Now, what's up?"

"It's funny. I'm not even sure if it was a man or a woman, but my gut reaction is a woman. Anyway, the person said if I was reporting on the Carrollton case, he wasn't all 'Godliness and cleanliness.' That part is a direct quote. The voice added, 'He wont no saint.' Another quote. That was weird enough but then just as I thought the person was going to hang up, they said, 'Lee wont neither.'"

"Sounds like a real redneck with those words unless the person was trying to disguise not only the voice, but also the type of person he was. Or she was, as you're surmising. Were you able to get a trace on the call?"

"Are you kidding? I'm a TV anchor, not one of your suspicious Homicide detectives. Besides it came directly through the switchboard and lasted about 30 seconds. I hung up and called you right away. Do you think this can help?"

"Don't know. I'll talk to Billy Joe about it and add it to our other information. We were just leaving for the day so let us think about it and call you tomorrow. Maybe you can get more definite about it being a man or a woman."

"I'll think about it, but I feel they were trying to be anonymous. Talk to you tomorrow. Have a great evening."

"That's the plan. Thanks, Dani. You're a good lady."

Wes repeated the conversation to his partner. They made a couple of guesses based on practically nothing, but agreed that this might lead to something worthwhile. Maybe another call will come. Maybe something will come up in the interviews that will make it fit together. Maybe.... Enough! Other than Billy Joe's quick email, it was time to enjoy a good dinner.

Wes walked to his car thinking about how well Billy Joe and he worked together. Not only was his partner dependable in a tough situation, he had a good sense of humor, which had often gotten them through tough times. His big, imposing body commanded respect from the raunchiest characters on the street even when there was a cynical smile across his face. Some of his adversaries would find it hard to believe that big, dark Detective LaCrosse was also a good father and a gentle husband.

Wes got into his car and opened his cell phone. He looked at his watch and hoped that it wasn't too late to catch Janeen. A few hours with his favorite woman, and he would initiate a meltdown from this crazy day.

"President's office. Janeen speaking."

"All right! What more could a man ask for? A dedicated employee that stays late enough to receive phone calls way after quitting time. A dedicated employee who might be willing to spend a few hours later with a very worn out and frustrated civil employee."

Wes heard a short giggle before Janeen responded, "You got yourself a deal."

Wes quickly told her that he had agreed to have dinner with Billy Joe and Eve as a gesture of camaraderie. Then he would be at her front door before his meal had time to digest.

"Great. I will leave the porch light on."

"I can find your place and you under any conditions. I'll be there soon."

．　．　．　．

Eve, Billy Joe and Wes arrived at the Roman Lily within minutes of each other. Wes looked around the neighborhood and remembered the term used by developers: transition. A short, almost-antique strip of shops housed an ice cream parlor, a second, third or fourth hand shop and the small restaurant. Directly across the street was a multi-acre construction project. It looked like the bulldozers had been commanded to remove any signs of living matter. Then the contractors were commanded to fill up the red clay wasteland with as many buildings as possible. Eve saw Wes examining the area. She told him that this would soon be the site of hundreds of luxury apartments.

"Luxury apartments? In an area that looks like it's barely hanging on to an existence? It's amazing what developers see that translates into money for them."

"It's going to be money for Roman Lily too. Think of all the hungry people who will be right across the street. Come on. We're some hungry people too."

"Hey, Raymond, it's me. I brought my partners from Homicide. You've heard me talk about Wes and Billy Joe."

"Hey, Eve. What're you doing here so early? We never look for you until closing time." A burley, red-bearded man walked toward them from back of the high counter. It almost hid the vast cooking area with a canopy of huge pots and pans hanging from the ceiling.

"Pull up a table and get ready to address some serious eating." Raymond turned away. Wes was surprised to see a tattoo that covered the back of his neck. His next thought was Ouch! This man probably doesn't mind going to the dentist either.

Wes, Eve and Billy Joe chose a table at one of the big picture windows that faced away from the developer's demolition. The window was surrounded by an eclectic collection of 'art' from pinball machines up on end, to very attractive tiles and a painting that Eve said was rescued from a trash can. Opposite the window on the high counter was painted many art deco faces of men that all looked like they were smelling the same odd thing. There was a very old, small memento case on the counter that had an assorted collection inside including an antique doll dressed for a party, a light bulb and lots of marbles. Certainly the décor had earned the word "fun."

Raymond came over to the table carrying two small plates, "Here, Eve and partners, try these new Bits and Pieces. On the house; because Eve is one of our nicest and most faithful customers. I think you'll love the Asian Shrimp. It's your kind of appetizer, Eve. The humus and pita chips you can all dip into while you are deciding on what's for dinner."

Eve thanked him warmly and gave him a hug around his neck. He patted her on her head and sauntered back to his hot stoves.

The three friends talked, ate and enjoyed being together away from the dreariness of City Hall East or a crime site. They talked some about their cases, but they also relaxed and argued politics and the ruination of Atlanta by the developers.

"Soon there will be no green space or quiet place to just take a walk without fear of bein' run down by the next SUV," Billy Joe said turning and looking again at the project across the street.

"But, Billy Joe, you forget that those developers are some of the anointed in this city. From politicians to the thousands of retail businesses, they see that more construction equates to more money for themselves and other business people. It will never stop until there is no more space anywhere," Eve said sadly.

Wes chimed in, "You know how I love to debate, but I'm ready to head out. We have too many other challenges coming up tomorrow like who shot two of those prominent men here in Atlanta."

Wes felt a twinge of guilt. Although what he said was true, he wanted to get back in his car and go see Janeen. She had been so patient with his ridiculous schedule. However, her good-natured personality may begin to wear thin. That would not fit into his recently made long-term plans.

Wes and Billy Joe split the bill and started toward the door. Eve hung back and said, "I'll hang around a while until Raymond is ready to leave. Then he can follow me home. He has told me often that he prefers to know I'm safely in my own place. Thanks for asking me for dinner."

The two detectives walked to the parking lot with its crumbling surface. Billy Joe turned to Wes and said, "Maybe those successful developers and contractors will spread some of their profit on this side of the street. I guess we'll never have to make those big economic decisions, but at least we haven't killed a tree yet for our own profit. I think I'll join the Green Party."

Wes smiled at Billy Joe's fast-track thoughts. He draped his arm around Billy Joe's shoulder and said, "Going to dinner was a wonderful idea. We should do it again soon. We need to put some fun in our too dreary days."

"Right! Now, I'm headed home. See the kids before they go to bed. Don't be late in the mornin'. We gonna be detectives first class. We gonna make Major Dilbert proud of our black and white asses." Billy Joe was still talking when he got into his purple Taurus.

Chapter 14

Janeen Newman Carson

Wes got into his car and opened his cell phone.

"Janeen speaking."

"There she is. A beautiful voice on my very own cell phone with a magnificent body attached to the voice. Just wanted you to know I was on my way to fill you in on all the Saga of APD Today."

"You can tell me all about the day that probably wore you out. I'll tell you about the 35 alumni who called to talk about Randall Lee. You would think everyone who ever passed through the campus knew that man. How about if we meet at my place? Then act like city folk and walk to the Caribou for coffee? I don't want to dress."

"I like the part about not dressing but would you wait until after coffee? Then I can help you take care of that part."

"Hmmph, you're too willing. I thought you might be harder to get. Now, get your mind on your driving. I'll see you on my porch soon."

"Yes, ma'm. I'll be there."

· · · ·

Wes pulled into a parking spot in front of Janeen's townhouse. The porch light was on. He noted that the little covered stoop had a large concrete pot on one side that held a funny swirl of some evergreen tree. He never could figure out why humans wanted to change the way that nature intended for things to grow. Straight up and down was OK for his esthetic eye. He looked at the other porches and noticed for the first time that there was something different on each one: a pale blue wrought iron love seat, a wreath of colorful silk flowers, a small table that held (really!)

a faux waterfall. He thought, I guess this is Midtown chic. They would frown at my porch: a bicycle, a green plastic chair from the drug store and bag of fertilizer that I was going to put on my trees but never did. Oh, well, maybe next weekend. I guess I'm not chic.

He stood on the little porch, rang the bell and took another sideways glance at the poor, tortured, twisted tree. He glanced at a few cars driving by. Wes wondered if any of those drivers carried a clue that would help him find the murderers of his two most recent cases.

Damn. Forget your day. Leave your baggage and your victim's baggage on Homicide's doorstep, not this one. Come on, Janeen. Give me something really beautiful to think about.

It was only a few seconds and the door seemed to pop open. She smiled when she saw him there. He reached into her stuffed mailbox as he passed it. Wes bowed slightly, handed her the pile of envelopes and said, "As a civil servant, I'm doubling as your mailman."

Janeen took two steps toward him and planted a kiss on his cheek, "I have never seen my mailman before. I think I should've been coming home earlier in the day. Maybe I should have written myself a few letters to be sure there was mail to deliver."

"Sounds like incentive enough to change my career. Maybe I'll try the postal system. If I do it right away, I won't have to find the killers of Carrollton or Lee. So let's go celebrate my future afternoon trysts with the resident who has a weird little tree on her porch."

"Afternoon trysts? I didn't know that was a part of the job description of a mailman. I have been spending too much time in the office!"

Janeen laughed so hard at the image of Wes being a postman that her eyes welled up. Wes grabbed her around the neck and pulled her head tightly against his shoulder. It felt so good to be silly; laughing together as they walked to one of Atlanta's popular coffee shops. Wes actually felt the stress melting from his head down through his body, perhaps leaving big, dark spots on the sidewalk behind them. He knew Janeen was good for him. She had changed his life in many ways in just a few months.

He was reminded of the old saying his dad used to tell him: It's not that you stop laughing when you get old, but rather that you get old because you stop laughing. His dad had a comment for every situation; sometimes two or three. He missed having his father to talk to at the end of the day when the old gentleman would tell him stories about what he and Jason had done.

Wally Wesley had taken in Wes and his infant son with no questions asked after Wes' wife announced that she preferred being an artist rather than a mother.

Wes had made an agreement with Linda Sue. For $10,000 she would not have an abortion. He would take their child and exit from her life immediately. He and his dad had raised Jason together for more than nineteen years with no regrets. Grandfather, father and son - or father, son and grandson - lived comfortably together. Jason learned important lessons from two generations. At times Wes would be his dad and at other times his grandfather would be his dad. Jason was happy to have them both even when his friends at school once asked why his "dad" had so many wrinkles and he answered defiantly, "Because all Wesley men hate to iron!"

Janeen had been watching Wes as they sat down in two overstuffed chairs by the fireplace, which was one of the charms of Caribou coffee shops. "Something's amusing you. You have a wistful look on your face."

"Wistful? I've been called a lot of things, but I don't think wistful was on that list until this minute," Wes' eyes twinkled, "I was thinking of my dad and how he enjoyed life. He was always there for me when I needed a hand or some conversation. He was a good man, Janeen. I wish you had known him."

"I think I know him a little through you. You're probably a lot like him, Wes. You're a good man too. You just haven't had enough time to give yourself much thought. With all the rough edges of life that you see every day, you've managed to be kind and positive about those around you. I think your dad did a fine job of raising you and helping to raise Jason. What a beautiful legacy Walter Wesley gave to his family."

The words brought Wes back to the present; to his cases that day, "Which reminds me, tell me about the calls you received about Ramblin' Randy. There's a man whose legacy wasn't what it could've been."

"From the different men whom I talked to today, it would seem that Randall Lee left more of a drama than a legacy. It's always interesting how opinions of people can be so diverse, especially when there's a hint of media coverage in the air. They hope they'll be quoted and enjoy instant celebrity.

"Yuk! America's love affair with telling all to the public is unbelievable. One alum who said he'd been in business at one time with Randy said he was a great family man and just adored his kids. He thinks that it was heavy social drinking that started his demise, his word exactly. He said that even after the Lee's divorce, he tried to keep up the same relationship with the children but when he repeatedly turned up at the door stumbling drunk or stoned, his ex put a stop to that. That was about three years ago."

Janeen watched as two women headed in their direction looking for a place near the cheery fire. She waited until they changed direction. What she was repeating was only for Wes, as a detective. Maybe it would help find the murderer.

In a moment, he broke the silence "What other opinions did you hear? You said they were different."

"It was interesting that the next one came almost on top of that one. It was venomous. This man must have hated Mr. Lee. He said he wasn't surprised that someone shot him. He was so egotistical and insulting to anyone he felt was not his equal. He said when they were at Tech, Lee and his friends were always talking about a secret group. You know, like they were special because they belonged and outsiders never would be considered.

He said they made it sound like it was only for a few; something even more prestigious than a fraternity. He said that the members were from several colleges, even the University of Georgia and Emory. They were all carefully chosen. The alumnus added that after a few months of that kind of boasting, he just stayed away from Lee.

"The other calls were mixed. Obviously, Lee had more than one persona. If drinking or drugs were his downfall, it doesn't explain the remarks of the former students who disliked him with a passion. Maybe something happened in his life which changed his character. What do you know about him, Wes?"

"Not as much as you do, but at the Union Mission they said he was never a problem except to himself. I would guess from what I know at this point that something did happen in his life, and that it was something for which he felt guilty. He carried a Bible and written over and over in the book was: 'I'm sorry, I'm sorry.' My first thought was that it was for leaving his family and making a mess of his business, but after what you have heard, maybe it was even when he was in college. Why would anyone be so hateful just because he was in some secret group?"

"Hmmm, if you don't get that one, maybe you aren't a Southern boy? Randy Lee could have thought he was a big deal if he was a skinhead or in the KKK. There are many groups based on hating others just because they can. It's a free country, you know," Janeen sat quietly and was about to apologize for lecturing when Wes slowly nodded his head.

"Point made. I guess I was being naïve, but from your observation you have given us another direction to investigate. Did Ramblin' Randy make enemies over a long period of time? Someone may have wanted to do this for years and patiently waited for the opportunity when his death would hardly be noticed. Ms. Carson, with your inquisitive mind, you just might make a fine detective if you get tired of serving the presidents of Georgia Tech."

Wes reached over and kissed her lightly on the tip of her nose,

"It's so nice to have you and your ideas close enough to touch. Let's finish our coffee and continue our discussion back at your place because the ideas I'm having now will get us thrown out of this place."

Chapter 15

Honeybun

The evening was balmy and Honeybun decided to take a walk. She wanted to think about her plan. How it would work out. Walking always helped her organize her thoughts. She realized that there were some loose ends, but she was sure that most plans for the rest of one's life didn't run smoothly.

She remembered how emphatically she had been told in her first year of high school by her physical education teacher that nothing of value was accomplished without a written plan. Of course, she was referring to exercise and working out, but she was right about all parts of life. Write it down and then follow it. Cross off the parts that are already done and do the next action. Yes, that's what she had remembered: it was called My Action Plan for Life.

She was barely a teenager when she knew exactly what she wanted to do. She just didn't know how she was going to do it. That had come much later. This was her gift to herself and to her sisters.

When her plan had begun, she had only memories of her two sisters who had been just a few years older than she. That thought was like a stab in her heart. The three of them had had good times together. They helped each other with schoolwork, played in the scrubby yard and often would hang out and just talk. Honeybun, Sunshine and Sweetie. Sure, they had real names but they never used them when they were together. They liked Honeybun, Sunshine and Sweetie.

One day Sunshine locked herself in the bathroom, sat on the cold floor and slashed her wrists. She was just seventeen years old. After that, Honeybun had begun reading about teenage suicides. She had never noticed before that it was not unusual. She remembered one article in the Atlanta Journal and Constitution that had a graph showing the statistics of teenager suicides. Well, her sister wasn't a statistic. She was her wonderful, alive sister, but only alive for a few years. No one even guessed that this could happen. Her mother didn't appear to notice that Sunshine was going to destroy herself. She never tried to find out why her oldest daughter had turned quiet. People didn't talk about depression so much then. It was more than ten years ago.

Sometimes, the three sisters would talk about feelings and lack of feelings. That was what bothered Sunshine the most. She said she never seemed to care about anything. She had compared herself to a flat line on an EKG as if she already saw herself dead. Honeybun couldn't remember when Sunshine had stopped laughing or even smiling, but she did notice that her big sister would either be silent or would cry when men visited their mother.

Honeybun and Sweetie stood at Sunshine's grave and hugged and cried. Sweetie said between deep gulps of air, "Sunshine didn't care about life. I care a lot, but most days I'm too tired to give it a thought. I feel like I always need more sleep."

Her younger sister looked at Sweetie's tear-stained face and for the first time noticed a strange pallor to her cheeks. She thought her eyes looked more deeply set in her face.

Sweetie died a year after Sunshine. Honeybun heard the word AIDS, but it meant nothing to her. Without medical care, Sweetie just quietly wasted away. At the end she was very sick. She never even tried to get out of bed for two weeks. One morning before Honeybun was leaving for school, she went into her sister's room to say goodbye. It was too late. Sweetie was dead holding her little panda bear named Hope. Unfortunately, there was no hope for her sister. Honeybun kissed her sister and whispered, "Good bye. I will never forget you. I'll never forget Sunshine. I know you're together. That's good."

Honeybun had stood in front of two graves: Sunshine's and Sweetie's. Kneeling between two small wooden crosses on which she had taped little school photos at the crossed pieces, she promised she would have a life plan for all of them. Now Honeybun thought that had been a big promise for a little girl. She remembered wondering how she could do it. And then she found the My Friends book.

Chapter 16

Wes T. Wesley

Wes, Billy Joe and Eve all arrived at the Homicide offices at the same time. Billy Joe had a wide smile on his face. His eyes sparkled. "Hey, Wes, ole buddy, you're lookin' good this mornin'. Musta been quite a pajama party? Put color in your cheeks, but left your suit all wrinkled."

Eve was wide-eyed, "Pajama party? Must be a code for something because I suspect that Detective Wesley doesn't even wear pajamas. Do you want to tell us both what Billy Joe is trying to say?"

"No, I would not like to do that. Why don't we talk about your visit to your mom? How's she doing, Eve?"

"Humph, funny, Detective. You were able to change the subject to something that I don't want to talk about either. It's too sad. You might say when you get to assisted living; you have a rather bizarre pajama party every day. So, Billy Joe, how can we annoy you now that we're on a roll?"

"Shit, I'm sorry I started this. Let's get to our doughnuts and talk about what we're each gonna do for the two big cases that're ruinin' our day. You mighta missed the news last evenin', but Dani Swain played up the Georgia Tech tie with the two murders. She said she wasn't suggestin' any relationship, but just that it's a busy week for the campus."

"I talked to Dani last evening. We were talking about research on the Carrollton shooting. She didn't mention Lee. Actually, I didn't think anyone much cared about his murder," Eve added.

Wes put his bags on the desk beside the others. Then he raised the cup to his mouth. He savored the hot, strong coffee and said; "There's always someone interested in another person's death. No one dies suddenly without leaving a mess somewhere. Lee's kids'll have to face cruel remarks from other kids. His widow will relive parts of her life that she's tried to forget, people whose lives he touched might cry or cheer, but he'll have left some lasting imprints on them. Maybe if we knew how to fill in some of those categories, we'd have our killer."

"I think what you're saying is that how he affected other lives would fill a larger box than the one we have with his material possessions." Eve looked at Wes for a moment. She saw a man who seemed to have strong convictions about humankind. She wondered if he gave this same scrutiny to all of his cases. She also wondered if these thoughts were helpful or harmful to him solving Homicide cases. If he became too embroiled in the psychology, would he miss the pragmatic clues that led to each person of interest? Would he want a guilty person to go free because of what he learned about the person who was killed? She asked, "Does it matter to your job whether he was good or evil?"

"Not to the job, Eve. We're given a responsibility that we must do. We do that every day. But, can it matter to me, Wes Wesley? You're damn right it matters. Some people don't deserve to live, but that's not my friggin' call. If we shot every damn child abuser on sight, would I care? No. Would I do the job and bring in the perp who just might get off on a technicality? Yes."

"This is too heavy for mornin'. On another subject, no response yet from the major except that Brassy responded to my e-mail sayin' she'd call. He added that money was tight. We might have to decide between a raise and more help. He's such a wuss. She probably won't call 'till she's checked out coverin' her ass as to whether this is her idea or ours. So let's get on the road. We can be finished before that woman has made those calls and combs her hair.

"I made an appointment with the ex Mrs. Ramblin' and she gave me the name of Mr. Ramblin's business partner. She wants me to come after she takes the kids to school so I'm gonna be in the middle of our shitty Atlanta peak time traffic. I just did it once to get here, now I can do it again to get there."

Wes nodded his head, "Yeah, but you didn't start in the beautiful, high rent district of Buckhead, so you get to see the traffic on the other side of town this time. Whatever Randy did, he did leave her enough money to live in the best part of town. I wonder if she still gets income from the business."

"I'll be interested in whether there was insurance on Lee. Maybe we can make this easy and have it be a murder of a homeless guy for his millions. Nope, no one would believe that one." Billy Joe was up and on his way. "Take care now!" He threw a big smile to Wes and Eve as he headed for his car.

"OK. We're left with the Carrollton case. Did you get a chance to do any research last evening? I know you didn't have much time, but I'm always hopeful."

Eve reached for her file folder. "I got lots of stuff. Some of it is what I called Dani about. Their channel has a good library of previous stories. That preacher man has the best PR. We could do a full 300-page book on Temple Carrollton, but what appears to have of value wouldn't fill a page. His 'Before Fame' life was either completely dull or very carefully hidden. I have to admit, Wes, I'm not sure which, but I would subscribe to carefully hidden."

They began reviewing the sheets of information that Eve had printed off the computer and some that had been faxed by Dani Swain. They went back about ten years. Photographs of Carrollton revealed a gradual change in style from a shaggy-haired, young, robust innocent to the sophisticated, carefully coifed and manicured actor who appeared on stage just two nights ago. Many of the stories had the same theme: Here was an almost heavenly being who could lead you to success and fortune. The implication was, "Didn't I do this for myself? Why not for you?"

Wes looked for the information that would fill in his life before he became an evangelist. There simply was none. The most personal note was that he had lived in Atlanta before he began his lucrative career. The detective noted that even that short mention was in a piece from an Atlanta Constitution feature that ran three days before his debut at the Robbie Cremins Coliseum. Wes was enough of a cynic to believe that this was added simply to get the attention of more Atlantans to boost more ticket sales. Where were those touching warm and fuzzy stories about this darling boy as he grew up, or where were the confessions of the brutal life he experienced at the hands of his family? Most "entertainers" told those stories to reel in their gullible fans.

"As you say, lots written about the good reverend, but I'm sure that all of it has been manufactured by his public relations team. If there was one fact here that said 'I am a real person,' I missed it. You did a fantastic job. Eve, but I think we're going to have to find our clues from his associates. And that's what should happen in about ten minutes. Matthew Christian is due here for a little chat."

"Sorry I'm going to miss that beautiful face, but I'm expected in class in thirty minutes. Maybe I'll skip class just to get another look at him."

"I had no idea that your head was so easily turned, young lady. I believe you were supposed to be smitten by his boss. You got the drill wrong."

"I don't think so. His boss held no appeal for me. I hate nasty phonies."

"Phony I can see but why do you say nasty? Every one of these articles talks about him being as caring and loving as Jesus."

"Oh, well," Eve hesitated as if thinking about her choice of words, "I say 'nasty' because of what he's done to so many innocent and naïve young people. He's altered or destroyed lives with his rhetoric and action. Why, imagine, Wes, how many people simply sent him money, then waited for everything to be right because he said it would be? Many of them might have lost their chances for their own successful lives because of him. And what abut the stories about the girls who were deceived by him? Those who followed him as his 'li'l darlins.' He did all of these things with no conscience whatsoever. He lived his life for ego and money. I call that 'nasty.'"

"OK. I see where you're coming from. We've already discussed that the murderer could have been one of his dumped lady friends. You may have just added another few hundred or thousand suspects: anyone who didn't get what they wanted after they paid and paid and paid for the Carrollton success formula."

They both heard voices across the tops of the office cubicles. Wes looked up and saw it was Matthew Christian. Although he was close enough to greet him, he made no move to get up. He always gave a new visitor to the Homicide offices time to be alone, take in the ugly, starkness of the stained and unraveling cheap carpets, dirty windows and overheard conversations that would definitely add a few new expressions to one's vocabulary. It all created an understanding that the visitor wasn't here for a pleasant chat or a business meeting. This was Homicide. By just being here, he might be in big trouble. If the visitor began to sweat or develop a nervous cough, Wes felt the wait was successful.

Chapter 17

Matthew Christian

Eve jumped up from her seat as she looked at her watch. "Oh no, I'm going to be late to class. As always, I'm a few steps behind."

"I would argue that point, missy. You're often way ahead of your elders here in Homicide. Get going. I'll see you later today."

Eve slowed down as she came to where Matthew Christian was standing, "Good morning, Mr. Christian, Detective Wesley is just about ready to see you."

"Thank you, Ms. ---. I'm sorry, I don't remember your name. I do remember seeing you last night, and I have to apologize for my behavior. It was a very painful time." The young man lowered his eyes, touched his bandaged arm.

"I'm Eve Zachary. No problem. You were probably in shock. I know you'll remember a lot more this morning than you did last evening," Eve gave Wes a quick wink "I'm out of here. See you later."

Eve smiled at both men as she almost sprinted across the foyer.

"She seems like a nice person. What's she doing here?" Christian asked..

Wes decided not to take issue with the question, "She's an intern. She's going for her degree in criminal justice. Of course, some people think that's an oxymoron, criminal and justice." He stood, looked the follower of the late Temple Carrollton in the eye and said, "Let's talk in the interrogation room." He wanted to see the reaction to the word interrogation.

The detective was not disappointed. As with most people, the word alone began to make the young man nervous. If he had used the word interview, the reaction would have been different. He knew if he had said 'Let's meet in the conference room,' there would be no negative reaction. He could safely bet his salary on these reactions. "It's the room there in the corner." Wes pointed to a scarred and unpainted door that was standing half closed.

He pushed the door open with just enough force that it slammed against the wall. Matthew seemed to tense up when he heard the loud bang, but still stepped into the room. His first reaction was that it was too awful to be a carefully planned environment. The windowless room looked barren Unmatched, cast off chairs sat askew as if they didn't want to get anywhere near to the beat up table, which was dirty, worn, abused and left to deteriorate. The uncovered light bulbs in the ceiling emphasized the dingy, gray walls and the cobwebs in every corner. It was a desolate area that anyone would have wanted to escape from as soon as possible.

"Sit over there, Matt. The chair at the corner of the table."

Matthew followed Wes' direction. The detective sat in another straight backed, metal chair directly in front of him. Matthew wanted to move back so he wasn't so close to the other man, but was sure that would not be a good idea. He sat stiffly, trying to relax. The torn, plastic seat cover felt lumpy under his butt. He tried to rearrange his position to feel more comfortable, but every inch of the cushion seemed to have either a bump or a hole in it.

"Well, Matt, how's the wrist? It looks like they took good care of you at Grady. Were you able to sleep last night?"

"Not hardly. How could I sleep?" Matthew answered, an edge to his voice.

Wes didn't blame him for being upset. It had been a bad night. "I get your point. So let's move on with our conversation so you can get some rest you didn't get last night. Matt, exactly what is your role with the Carrollton organization?"

Christian hesitated just long enough for Wes to note that there was something important in this rather innocuous question.

"I'm one of the Carrollton Lieutenants. There are twenty of us. We're there to do whatever has to be done. Our most visible job you saw at the event. We're there to be the contacts with the followers and as security if someone goes postal."

"And, of course, you're there to collect the money and mementos from all of the followers."

"Yes, that's part of our job." Matt agreed in a low voice, "It's important that the followers demonstrate their belief in Temple's power. Giving to help maintain that power is critical to their success."

"Knock off the commercials, Christian. You're not going to convert me. Besides, it's too late."

"I speak the truth, Detective Wesley. It's been shown to work for thousands of people. And it's not too late. Someone else will come forward to fill the place of Temple Carrollton. He may not be in the same league yet, but he can grow into it if he follows the teachings of our first leader.

"Oh, really? Who might this new leader be? Are you a candidate?"

Matthew Christian sat a little straighter in his chair, looked at Wes with a slight smile on his lips and said with a dignity that may have never been seen in the mean, ugly, interrogation room, "I am probably too young, but I am certainly a consideration."

Wes was shocked. He thought of the Temple Carrollton he saw just two nights ago on the stage speaking and swooning for his audience. He looked at Matthew Christian. He saw a fresh-faced, handsome youngster. He wondered why he would think he was a contender. Wes asked, "How many are being considered?"

"Actually three of us. Now, I guess the group will have to decide. Before last night it would have been Temple's decision. He had no reason yet to choose his successor. Obviously, he thought he had time to watch us and name his choice. We all knew that one of us would lead some day."

"Oh, and what would the other two do when that happens?"

"Continue to serve the beliefs of our great, spiritual

commander."

"Might that be a problem for those two? Won't they want to be the top dog? Would it have bothered any of you to have learned that perhaps Carrollton had already made a decision?"

"It would not have bothered us if it had been Temple's decision. We all knew that he made the right decisions. We serve because we want to. Because we believe that he's all that he says he is."

Wes continued to be surprised. He had heard about complete dedication to a person or to a cause. Sure, he knew about Waco and the Kool Aid episode in Guyana, but he'd never actually met anyone with the unwavering loyalty that was being shown here.

"Why are there only three candidates for the position of leader?"

Matthew waited. He obviously was carefully considering his response. His sparkling blue eyes seemed to fill with tears. His face showed no emotion, but behind that face Wes believed there was a multitude of thoughts that Christian was trying to sort. The room was quiet while Wes waited for an answer.

"There are three of us," Matthew replied in a low voice. "Temple Carrollton had three sons. I am the middle son."

The quiet of the room became more pronounced. "You were going to find this with your investigation so I might as well tell you now. I must ask you, beg you, to not make this information public. If the media gets hold of this, they will go crazy. They will make it sordid and dirty. That's as far from the truth as can be. Our father was a pure and good man. Nothing he did was wrong. He had been preparing all his life for this calling. He knew that it was important to have his own children, but he was too dedicated to his mission to spend his time establishing a family, a home.

"He's always taken care of our mothers. The only thing he asks from them is to never tell about their relationship to him. For that, he divides a million dollars and gives them each a third every year. He has raised us, educated us, loved us and set us on the right path. He said that we prove that he is good and that he was smiled upon by the Creator. If he had made wrong decisions in his life, he would not have his three perfect sons and his followers by the thousands."

Wes listened intently to the confessions of Matthew Christian. It was a story just made for media frenzy. He wouldn't offer the information to the public. He wouldn't add to the new attitude that everything should be for public consumption. There are many events in each life that should be kept private. He believed that. He tried to protect information. It was part of the case. Not a part of the six o'clock news. He wasn't sure if this would somehow become media fodder, but it wouldn't come from him.

He thought of his own life. Would he want the media to decide how to handle that he had made a $10,000 deal with his own wife to not have an abortion? No, absolutely not! That was his business. Did he, Wes Wesley, want to be responsible for messing up the lives of the women who were taken in and taken care of by Temple Carrollton? Did he want three young men to become the subject of the talk show hosts who glory in smut and dysfunctional people? No, absolutely not!

Wes wasn't sure yet how this new information fit into their investigation, if it added more suspects to his file. It was for Homicide to figure it out, not the damn media and scandal-seeking public. If Temple had mentioned to the boys that he had decided who would be the 'anointed,' did the other two retaliate before it became known? Did one of the mothers want more than her third? When it didn't happen, got angry and killed him? Didn't sound like a plausible scenario, but stranger things had happened. After all, it was apparent that whoever shot the man was someone he was comfortable with and did not fear. The hotel suite was too clean, too neat.

"Matt, the media won't learn your secret from Atlanta Homicide, but when they start digging, it's amazing what they find. Your information becomes part of our files. It will be treated with the same privacy as our other cases. Let's get to a few more details. Where were you when Carrollton was killed?"

"I was in the hotel, as were most of us. We had all returned from Georgia Tech and were doing our usual job of counting the contributions of the night. I guess that's going to give most of us an alibi. We were all together in one of our suites."

"I'll need a list of who all was there, what relationship each has to the organization and to Temple Carrollton. Which reminds me, what are the names of your brothers? I will want to talk to each of them too."

"I'll get a list for you. No problem. My brothers are Mark Bible and Luke Altar. I guess that sounds weird or hokey, but our father felt that it was important that our names relate directly to the things that he believed were sacred. It may be silly to others, but that's how we got Matthew, Mark and Luke and Christian, Bible and Altar. Maybe he was planning on a John but we haven't met him," he smiled as if to say, but there could be one. "And as you see, the last names he chose all related to his spirituality. He used to call us his lucky charms. It looks like we weren't lucky enough to help him."

Tears were welling up in his eyes again. "I know people like you think my father was a fake, but we knew him best. We think he was another promised son on earth. He's always lived his life with no regrets. The idea that someone wanted to kill him is positively unthinkable." He lowered his head and a few tears dropped into his lap. His shoulders began to shake. He covered his face with his free hand and sobbed.

His words came haltingly, but were easily understood, "I guess the reality of it all is beginning to finally get to me. My father, my spiritual leader, is gone. Since I don't know my mother well, it's like becoming an orphan and a lost soul in one night."

Wes thought of his son, Jason. He and Matt were close to the same age. He thought of his own father. How much he missed him. He reached over and laid his hand on the young man's shoulder.

"That's enough for today. If you can get that list to me,

Detective LaCrosse and I'll begin interviewing the others. We need to get as full a picture of what we're facing. There are no suspects so far."

Chapter 18

Billy Joe LaCrosse

Billy Joe was slowly driving through the beautiful streets leading to Mrs. Ramblin' Randy's home. Long, undulating, green lawns reached flawlessly from the street to outrageously large homes. They were framed by impressive plantings and trees. They could all be movie sets built just yesterday. They lacked any sign of human occupancy. Surely, Billy Joe thought, someone must spend many hours keeping these lawns in perfect condition. So why isn't someone working on the grass and shrubs? Where were a couple of toddlers enjoying the early morning sunshine with their mother? Oops, he corrected quickly, maybe with their nanny. He noticed no shouts nor boom box music coming from houses or cars that passed him.

He smiled and thought of the contrast of his own neighborhood. It had tiny lawns fronting neat small houses that were close enough to speak to your neighbor from your front porch. That's how he grew up and that's the way he believed a neighborhood should be. Even though there were times when it got too noisy, like on a Saturday night, he liked hearing the music and the voices of his friends and people who lived on his street. He admired the beautiful neighborhood that he was seeing but did not covet the lack of activity and life. He laughed and wondered how the residents of Valley Road would react to his car jacked up on the curb while he worked on the motor; his two kids bringing him the radio and a beer to make brownie points with their dad. He decided that everyone lived the way that was comfortable for him or her and this is how it should be.

He found the Lee home, turned into the property and swooped up a graceful driveway. As he followed the carefully trimmed asphalt ribbon, he almost felt like he was gliding toward a fantasy world. Yes, old Ramblin' Randy did not scrimp on taking care of his family. Looks like he did something right. So why did his life go so wrong?

Billy Joe stood at the front door looking down toward the street. The view was almost as attractive as from the other direction. He waited for the ringing of the bell to be answered. With maybe 15,000 square feet of house, he imagined it could take a few minutes for someone to appear. Hmmm, he thought, 15,000 square feet would allow him to put more than ten of his homes inside these walls.

The door opened. Billy Joe saw whom he assumed to be Mrs. Lee. She could be described as just plain vanilla – about five feet five inches tall weighing close to one hundred and thirty pounds with medium brown hair and medium hazel eyes. Her slacks and lightweight shirt were both shades of beige to emphasize Billy Joe's opinion of just plain vanilla.

"Detective LaCrosse? I'm Deanna Lee. Won't you come in? I think we will sit on the sun porch where we can enjoy the morning sunshine."

"Wherever you're comfortable, ma'm. We just need a place where we have some privacy." He would often add, 'and where it's quiet,' but he knew there was no reason to say that. He felt like he was in church just before the preacher started to pray.

"There's no one here but you and I. As I mentioned yesterday, I've taken the children to school and the morning is set aside to talk to you. Then my sister, Lana, is coming to pick me up for lunch. She said I'll need a break after your visit, but I really think she wants to get all the up-to-date news. Lana certainly had not been one of Randy's fans. She always says that only a stupid s-o-b would trade an outstanding living to become the living dead." Deanna Lee shook her head, "My sister doesn't sweeten her thoughts when she puts them into words. But she's my sister. Now, if I believe what I see in the movies, I guess I should ask for identification."

"Here's my ID. It's a good habit to be sure you know who you're invitin' into your house. Strange things can happen."

Deanna Lee glanced at the badge. Although she didn't think it was necessary. She recognized his deep, bass voice from the telephone. He was here precisely at the time he said he would be. There was no question in her mind who he was. He did look exactly like what an Atlanta Homicide detective should look like: big, strong, tough, with a slight frown on his face that broadcasts no nonsense from Detective LaCrosse.

"Would you like coffee? I have some that's still hot."

"No, ma'm. I had a doughnut and coffee while I inched along in traffic."

Deanna laughed, "That is too funny. While I was waiting for you, I had this thought: I guess I should offer the man doughnuts and coffee. That's what they're always consuming on TV."

"Where do you think they get their ideas for those programs? Right from us. We do it. They pretend to do it. I have a partner who's stopped at Krispy Kreme every workday for more than 15 years. He says that it was part of his Police Academy examination to name all the doughnut shops in Atlanta."

"Actually, I think my eight year old son could do that, too, Detective LaCrosse. While most kids ask to go to McDonald's, he has always wanted a Krispy Kreme. Maybe I'll suggest he should consider police work since he already has the answer for part of the test." Deanna Lee smiled broadly. Billy Joe realized that her personal confidence even in a stressful situation raised her quickly above just-plain-vanilla. She was warm and friendly.

"You mentioned children. Is your son the oldest?"

"Yes, Andy is in third grade and his sister, Leeanna, is just a year behind him. They can be a challenge. Do you have a family, detective?"

"Yes, ma'm. We also have a boy and a girl. They really are good kids but they definitely belong to this generation with their rap music and crazy fads. Could I ask you about your late husband? I don't want to take too much of your time."

"Of course, that is why you're here. First, may I ask whether you have any suspects? Randy had become both an enigma and a stranger to us, so we have no notion who might have wanted him a-a dead or why. There were days when I thought I wanted him dead, but now that it has happened, I really feel rather sad."

Billy Joe mumbled, "Yes, I understand," then he added, "We have no suspects at this point. The murder scene is still being investigated."

LaCrosse saw Deanna Lee wince at the words murder scene. That was not surprising. They were talking about the man she had once loved, was the father of her children and who left her financially safe.

"Your husband had been stayin' at The Union Mission for only a short time before the shootin' occurred. The staff there said he had no obvious enemies but that he frequently disappeared for days or weeks or months at a time. When he returned, he was usually a mess both physically and emotionally. Mrs. Lee, can you give me any reason for what changed his life so drastically?"

"Detective LaCrosse, I have asked myself that question a thousand times and have come up with no reasonable answer. It's not that I don't come up with answers, but then I reject them. It had to be more than my guesses for a man to give up absolutely everything he had – family, business, respect, love, friends, status in the city, financial security, material possessions, good health and on and on. Could he have ever known how his decisions would hurt his children who adored him and he seemed to adore them? What could turn him into another person? It has to be more than simply that he started to drink too much. We could've worked that out together. The four of us could've done it. I know we could've. It had to be something else."

Billy Joe had heard these statements from many people in similar situations. Often they were fooling themselves, but he felt that Deanna Lee really had no idea what had ruined the life she thought she had. If the shooting was not simply a random act, he felt that if he could find some tie to the mystery of Randy's fall, he might have the first clue as to why he was killed.

"The one memory that I have never been able to explain or was never able to get Randy to talk about is that he obviously had a deep, overpowering sense of guilt. What about I don't know. I always felt if I knew, I would understand why my husband walked away and became a stranger to us all."

"I understand that he did come back here from time to time. Maybe to see how you and the kids were?"

"I see you've already been doing some investigating. You're correct. He did come back. Once he stayed for almost a week. Then just went out one afternoon and didn't return. After that, he would turn up at any time of the day or night, always unannounced and always drunk out of his mind. He just wanted to talk. Then he would take off. Once I found him in a heap right there on the front porch beside the League of Women Voters public relations committee chairman. Another time, he arrived just as Leeanna was leaving for a dance class with her friends. That was the last straw. He wasn't really trying to reclaim his life. He was a terrible embarrassment! He was destroying our piece of mind each time we seemed to get ourselves under control."

Billy Joe listened carefully. Deanna paused and was silent for more than a minute. He spoke up to keep her talking. "I understand your husband was a real estate developer. What has happened to the business?"

"I'm now involved in the business that Randy and Emory Mercer started. My experience as a manager in retail, fit into the corporate need for a business manager. That's what I've been doing for almost three years now. It works and I feel that I'm contributing. I've become close to Emory. We have been seeing each other for a about a year. He's as baffled as I am about Randy's life. One thing we both have agreed on is that something was seriously bothering him before he started drinking."

"Let's talk about what you may know about this guilt feelin'. We've seen his Bible and in it was written; I'm sorry many times."

"His Bible?" Deanna exclaimed, "Randy never had much interest in religion. I don't think he even looked at the Bible when he lived here. That's quite a surprise for me but the 'I'm sorry' is no surprise at all. There would be times when Randy had troubled sleep. I would hear him mumbling those same words. Of course, when things started falling apart for us, I assumed that it was another woman. I tried to talk to him about that possibility. He always assured me that there was no one since we were married. He would laugh and say that he had done all his wicked living before he met me. Now I was his only vice. I thought it was rather cute at one time. It doesn't seem so cute anymore. Could that reference to his wicked living really mean something instead of just being a cute response?"

"We believe that one of the tracks we want to investigate is his life even before he walked out. We want to talk to his business partner."

She looked surprised for just a moment and then said, "I guess that makes sense. I can assure you that Emory has no kind words for his ex-partner. Randy left him in the middle of some very important negotiations and took enough money that Emory had to talk to another venture capitalist about a short-term loan to complete the deal to buy a huge tract of ground adjacent to Peachtree Industrial Park. Since this cost the company big money, Emory blames it all on Randy taking off at a critical time. He also has never forgiven Randy for taking his share of the profits. I don't agree with his strong feelings, because I don't think Randy was rational at that time. It was his business too. Much of that money he would have considered his. He didn't touch our savings or investments, which if you notice how we live amounted to a considerable amount for the children and me."

"Emory and I just don't talk about what happened with Randy. Maybe that's why we aren't married. I don't think I could live with a person whom I have to skirt around certain important subjects. Oh, detective, I think I've gotten way off track. I didn't mean to present our lives like some soap opera. I just wanted you to know that I don't think Emory will be friendly to your questions."

"Don't worry about what you've said. The more we know the better chance we have to findin' the perpetrator. That's what we want to do."

"I guess it's hard for me. I only knew Randy as a thoughtful person and Emory is just not that type. He's all hard-ball business."

"Was there anythin' special that your husband kept secret? An address book? A locked box? A hidden cache behind a picture?"

Deanna Lee smiled broadly. Her eyes twinkled. She looked completely relaxed for the first time since LaCrosse had arrived. "Now you sound just like a detective. Like: let's get to the mystery. I hope you don't mind that I'm amused. Perhaps, I should be more serious, but I find in the past few years, the only thing that has kept me sane is being able to put the problems aside from time to time."

"No problem, Mrs. Lee. I welcome anythin' that can help you relax. You have a better chance to remember what might be the clue to solvin' our case if you aren't all stressed out because I'm here. So, no secrets?"

"Funny, but there was only one item that I could say popped into my mind when you asked those questions. Randy had a certificate that he seemed to cherish. At first I didn't pay much attention to it because it hung in his office and I really didn't spend much time there. I asked him about it only once. He laughed. Said it was a fraternity commendation from an old group that he used to belong to.

"Randy said everyone in the group had one as a link to one another. That was good enough for me. I personally think fraternities are rather juvenile. But the strange part of this story is that several months later, it could have even been a year, when I was in the office to pick up Randy for a dinner, I noticed the certificate was gone. I didn't mention it because I thought that maybe he'd decided it was juvenile too. It really was no big deal, but you reminded me of it with your questions."

Billy Joe was reminded of something too. He wanted to go back to the office and take another look in the box of Ramblin' Randy's possessions. He felt maybe that strange little, old, worn piece of parchment might be what was left of the cherished certificate. Could this be a clue leading to who wanted Randall Robert E. Lee dead? Was that possible after all this time?

Chapter 19

Wes T. Wesley

Wes had spent the afternoon interviewing many of the young attractive Carrollton 'lieutenants.' His notebook was full of words and quotes from the individuals, but he could have used carbon paper for the first interview. Not only did they physically resemble one another, they sang from the same hymnal or spoke from the same script. Obviously, the evangelist had an image that he wanted portrayed. The young men had predictably handsome features, hair that ranged from brown to blond, cut just long enough that if there was a curl or two, they would lay on his neck above their collars. All had clear innocent blue or gray eyes, were physically fit, and with no exception, flashed bright, dazzling smiles with perfectly, strait teeth. Each one looked like a well-mannered and intelligent person that folks would easily welcome into their homes and wallets. Wes thought there is much to be said for the All-American look. It exudes confidence.

Mark Bible and Luke Altar fit into the mold. Although they had three different mothers, the resemblance to Matthew was striking. The three men were close. They each had told exactly the same story of their lives and the arrangements with their mothers. They had all lived briefly as youngsters in their mother's homes then moved with their dad when each turned ten. They immediately began a training program controlled personally by Carrollton. The school-like direction had lasted until his death just a day ago. They were being carefully groomed by Temple Carrollton to take his place and run the organization. The only change in his plans is that the time had come many years before he had foreseen.

Mark Bible was the oldest by two years. He had an air about

him that said to Wes, 'I will be the one to follow in my father's ministry.' He had referred numerous times that he was the eldest and he was closer to his dad in many ways. When Wes asked what ways, Mark's response verified his attitude, "I was my father's intimate confidante. We discussed many critical issues like finances, new recruits and where were our best markets. Matthew and Luke knew this is how it had always been and would always be, because I was the firstborn. My brothers would be important to our organization, but I was being groomed for my father's place. Of course, the magnificent man felt he had years to do this until someone ended the most precious life since Jesus."

Luke Altar, the youngest by only five months, was more like Matthew than Mark. He said that whoever followed in their father's steps would be the right person. Even from the grave; Temple Carrollton would help make this appointment. Luke said, "Our father had many conversations with Mr. Warrenton about how each of us was learning and developing the best attitude to be the leader. We weren't supposed to know this, but we would listen to their rather quiet conversations when we were traveling in our bus. They agreed that whoever it was to be would lead strongly and would have the support of his two brothers. So the choice will be controlled by my father's opinions."

Wes was struck by the complete devotion that Matthew and Luke voiced. He thought about other cases where brainwashing about religion and cults overpowered any sense of reason. Leaders in these groups could get the followers to do both simple and complex deeds. They could instruct them to commit criminal and immoral acts. He wondered if this blind dedication had anything to do with the murder of Temple Carrollton. He made a note in his book and underlined it.

Although Wes was ready to call it a day, he still had two appointments. He looked at his watch and was surprised to see that it was almost six o'clock. He had done his job but was closing up his interviews feeling that he had accomplished very little. Matthew had told the truth that many of the Carrollton lieutenants had been together well into the early morning hours counting their loot. They had chosen one of the suites on another floor from their leader to do this. No one saw or heard anything unusual until all hell broke loose and the news of the shooting had reached them. They had quickly put away the money and the pile of mementos in the hotel-provided safes and ran to the penthouse floor. It seemed that since that time they had been preoccupied with two tasks: talking about what had happened and talking about what was going to happen next.

Wes had learned that there were two managers, finance and business, who traveled with the group. They made most of the tactical decisions and mapped the strategies. They gave the orders to the many lieutenants who reacted much like slaves. "Yes, sir. Yes, sir." Wes was envious. These guys were better to have around than even the Homicide interns who often were willing gofers but certainly never slaves. He smiled at his thought and decided that Carrollton was better with his training program than he and the other detectives were.

Wes sipped a Coke while he waited for the business manager. He was comfortable in the small conference area that the Marriott manager had provided for him. Canton Roswell was making everything as easy as possible for Wes in the hopes that he would soon complete the investigation, announce a suspect and disappear from their premises immediately. Already the hotel had lost almost twenty five percent of its guests. To give the manager credit for acting under a difficult situation, he had been gracious and even helped the fleeing population find rooms at other downtown hotels. He was smart enough to know that his assistance and understanding attitude would be a plus in the future. After the hysteria, the same people would come again and then talk about how they were there when Temple Carrollton was murdered in cold blood. Oh, yes, it will become part of the lore of the hotel. Of course that would only work if the murderer was found soon. So, Mr. Roswell had provided lunch, telephone service, a computer, staff who dropped in quietly to refill supplies, and a conference room tucked out of the sight of most guests and tourists. His graciousness was good business.

Wes was lost in thought when a deep, male voice said, "Detective Wesley, I'm Thomson Warrenton. I'm the business manager for Carrollton Enterprises."

Thomson Warrenton stood with his hand extended. Wes rose and shook it, "Thank you for meeting with me, Mr. Warrenton."

He was surprised at the strength in the man's hand. Warrenton must not have been any taller than five and a half feet. If he weighed more than 120 pounds, it would be a surprise to Wes. His curling black hair was cut short, his dark eyes framed with silver-rimmed glasses. The brown of his suit material was just a shade darker than his skin. Having worn a starched white shirt and dark maroon tie for their appointment, it looked like he was ready to conduct a board meeting for a local bank.

"Let's sit at the table. I have my notebook and tape recorder there. Also the hotel has provided a choice of just about every non-alcoholic drink available to man for our pleasure. Help yourself to whatever you want. I must admit that your 'boys' can put away gallons of soft drinks. I believe our soft drink supply has been refilled several times today."

Thomson Warrenton smiled as he reached for a can of Coca Cola. "Aren't we obligated to drink Coca Cola while being in the shadow of their headquarters? I think I heard that it's a requirement if you stay more than a day in Atlanta."

"Well, it's not quite that rigid, but Atlanta does have a preference to a bright, red can. Make yourself comfortable. Then let's talk about Carrollton and your relationship to him and the organization. As I've asked all of your young men, where were you last night after the event at Georgia Tech?"

"I'd gone to visit with friends. They picked me up right at the coliseum and we went to a restaurant close by. I lived several years in Atlanta. I worked for both the M L King family and the Urban League, so I still have people I see when I'm here. You know me as a business manager, but I started out my career as a minister. I think it was the combination of the spiritual and the practical in my life that attracted Temple to invite me to join his organization."

Wes noticed that at the end of that sentence, the Reverend Warrenton dropped his eyes and fidgeted with his Coke can. He made a note in his small book: Something more here? Don't lose this. The detective was sure the other man's eyes were just a bit moist.

Wes was ready to ask if he wanted to pause for a moment, but Thomson Warrenton went right on without looking up, "I've worked for Temple for about ten years. I've been traveling with the group almost that whole time. I have a family that lives in Los Angeles and this life is hard on them. I do get back there at least once a month. When we're between appearances, sometimes I even get to stay three or four weeks." He hesitated and smiled, "My kids do know my name, Detective, and have no problem calling collect for conversation, advice or extra funds. My wife sometimes joins me when we're going to be in a place that interests her. Atlanta isn't one of those places."

"How close were you to your boss?"

Warrenton dabbed his eyes with a sparkling white handkerchief. He was not quite crying, but he was working hard at being in control of his emotions. "Temple and I were the best of friends. We were both passionate about his cause, and we shared several avocations like golf. When we were in any location that had a good course, we always found a sponsor at a club. That wasn't hard, as you can imagine. People loved having the great Temple Carrollton play their course. They would talk about it for months. Some of those sponsors had even been followers of Temple's ministry since they were students. It was so gratifying to see them doing so well."

"Did they still support the cause?"

"Yes, many of them did. They understood that their successes were not only because they worked hard and took advantage of opportunities, but that many of the opportunities came because of Temple Carrollton's prayers and concern. He worked for them all every day. They believed what Temple believed. That he was the impetus for thousands of our country's successes. He was the inspiration that got them going toward reaching far beyond their original goals. We must continue his way. It is critical to his followers."

Wes watched the face of Reverend Warrenton carefully. Was he putting him on? Could he be stringing him along? Surely many people needed all the steady guidance that was available but the 'Carrollton Success Factor' seemed a bit extreme. The surprising thought that Wes was having was that Thomson Warrenton seemed to truly believe the power of his friend and boss. The whole organization was steeped in the mystique of this pay-your-way-to-success scheme.

"Do you know of any enemies that Mr. Carrollton had? Did he ever receive threats or were there demonstrations at the various places he appeared?"

"I can respond to those questions very strongly. He had no problems with his ministry or his followers. They knew they would benefit from his blessing. A few times we've received letters or even calls from people who were not enjoying the good life that they felt he promised them. These were never serious and were handled by one of our lieutenants taking that person under his wing and talking sense to him. You probably are saying, "Those young kids?' They are young, but they are masters in representing Temple's philosophy and his personality. That is why we chose them and trained them so carefully Age is not the point, belief is."

"And was that talking sense contributing to the cause?"

"Of course, that was part of it. That's the heart of what makes Temple's beliefs work. He gives his mind, body and power to their success and in return, they contribute to him. He did not have this power when he was a struggling young man trying to make a living. He faced his own challenges and demons. Without the voluntary gifts, his energies would have been used up on his own financial survival."

Wes felt that Thomson Warrenton was too ready to justify the financial support of the organization. Usually if a person talks a lot during an interview, he is trying to stay away from another topic that might not be quite as positive and in his case inspirational.

He decided to take a new tactic "Reverend Warrenton, how well did you know Carrollton before you joined the organization?"

Thomsons's eyes shifted to looking at something on the wall past Wes' head before he answered. "As I said, I've been with Temple for almost ten years. We knew each other very well."

"No, how long and how well did you know him before you were asked to join the crusade?"

A response was coming but again, there was a hesitation, "I knew Temple for about a year before he asked me to be his business manager."

Wes noticed that now there was no elaboration. Just the facts. He knew he was skirting around something that Warrenton didn't want to talk about.

"How did you meet and get to know each other well enough to be asked to fill this important position?"

The minister-business manager looked down at his hands and seemed to be in deep thought. Then he looked back at Wes, "I met Temple by chance one night in church right here in Atlanta. I had agreed to fill the pulpit for a friend who was on vacation. I was in the church the night before to get comfortable with the environment and Temple came in. He was trying to make a big decision in his life. He'd been trying various pursuits to arrive at the right answer. Other counsel that he had was not right for him. We talked for hours that night. I continued to be his advisor for months until he followed the call to his own ministry."

Wes now observed that the man was beginning to perspire. He had wiped his forehead with his handkerchief. He no longer seemed comfortable in his chair.

"What was the other counsel he had sought that didn't work?"

"Well, he was young and he had talked to other young men. They told him that the best way to become successful was to belong to the right group, know the right people. Groups always helped each other and stuck together. Temple had wanted to believe them because he wanted to have friends and be successful ASAP. Well, as you and I know, it isn't that easy."

Wes was listening and watching intently as the man spoke. He always watched body language or facial expressions.

The interview continued and Thomson Warrenton sipped the Coca Cola as if it was a fine wine. Wes expected him to swirl the liquid in the glass and look at it intently. He had the feeling that the man wanted to do anything to erase some of his private memories.

Chapter 20

Augusta Martinez

It was quiet. Wes sat at the table sipping on his third Coke. He was still thinking about Thomson Warrenton and what he probably had not said before the surprising announcement made as he was leaving. He replayed the conversation in his mind because he felt it was such a contrast to everything else he had learned about Temple Carrollton Enterprises.

They had been shaking hands when Wes added, "I have an appointment with your financial manager now. What's he like?"

"He's like a young woman."

"What?"

"Actually, he's not like a young woman. She is a young woman, Augusta Martinez." Rev. Warrenton smiled, enjoying his little joke and watching the surprise on the detective's face. "Why is that such a surprise?"

"Because it had appeared up to this point, that Carrollton had built his organization in the masculine mode. I'd assumed, which, of course, I should never do, that it made it easier to keep the enterprise managed with all the traveling and togetherness that seems to be necessary."

"I must say that I, too, shared your assumption, Detective, until Temple convinced me that this could work. He was right. Having a female vice president has not been a problem. Augusta has done a tremendously professional job. She looks like a kid, but she has the financial mind of someone with many years experience. Guaranteed, you will enjoy your conversation. I don't want to hold you up so I'm on my way."

Being deep into his thoughts, Wes hadn't noticed the first soft greeting that the young woman had spoken. The second time she spoke louder as she entered the room, "Hello, I'm Augusta Martinez. Am I in the right place?"

Wes stood up. "Yes, yes. You are. I'm Detective Wes Wesley. Thank you for meeting with me at such short notice."

"Wes Wesley? An interesting name. Is it really Wes or is it a repeat like Wesley Wesley?"

"Nope, just plain old Wes."

He took the opportunity to study the woman standing relaxed in front of him. She was certainly young. He guessed not more than early twenties. She had long, dark hair that flowed like lava almost to her waist, a clear, smooth, olive complexion and dark, brooding eyes framed with ebony lashes. Augusta Martinez was petite, dressed in jeans and a T-shirt like she could have been still in her teens. She almost frowned when she looked Wes in the eyes. Everything about her appearance announced that she was young except her eyes. They said, "I am a mature and competent woman." They also seemed to announce, 'Don't push me.'

"Do sit down. Have a drink or a snack. The hotel has been very generous so feel free to help yourself."

"I guess they want you to find the murderer and let them have their hotel back. Can you imagine what this is doing to their bottom line? I've been totaling up the lost profits each time I've seen a guest packed up and standing nervously at the front desk. This tragedy is very personal to us, but it's just plain dollars to them. I'm sure they thought they were lucky when we booked our entourage here. Lots of rooms, meals, extras and visibility."

Wes wasn't surprised that she would notice the lost dollars in each packed suitcase. All the financial people he knew were quite the same; absolutely fixated on the profit/loss statement. He was lucky if he could get his income tax forms filled out correctly each April.

"I know that's right. But I agree with them. We want to get this perpetrator too. The visibility of Temple Carrollton works against us too, if we aren't performing immediate miracles. Let's talk about you and your role with the organization?"

"Sure. That's easy. I'm the financial manager and responsible to keep us operating in the black."

"In the black? I don't see where there's a problem. Everything I hear about this operation sounds like the blackest of the black."

"We do fine, Detective Wesley, but we have huge expenses too. It takes some finesse and careful planning to keep everyone happy."

"May I ask where you've gotten your expertise? You look like you should still be walking across a campus trying to remember a debit from a credit."

Augusta laughed lightly. Her eyes changed from the serious, mature woman to more the person Wes was seeing. He thought she even look younger with the wide smile on her face.

"Do you know how many times I've had to respond to that question? Of course, even Temple asked it when I interviewed for this job. He laughed when I told him to look no further. I was the person for the job. Later, he admitted that I was correct," the young woman seemed to be enjoying this moment of putting another man in his place. "Who said you have to be old or male to be a professional?"

"Oops, sorry. I didn't know that this was such a tender subject. Let's get back to the question: Where did you get your experience that you have this position?"

She gave him a hard look without any hint of the mirth that was there a few seconds ago. "I began working in a CPA firm when I was twelve years old. I was always good with math but my expertise was gained through working. My dad was the partner of a top CPA firm in Washington. My Uncle Jack was a partner in one of the largest law firms specializing in tax law and my other uncle, Jeb, was a financial consultant for dozens of the big deals in our Congress. I definitely was born with black ink in my veins.

"I started working for my dad to help out during tax season and continued to do more while I finished high school. Then

I moved over to my Uncle Jack's business during the summer before I was to start college. I never got there. I stayed with my uncle's law practice, except during tax season, when I went back to my dad's firm, I took special courses, went to lots of seminars and passed every test ever offered for certification. That's how I got my education, and that's what I did until I joined Temple Carrollton Enterprises."

"Why did you make that change?"

Augusta Martinez hesitated just a moment. Wes was sure that she had been asked the same question many times, but maybe she gave different answers depending who asked. She took a small sip of her soft drink and then said, "I usually say, 'I was captivated by Temple's ministry and made a commitment to become a part of it,' but I actually wanted to get out of Washington and see the real world. It doesn't matter now that Temple is gone to tell you confidentially that I wasn't wholly committed to the cause, but it was my opportunity to do what I wanted to do."

"Why weren't you committed? It seems everyone else is who is connected."

"Many are, that's true. Others see it as a way for good money without very hard work, a chance to travel in style and with some celebrity standing. As you know most of us are young and it's easy to get immature people, mostly men, to agree to a non-traditional life."

"You say 'mostly men.' You're the only woman that I've met."

"I was the only woman for about a month. Then Thomson and Temple decided that it would be easier to have two. You know, we could room together, pal around, help each other with things 'the men' didn't want to do and have each other to talk to. I think they thought, too, if we were together most of the time the guys wouldn't be hitting on either of us all the time. But guys are guys. So when the arrangements position opened up because the last director was getting married and his fiancée wanted him in one place, they looked for a female replacement.

"I'll give the two old boys credit. They had me interview every candidate and the final word was mine. I was supposed to single out the woman who could do the job, and I could work and live with. Annie filled the qualifications. She is a pro when it comes to figuring out all the many things that need to be done moving from city to city, and she has been no problem as a roommate. The rest of the time, she goes her way and I go mine. It's like having a sister whom you respect."

Wes wrote down the name 'Annie' and went on to another question. He found Augusta's history intriguing, but he was ready to get back to the present.

"Where were you last night after the event at Georgia Tech?"

"I stopped at the Varsity, got a chili dog and onion rings, came back to the hotel, popped a beer and pigged out. If you're at Georgia Tech, you can't pass by the Varsity. Annie had gone out with two of the guys. They said they were going to find out what the nightlife was like in Atlanta. She is more a party girl than I am."

"I'm surprised you know about the Varsity. Has its reputation traveled to DC?"

"In my family it has. Our roots are here in Atlanta. My dad followed his brothers to Washington when I was about ten. They convinced him that there would be more opportunity for him there and they were right."

Wes noted 'Atlanta roots' in his book. He found it interesting that Temple Carrollton also had roots in Atlanta. Although it was a different location and a different reason that brought them together. He asked, "Do you think with both you and your boss having Atlanta ties, that had anything to do with you getting the job?"

He watched Augusta digest the question. She was momentarily in deep thought like she was reaching for a buried remembrance, "I don't think we ever talked about it. If we did, it's long gone from my memory. I don't know if anyone has mentioned to you, but Temple never spoke of his life before he became a preacher man. If you wanted to, you could believe that he was born with his beautiful robe swirling around him and his hair already blow-dried. He was a self-made man. I mean self-made. He created the persona of Temple Carrollton."

"You sound like you didn't like the man."

"Oh, no. The man he created was likable enough. I'm saying that he wasn't what he presented. He was what he created for his profession of caring and love. In my opinion, that wasn't the real Temple Carrollton."

"Based on what?"

Augusta didn't want to justify her opinions. She wished that she had not added her evaluation of her boss. As long as she had been with the organization, she had kept her thoughts to herself. Unfortunately, this man had talked her into letting her guard down.

"Mostly gut reactions. Don't even give it a thought. I just didn't see him treating his staff like he treated his followers." Augusta then asked her own question, "Do you think that the murderer was at the event last evening?"

Wes watched Augusta smoothly change the topic that had been on the table. He would not pursue her 'gut reaction' now, but depending how the investigation proceeded, he might come back to it again.

"Probably not. This wasn't a casual, spontaneous shooting. The killer would have had to have more information than the public audience would normally have. Of course at this point, we aren't rejecting any possibilities."

Wes glanced at his watch and then slipped his card across the desk toward the young woman, "It's getting late. Let's call it a day. If you think of anything else that could be helpful, give me a call. I may want to talk to you again, so if I could have your card, it would make it easier to find you. Just jot down the hotel telephone number."

"No problem. Now, I may just head for the Varsity again. I

think my dad used to call this a grease attack!"

She was ready to leave the room, but she was also pleased that she had been able to change the subject. Her opinions are none of his business, and she was furious with herself for mentioning the issue. She decided the stress of the whole situation was getting to her.

Chapter 21

Honeybun

Honeybun turned and locked the door, plumped up the pillows against the headboard, took off her shoes and bounced into a comfortable position on her bed. She closed her eyes and clasped her hands between her breasts. She could feel her heart beating faster than usual. She took several deep breaths. She wanted to be calm, even serene, before she touched the My Friends book. Just feeling it in her hands made her blood pressure rise like a rocket. She didn't want to have a stroke. She still had things to do. Sometimes she would even do a short meditation before she looked at the book.

She waited. She repeated over and over again a mantra that she had chosen for herself. She was already feeling better. She wiggled her toes and shook her hands. She took an extra deep breath and thought, 'I'm fine.' She felt good.

In taking the book out from under her mattress, she leaned over and checked out the locked suitcase under her bed that held the Barbie doll case. Everything that was important to her was right here in this room. She had carried the case with her for more than ten years. She had carried it inside the suitcase now for just a few years. She would get too much attention if she were seen carrying a little girl's play box now that she was no longer a child.

The book had belonged to her for only a few years. It became hers when she found it packed away in a box of old clothes and papers that were in the attic of the house where she had lived with her sisters and mother. Finding it had changed her life and had initiated her life's plan. As she read it many times and finally understood what she had found quite by accident, she knew what she would do. Well, maybe not by accident. Was any of life by accident? She believed that she was supposed to find the book and then she was silently guided to work out what to do about it.

She opened the pages as she had done hundreds of times. She looked at the names and other information: the dates, names, dollar amounts. It could almost have been a timesheet. She saw her own newer markings. Some check marks, lines drawn through names and several stars. Oh, yes, these were her stars. They had changed her life and she was changing theirs. She traced her finger across each name and felt a tingling that reached to between her eyes. She felt a headache coming on, but it pleased her to feel the pain. She wouldn't feel the pain much longer. Her plan was coming together.

Chapter 22

Franklin Raub

It was almost 8:30. Wes had dragged himself out of the car, stopped at Checkers to pick up a hamburger and spicy fries and had eaten them sitting on the edge of his bed while he watched CNN tell him what had happened during the day. It was like the old days "BJ" (Before Janeen). He knew this was her evening to meet with Special Olympics as a volunteer, so he reverted back to his old habits: fast food and television. He leaned back on the pillows. He let his eyes close. The next thing he heard was the telephone ringing.

He looked at his clock and was amazed that it read 2:37 A.M. He was still dressed and the bag that held his meal was now on the floor. So much for gracious living. Martha Stewart would never come to him for advice.

"Damn, who's calling? I hope it's not Jason with a problem," he said as he reached for the phone.

"Wes! Are you awake?" It was Billy Joe and he was excited, which always made him loud.

"I am now. What's up?"

"Big news. You've gotta meet me right away. Franklin Raub, president of City Council, has just been found in his driveway shot dead!"

"Shit! Franklin Raub? What next? We have two big cases without any suspects. Now we have another well-known man shot. What's going on in Atlanta? Where are you? I'll meet you there."

"I'm headed toward his house now. You know where it is?"

"Sure, close to Monroe. On Amsterdam, right?"

"Right. I'm just about there. Lots of activity already. Place looks like a Wal-Mart parkin' lot on a Friday night. Get here fast. This is gonna get everybody's attention." Billy Joe was gone as fast as he had appeared. Wes was already headed for the bathroom. A quick stop there and he was gone. He sniffed his shirt and said to his reflection in the mirror, "Good enough for a murder site."

No traffic and 60 miles per hour speed through semi-residential streets got him to the Raub house in about five minutes. It was a wild scene. Probably even more people and official vehicles than when Billy Joe called just twelve minutes ago. He recognized the mayor's chauffeured Lincoln and groaned. They were in for a bad night and day and night and ..... Hell, it's just a bad week!

"Wesley, over here!"

Oh, no. Just as he had thought his week couldn't get worse, he saw Brassy standing next to Major Dilbert. Was the whole damn City of Atlanta here?

"Hey, Sergeant and Major Dilbert. How'd you get the news?"

"The mayor called the chief and we got a call right away. Your partner is already here. I'm surprised you're so late." Dagmar Dilbert growled. Even at 2:30 in the morning, she looked like someone had dipped her in starch. Her uniform was flawless and not a hair out of place. Wes wondered if she slept wrapped in tissue paper already dressed and ready for a call to action or another chance to read the rules to anyone close enough to listen.

"I got Detective LaCrosse's call exactly fourteen minutes ago. An earlier call from you, Major, would've gotten me here sooner."

"Don't get smart with me, Wesley. Just go do your job. And keep me informed about everything you learn. I want no surprises and I want to be able to pass on full, detailed reports to the mayor often."

Wes nodded his head toward his boss and went in the

direction of the yellow crime scene ribbon. It was easy to see big Billy Joe in the middle of a kluge of uniformed police and other people in a motley array of quickly grabbed outfits. Several, Wes was sure, had been chosen in the dark hoping not to waken wives, husbands, family or girlfriends. He decided that he looked quite good. It paid to not take off his suit when he slept on his bed!

"Shit, Wes, this is a disaster. Homicide is gonna be on the hot seat until this is over. The fuckin' mayor's runnin' around like a nut demandin' that the police find this monster, his word not mine, immediately. Like in half an hour. Why don't we declare it was Major Dilbert? She was here before any of us. Maybe she was just tryin' to leave the scene rather than come to it. Then we could all go home and get some sleep and get rid of a pain in the ass at the same time."

"I like the idea, Billy Joe, but it's not going to work. She doesn't even know how to shoot." Wes was being careful to speak softly so only his partner could hear him. He was afraid that he could start a whole movement in the police force, "Now let's get serious. What do you know by now and how did you get here so fast?"

"I fell asleep early after eatin' one of Cleo's fried chicken dinners so I was wide awake and up readin' at two o'clock. Of course, I had my radio on. I heard the first call come in. Raub was found by his son returnin' from a party. He immediately made the call to 911 on his cell phone.

"The body is over there by his car. I would say that someone got him as he got out of it. The car door was closed, but he still had keys in his hand and his briefcase is under the body. No sign of a struggle. Two nice clean shots. One in the head and one in the stomach. I doubt whether he even saw it comin'. The killer might've called to him or made a noise that got his attention. When he turned toward the person, zap! That was it. Time for a new president of City Council."

"Did his son see anyone? Did he hear anything when he arrived?"

"He's way out of it, but so far it seems that he didn't. He did touch the body and said it was still warm. So we've an idea of when it happened. I don't know if it was good or bad that the son arrived when he did. He might've been shot too. Or, if he had arrived earlier, would the shooter been scared away?"

"Let's take a closer look. Think of all the Atlanta residents who have said from time to time, 'I'd like to shoot the son of a bitch.' We probably have about 50,000 suspects for this murder."

Wes and Billy Joe made their way through the crowd. Some folks seemed to be in a daze. They were simply standing, staring. Some were talking to the person standing beside them. A few actually appeared to be doing a job. Filling a purpose. One thing was evident, the mayor and his staff had been busy making calls. His public relations people were there, police officers from uniforms to the top brass and many of the folks who were always hanging around the mayor's office. Who, for some reason, had earned the right to draw a regular check for adding body heat to a room. If they ever did anything else, it was very cleverly disguised as loitering.

The two Homicide detectives stepped over the crime scene tape, nodding to the uniforms who were posted to keep out the masses. They stopped and looked at the scene from a distance. The body of the president of the city council was covered. It was to the left of the driver's side of a new dark blue Lexus just a few feet from the closed car door. The garage door was open and a small sports car could be seen in the right-hand space. Probably the son's car that he had just put away before finding his dad. The house was lit up like the family was expecting guests to arrive for a festive event that was never going to happen.

"Let's take a look at the body. From what you said, there isn't going to be much to see."

"You're right. It looks like a hit and run to me. No time spent hangin' around or takin' a chance that Raub might fight back or yell for help. We want to find out where he'd been. Who he was with. It might be important." Billy Joe hunched down and lifted the edge of the blanket. He noticed an immediate hush from the crowd behind him. They seemed to be poised for a revelation. Billy Joe was careful to use his own body as a shield between Franklin Raub and the assemblage. He didn't have to look, because he knew there were cameras pointed and ready to flash. The media was on the spot as well as the thrill seekers and ghouls. He was so tired of killings and wasted bodies, but it seemed that the public never had enough.

Wes began ticking off what he saw, "Still dressed for business. Nice suit. Kinda matches the car he drove. Shot facing the shooter. Right in the forehead. Very neat from this view. Another shot in the stomach. Looks almost dead center to me. Not random shots. Very definite and very precise. No gun close by, but maybe the killer dropped it somewhere in the neighborhood just to be good to us. Wallet is here in his hip pocket. If it was robbery, perhaps his son's arrival scared the perp off. You said that the son didn't see anything or anybody?"

"That's his story now. I think he's so upset that tryin' to get him to account for those few minutes is gonna be impossible."

"While our crime scene tech guys are working, let's give it a try. He just might have a clue that we need to know." Wes was already headed toward the house with Billy Joe at his side.

He knocked lightly, waited and knocked again. Then he tried the doorknob. The door was unlocked so he opened it and looked inside. A woman about the right age to be Franklin Raub's wife was hurrying toward him.

"Who are you? How did you get here?" she demanded.

"Homicide detectives, Wesley and LaCrosse, ma'm. Sorry to bother you. We want to speak with the young man who found Mr. Raub."

"Homicide? Oh, yes, of course. I'm Laurel Plitz. I'm Franklin's sister-in-law. His wife's sister. Little Frankie's aunt. Come in and close the door before some of those media vultures fly in. They've already pushed a microphone in my face screaming for a statement of how did I feel about what has happened. I don't know how they did it, but they already knew my name!"

"Ms. Plitz, do you live here?"

"Oh, no. I do live just across the street. Iris called me right away and I ran over. As you can see, I didn't even wait to dress."

Now that she had drawn his attention to herself, Wes took a look at the woman's attire. She had on some long shirt that reached to just above her knees, Indian moccasins and a colorful, warm-up jacket. Her dark, brown hair looked like she had combed it with her fingers, her dark eyes had smudges under them as if her mascara had been misplaced. Even without makeup, her chocolate brown face was attractive.

"Iris is your sister and Franklin Raub's wife?" Wes repeated what he had heard to be sure that he had the characters in this drama correct. She nodded and Wes continued, "Where are Iris and her son?"

"They're in his room. I'm not sure who's comforting whom. Little Frankie was hysterical when I arrived, but after seeing how upset his mom was, he seemed to get under control and was being her support. He's a nifty kid. A lot like his parents. Why would anyone do this? What awful person would wait at two in the morning to shoot a family man and a leader in the city?"

"It could be, ma'm that he was shot because he was a leader in the city. Lots of people always have problems with what's bein' done in Atlanta," Billy Joe said.

"Yes, you're right, Detective. I certainly have heard my share of what Franklin is or isn't doing. Even just being his sister-in-law, I get calls now and then saying 'tell Raub this or tell Raub that.'"

"Could you get Frankie to come out here so we can talk to him, please? We don't want to hold you up anymore, Ms. Plitz." Wes wanted to get on with talking to possibly the only witness.

"Yes, I'll be a minute. Let me see how they're doing." Laurel Plitz turned quickly and was out of sight in a moment.

Chapter 23

Franklin Raub

It was absolutely quiet in the house. Billy Joe and Wes continued to stand just inside the door because Laurel Plitz had not invited them to do anything else. They could see into a living room. It was tastefully furnished in "Nice Family," showing that the Raubs enjoyed their home and each other. In the other direction was a contrasting formal dining room. Billy Joe wondered where they put the enormous flower arrangement that was on the table when they gathered for a meal. He was amused at his inspection of the décor of the Raub house. It was just hours ago that he was making a similar evaluation of the Lee house. They were many miles and many levels of cost apart, but both homes were warm and comfortable.

Laurel Plitz came slowly down the stairs, "Gentlemen, Frankie will be right out. Why don't you wait in the living room? I think that will be a good place for you to meet. Iris is resting so I hope you won't have to see her now too."

"The living room will be fine. We can wait until later to see Mrs. Raub. Unless she was with her husband, she probably didn't see anything. But we'll ask her later." Wes began walking toward the arched entry to the room. Before he had stepped onto the plush carpet, a teenage boy came down the hallway.

"I'm Frankie. I hope you're going to find the sleaze-bag who did this. Too bad there're a lot of crazies out there." Frankie Raub took a deep breath, "My dad was always careful. Why should he have to be looking for trouble in his own driveway?"

Wes looked at the anguish that was so obvious in the young man's eyes. He saw that they were light brown and his face was about the color of coffee au lait. His hair was quite long and full, just touching the shoulders of his Woodward Academy shirt. It wouldn't surprise Wes if Franklin Raub's son were an athlete at his school. He was built like he spent hours each week working out staying in shape.

"We're here to find the murderer and hope that you might've seen something that will help. Did you see any cars or people when you were approaching the house?" Wes watched the boy's face to see what reaction he had to the question.

"I've been thinking about that. Sometimes I'm not paying attention to what's around. I'm so used to this neighborhood that I really don't look at it. It's just a place to live. But I really don't think I noticed anything. Seeing someone walking would have been noticeable. No one walks around here. I know I didn't pass another car after I turned off Monroe.

"I noticed my dad's car when I turned into the driveway and wondered why he hadn't put it away. The garage door was up but the light was off. I think it stays on about five minutes. I've never paid much attention to that either. I just get my car into the garage and head for the house. You know I can't explain it, but I didn't head for the house this time. I decided to check out dad's car. I don't know why."

He hesitated and dropped his head in his hands, "I must admit I was hoping to find him asleep or bombed so I could give him a hard time." He rubbed his eyes as if trying to erase what he had seen. "Then I saw him on the ground. I thought heart attack. He works hard. When I leaned down and touched him, I, uh, I, oh—" His voice cracked, "I saw the blood. I still wasn't thinking that he was, uh, dead. I thought he'd fallen getting out of the car."

"Was the car door open or closed?" Wes asked.

"It was closed. Otherwise I would have seen the light even when I turned into the driveway. No, it was dark."

"Then what did you do?"

"I touched my dad, maybe kinda shook him. He was like a lump. I think I knew right then that my dad was dead," Frankie had been courageous up to that moment. Now they noticed tears on his cheeks, welling from his eyes. He didn't sob nor make a sound, but the tears were flowing down his cheeks and onto his shirt. "I just don't know anything else. Do you think if I'd come home earlier, I might've saved him?"

Wes could feel the torment and guilt that Frankie was experiencing. That question would always haunt him, "Probably not, Frankie. This wasn't a random attack. This looks like it was intentional."

The boy looked at Wes. Was there relief in his eyes? The detective was glad that he had said what he had. Then he saw the boy's eyes focus on something else and Wes turned. He thought it was Laurel Plitz standing in the doorway. Then he noticed that this woman was dressed differently and had her hair pulled back in a thick braid.

"I'm Iris Raub. My sister said you were in here. Please don't upset Frankie anymore than he already is."

"I'm OK, Mom. I want to help if I can."

"Your son has been brave and has definitely helped us. He's the only one who was right out there. He has some observations that might be helpful. Come sit down, Mrs. Raub. If you're feelin' up to it, maybe we could talk a bit." Billy Joe took the woman's arm and led her to the nearest chair.

Iris Raub felt almost fragile under Billy Joe's hand. Her bones were pronounced against the soft material of her bathrobe. Her eyes were puffy from crying, but it was easy to see that normally they were beautiful light hazel color; almond shaped with a slight, exotic lift at the corners. He had seen many photos of Iris Raub standing next to her husband, but he had not realized that her true beauty was in her lovely coloring that started with her unusual eyes complemented by a smooth tan complexion.

Wes and Billy Joe had often talked about this part of their jobs. They had never gotten used to having to talk with a victim's family or close friends. There was no easy way to do it. No magic words to make the encounter more comfortable. Wes always wanted to give sympathy; let them cry or rage. Billy Joe once said that he would probably be arrested for molestation if he did what he wanted to do. He wanted to put his arms around the anguished person and hug them close. The feeling was the same with Iris Raub. He thought, "She looks like she would break if she were even squeezed a little."

"How many times I've read in the paper about things like this happening and just glossed over it like it wasn't important. Now it is important. It's real. Why would anyone do this to Franklin? He didn't please everyone with decisions made by the City Council but certainly someone wouldn't kill him over a city project or something."

"Do you know of any threats, strange telephone calls or even hate mail, Mrs. Raub?" Wes asked softly.

"Franklin didn't mention anything in particular. There were always confrontations. It would be the same for the mayor or the governor. Can't please everyone."

"Had you been out with your husband tonight?"

"No, this was his night to meet people at Manuel's. Of course, you know what a political hangout that is, because it's a police hangout too, right?"

"Yes, ma'm, it is. I've seen Mr. Raub there several times."

"Well, that's where he was and that isn't my idea of fun. I've done that enough in my younger life. Franklin felt it was important to meet people and relax over a few beers. It always stretched into the early hours but he never had trouble getting up. He seemed to thrive on it."

"So it wasn't unusual for him to get home from Manuel's as late as two A.M.?"

"No, not at all. I didn't hear a thing until Frankie came in. The sirens followed almost immediately."

"That's because I called 911 with my cell phone from right there at the car. I still hoped there was a chance that someone could help dad."

"Mrs. Raub, we're going to let you get some rest now.

We'll be checking back as we go ahead with the investigation. We'll want to talk with people who were at Manuel's and others like office staff. If you think of anyone you feel might know something about why this has happened, would you jot down those names and we'll get to them. At this point, we welcome any new information. Detective LaCrosse or I will be available to you," Wes handed her his card, "Just call either of us at this number."

"Thank you," she looked at the card, "Detective Wesley, I'll try to remember something that could be a clue for you. It won't bring back my husband, but it might find the person who's responsible."

"Frankie, we'll probably want to talk again. Keep this card in case you want to be in touch before we call you."

"Yes, sir, I'll see you again, I'm sure. I can always get to your office or wherever. I suppose you've guessed that I'm at Woodward. You can get me there too." Frankie extended his hand and both detectives shook it as they turned to leave the house.

Wes thought that probably right now on this councilman's driveway, the city of Atlanta had at least 300 years of experience represented. That estimate may be low, but he knew the skills and talents were impressive. The team was on the job, and the mayor will be on their backs.

"Wes, I have a funny feelin' about this shootin' and its timin'. Three men whose ages are fairly close, each has had a taste of success, all shot with no struggle, no dumb mistakes yet by the perp, and each shot in the middle of the night. These could all be coincidences, but you know how we feel about coincidences. There just ain't many in this crazy world of ours. Maybe it was an advantage that we got the ultimatum from the Dreadful Dilbert to show up at every homicide site, because if I wasn't standin' right here thinkin' about our week, I might not have put these together."

"Yeah, I know the feeling," Wes replied. "My problem so far is that I don't see the connection among the victims. I think we need to do a deep, intense background search. Where might there be a place where some tracks cross? We need to get some hard evidence that these shootings could be related. Or forget it and work on some other theories. All we're both going on now is our guts. Some might say that it's just too many doughnuts. Do we have our report back on the weapons? It would be great if we found the same gun was used for each shooting."

"Don't' count on that. I called "Irish" Finn at the lab. He said it was a Loren 9 mm that killed both of them but the bullet markings were different. Still doesn't mean those guns weren't used by the same person. If it's the same killer, maybe he's smart enough to not use the same weapon. Lorens are easy and cheap to get. So far, whoever has done these shootings has been either very good or very lucky. Different guns could be planned, too."

"Sounds like premeditation rather than spontaneous killing. One or two or three killers, each one has left a clean crime scene. Let's think about this and look at possibilities in the morning."

"Mornin'? Man, what do you think this is? Can't get more like mornin' than this. But, I gotcha. We both need a shower and a clear head. See you at the office when the sun comes up." Billy Joe was already heading for his car.

Chapter 24

Danielle Jarvis Swain

Dani Swain couldn't believe that she was on her way to the murder scene of another well known man in Atlanta. She had been awakened about four A M with a call from one of her regular volunteers who thought there was nothing better to do than listen in on police calls. Usually there were not a lot of calls that were of great interest to the television newswoman. This week was completely out of control. She was almost beginning to wish that the telephone would not ring. Almost! Certainly she did not want to lose out on a big story. And this one was a big one: Franklin Raub was dead.

Dani arrived at the Amsterdam Avenue address just as Wes and Billy Joe were pulling away. She tried to get their attention but she could tell that they were not planning to hang around for anyone. She wondered how long they had been there. What did they already knew? She would call Wes at the office later, or was it really earlier? She would have been able to talk to him here if she hadn't stopped by Channel 22 to do a BreakIn! segment before leaving with Loretta, her camera operator. She felt sure that they had been the first to present the news of this latest killing. When she ran out to her car, she left another staff person behind with directions to get some good background information while they got the footage to be on camera.

"It looks like the opening day for the Braves baseball season. Look at all the flashing lights and cars everywhere," Loretta said as Dani parked her car in a neighbor's driveway. Jumping out of the car, they were half way up the street in a minute.

"Even the mayor is here. I see his car and his driver. Wouldn't it be nice to just sit in the back seat and never even think about having to navigate around grid lock? Loretta, I wonder if Franklin Raub had a driver. The report said that he was found beside his car."

"If he didn't, maybe another reason to have a chauffeured car has just been brought into the spotlight. I don't get it. If people want to steal a car or whatever, why can't they take it and leave? Why do they kill the owner?" Loretta was talking as she was checking out her camera equipment. She and Dani rarely had time for much conversation. When they were together, they were chasing a story.

Loretta started filming as soon as they approached the Raub property. She panned across the New Orleans style, wrought iron fence that ran along the street side of their yard. Several patches of colorful flowers clustered at the corners surrounded by carefully trimmed grass. A curving sidewalk, a narrow sliver of concrete, stretched from the driveway to the small front porch. The yellow crime tapes were gently undulating on both sides of the driveway in the early morning breeze. Until a few hours ago, she was sure this scene had been like most any other middle class home in the metropolitan area. How fast lives can change.

Leaving Loretta to get plenty of footage to edit later for the next news broadcast, Dani looked for people who may know something that she could use to make her report more compelling than her competition. Her attention was immediately drawn to the front door. It was partially open and a woman was standing with her back to the street. The woman turned, walked off the porch and began to cross the lawn. The television anchorwoman decided that she would head directly toward the porch knowing that her path would intersect with the woman who was bundled in a heavy coat. As the two women approached the same place in the yard, Danielle realized the other woman was staring at her. The woman smiled. "I know you. You're on Channel 22," she said.

"Yes, I'm Dani Swain. Thank you for watching our newscasts. I don't believe I know who you are."

"I'm Laurel Plitz. Franklin Raub is my brother-in-law."

Dani noticed that Laurel said 'is' rather than 'was.' After a sudden and violent death, she knew that it took awhile to change that. She also noticed that Laurel turned her head and looked at where the car was still parked beside a chalk drawing of a body. That rough silhouette was the last connection to life for Franklin Raub. She turned back to Dani and there were tears in her eyes.

"It's not 'is.' It's now 'was.' My brother-in-law is simply a memory and a few marks on the driveway."

"I'm so sorry about this. Please accept my sympathy and empathy. I understand that Mr. Raub's son found his father."

Laurel Plitz hesitated. With the back of her hand she swept away the tears that had trickled down her cheeks. She took several deep breaths to compose herself, raised her head a little higher hoping to discourage more tears from overflowing and said, "Yes, that's true. Poor Frankie. He'll never forget this terrible night. The only way that it can be made better is for the murderer to be found. Franklin had said many times that more and more killings go unsolved. I pray this will not be one of them."

"May I walk with you to your car?" asked Dani, not wanting to end the conversation.

"I don't have a car here. I live across the street. When this all happened, my sister called. I came right away. It was already too late to do anything for Franklin, but I hope I helped Iris and little Frankie. But, what can one do? We all liked Franklin. We all campaigned for him, gave money and then voted. Maybe if he had lost the election, he would still be alive."

"Why do you say that, Ms. Plitz?"

"Well, it has to be someone who didn't like what he was doing as president of the City Council. He would receive nasty telephone calls or notes after different votes. He used to laugh about the notes. Called them 'my loving poison pen letters.' He would say that only people who cared about the city would take the time to react and write letters. Iris said he tried to answer most of them. He knew that even if he believed in a specific action, there would be those citizens who hated it."

"Do you remember any recent letters or calls that could help direct the police investigation?"

"No, I can't think of any. I really was speaking only as a generality. Franklin just didn't have enemies outside the political arena. He had lots of friends. The family was very well liked. Why not? They were all nice people. My sister is a gem. Her compassion created an openness that went far beyond her family and neighborhood. In fact, just this week, she was talking about the poor families of the men who were murdered recently here in Atlanta and wished that she could help them in some way. Do you think their families will think of her?"

Dani and Laurel had been slowly walking across the street. Laurel stopped when they reached the curb. She seemed to be saying, "This is as far as I want you to go. I'm going home alone."

Dani felt Laurel's hesitation and knew that it was time for her to end this conversation. She had other people to talk with and a deadline to keep in mind. She was ready to say goodbye when the pretty woman turned and added, "Franklin was a very attractive man with wonderful charisma. One of my roommates would kid Iris that if she ever got tired of him, she would be happy to take him off her hands. I think his personality was what captivated so many voters. This has to be a random attempted carjacking. Even though I have been thinking about a political crank, I don't really believe that someone would go this far over a water or sewer or traffic issue. That is just too bizarre."

"If you think of anything that you believe could be helpful information, here is my card. Feel free to call anytime. Sometimes the smallest clue is what breaks the case."

The two women said goodbye and waved weakly as they turned away from each other. Dani decided she would follow up later in the day and see if Laurel Plitz might have more ideas or remember earlier conversations that might open a new direction for Wes and Billy Joe. That reminded her of the call she had received about the Temple Carrollton case. She wondered if they had found out anything about the caller. She could not decide if it was from a man or a woman.

Chapter 25

Janeen Newman Carson

Something was blaring. It just wouldn't stop. Wes heard the alarm go off, but he didn't move. After just two more hours of sleep, he wasn't ready to hit the streets. Maybe the Franklin Raub business had been a bad dream. He'd gone to bed last night, and here he was still in bed. Why not a dream? Yeah, right. He wished it were that easy. Like it or not, he had to get up and think about Raub. What a downer.

A second thought raised his spirits: Janeen. A few minutes with her could help toward an attitude adjustment. He jumped out of bed, went directly to the bathroom and turned on the shower hot water. He was going to clean up then call his favorite person.

Wes waited only two rings. His special girl answered the phone, "Are you up?"

"Yes, I'm up. I was about to make some coffee and look at my calendar for the day. What's wrong? Why are you calling so early? Are you OK?"

"Too many questions for so early in the morning, but I have one of my own. May I stop over to say good morning in person on my way to the office? It's been too long since I saw you. I need a Janeen fix."

"You crazy guy. It's not been two days."

"Seems like two weeks. Let's not waste our time talking from a mile apart. I can be in the car in five minutes. Less if it's OK with you."

"If you can't move faster than that, just forget it. You implied you were anxious to get here. Now you're backing down to not even leaving for five minutes." Janeen started to laugh. Wes

Wesley was unpredictable and a tremendous boost to her ego. In a world where most people are taken for granted, he seemed to always want to show that she was special. A call at 6:30 A.M. was certainly not expected.

"I'll lock my door in one minute. I might be there before you can unlock yours. See ya', love of my life."

Janeen took a quick peek in the mirror. She was glad she had chosen her forest green pants suit, a soft, ruffled, pastel green silk blouse and long, single strand of pearls. Wes made her feel very feminine and she liked to look that way for him. Her hair was glossy from just having been washed and blown dry for a casual, stylish appearance.

Janeen plugged in the coffee maker then went to the front door. It was not going to be locked when Wes arrived. She would watch for him and open the door before he ever got to the porch. She thought about his enthusiasm when he called. She knew she felt the same as he did. After many years of being a widow and not dating a lot, it was a joy to have a relationship with a man who was as attentive as he was attractive. How lucky could she be? She believed every single woman over 35 dreams of such a gift.

Janeen watched the car turn off Juniper Street into the narrow driveway that served the entire row of townhouses. It never ceased to amaze her that the Atlanta developers could build dozens of houses in a space that had originally been for only one, elegant in-town home. The "old days" certainly had a quiet class to them, but in today's economy, who could afford to live that way? She still considered herself fortunate that she found this little strip of sanity that was now being encroached on by high rises completely clad in glass and concrete.

Wes came charging around the corner of the building. He checked his watch as he bolted up the short walkway, "Ah, ha. Here I am with all my anticipation plastered across my face." He put his arms around Janeen's waist and pulled her close. "How could you say it was only two days since I saw you? You really know how to hurt a guy. I'm wounded and may never recover."

Janeen's smile evolved into a laugh that sent a tingle through Wes' whole body. He loved that laugh. It was one of the reasons that he liked being with this lovely woman. She even made his little jokes appear to be much bigger than they had a right to be. He had dated many women since his divorce more than eighteen years ago, but not one of them ever made him consider taking another chance on marriage. Now, he actually played the words 'I do' over and over in his head.

"Shall we stay out here and start all my neighbors' days with a goal of what to do before the sun comes up? I think not. Come on in, Wes. I'm willing to share my coffee with you, but I must confess that I have no doughnuts."

"That works for me. Actually I hadn't thought about doughnuts. That happens mostly when I turn onto Ponce de Leon Avenue and the car automatically heads toward the parking lot that surrounds the sign that says Hot Now."

They closed the door behind them. Wes again gave Janeen a hug. He buried his face in her soft, clean hair. "This is heaven in Atlanta. I thought that our city had long outgrown such a possibility. I see more of the opposite – all the hells of Atlanta. Three minutes with you and I can almost forget that I was out most of last night because of the shooting of Franklin Raub."

Janeen gasped, "Franklin Raub, like president of our City Council?"

"The same. He was shot in his driveway as he returned from Manuel's. I hope he enjoyed his last visit with his faithful voters."

"Last visit?" Do you mean he's dead?"

Wes nodded his head as he gave Janeen another light kiss on her lips. He wished he could forget last night.

"Wes, you're really having a bad week. I can't believe that in just a few days there have been three murders of men who all had prominence in Atlanta. Do you think it's a conspiracy to get rid of men who have made a place for themselves here and at various times made a difference in the city?"

146

"It could look like that although conspiracy sounds a bit dramatic. Billy Joe and I are going to do some investigating to see if there's a connection. At the same time, we're hoping that whoever is behind this has run out of community celebrities. The city is soon going to go bonkers. The mayor is already checking us out. The chief is breathing down our necks through Major Dragon Lady, You're right, it's not been a good week. Since both Lee and Carrollton sorta relate to Georgia Tech, do you hear anything new around campus?"

"Not really. Of course the two shootings are in everyone's conversation. And that brings back the rehashing of Andy Dren's murder."

"That reminds me, I ran into Walter at the Union Mission. He said he's available to be a dep-u-ty, if I need him. He knew Ramblin' Randy. I'm going to meet him at Manuel's tonight for a couple of beers. It's just for old times but who knows, he may just be carrying around a clue again. We sure do need one." Wes suddenly looked tired. The week was taking its toll.

"You need some sleep and some time away from the office. That's a funny thing to say when I relate it to your job. Since we're about to start the weekend, I think you need to spend a big part of it in bed."

"Yes, ma'm. If I bring my teddy bear, may I sleep over?"

Janeen's eyes twinkled. "Wes, you're too much. Why don't you just pick up that teddy bear on your way back from Manuel's. We'll have dinner here where you can relax and even fall asleep before dessert? But, right now, I have to get moving. Can I put your coffee in a plastic cup? Take it with you since we didn't even get to the kitchen?"

"I don't need the coffee. I really just wanted to see you. Your plan for tonight sounds great. If I get a little nap before dessert, maybe I can stay awake long enough to show you how wonderful you are. I know just the way, but I'm going to keep it a secret until tonight. Try to imagine it during the day. Keep your mind on the two of us alone, a little music in the background, my arms around you, my lips finding exactly the right place to drop a soft, wet kiss and then…"

"OK. Enough of your scene setting. I've got the idea. How will I keep my mind on my work? I'll only be thinking of tonight."

"Yes, that's the point. Remember. When you see me next, I'll be unbuttoning your blouse and then…" His voice had become very low.

In a husky whisper, Janeen added, "And, then I'm going to make you lie down in my bed so I can help you forget this horrendous week. Good bye, sweetheart. I'll see you tonight."

"How can you push me out on the street in this condition? Have mercy on a poor, old, broken down policeman." Responding to Janeen's gentle shoving, Wes was already half way out the door. Janeen looked at her watch and said, "Out. See you later."

Chapter 26

Matthew Christian

Matthew Christian was waiting for Wes. He stood up when he saw the detective come in doing his usual juggling act with his briefcase, pungent doughnuts and coffee container. He rose carefully favoring his arm, which was still supported in a sling. His face was rather pale reflecting the hurt that losing his father had created. His handsome features looked younger and more vulnerable than at the exciting evening in the Robbie Cremins Coliseum or even when he attacked Officer Giles at the Marriott.

"Hi, Detective Wesley. I hope I'm not bothering you. I brought something that is strange. We found it last evening."

"Come on in, Matthew. I'll share my Atlanta breakfast with you. It might make you glad that you were raised somewhere else. Where was that, by the way?"

"I lived in Birmingham until my father decided it was time to join him on the road. That's where my mother still lives. Of course, now she's here in Atlanta. She came over to be here for the event and to spend some time with me. We never told my father because he wouldn't have liked that one bit. He had no idea that she'd visit when we got close to Alabama and that she knew many of the people on the staff. Now I guess it doesn't matter."

"Your father wouldn't have liked her to visit with her son?"

"Probably not. We weren't willing to find out, but she's real popular with some of my friends. Especially Augusta and Annie. They're funny because sometimes the three of them would go out club crawling. You would've thought they were all the same age. They used to call themselves Sisters in Crime."

"Why Sisters in Crime?"

"Because they felt that they were breaking Temple's rules. They loved the thought of doing that. Detective Wesley, my father was a tremendous person and all that you saw in public was real, but he was a tough taskmaster. Very hard to please. The rest of the crew would say that. Then they would add 'but he pays well.' I'm sure they had more to say when Mark and Luke and I weren't around.

"Well, you know in the U S of A, one of our favorite topics for conversation is boss bashing." Wes smiled as he watched Matthew sit gingerly on the edge of the chair. "You're right to be careful when you sit on these chairs. They've been mistreated and abused by both police and perps. Atlanta hasn't budgeted for an upgrade in our offices in about fifty years."

"Actually what the other staff members say is true. It isn't boss bashing. My father was a rigid taskmaster, which brings us back to why we didn't tell him everything."

Wes was pleased with this opening conversation. He decided that the young man was facing reality more squarely this morning. That could be good for learning some worthwhile information. He noticed for the first time how well dressed young Christian was. He could have been advertising GQ magazine in his beautifully tailored, gray cashmere sports jacket, opened-neck pale yellow shirt and darker gray slacks. Even with only one arm, he had managed to look elegant from his blond curls to his polished loafers. For a moment, Wes felt he should have taken more time in putting together his clothes this morning. He was glad that he had worn his favorite striped red and blue tie.

"Lots of doughnuts there for you, but in between bites, what is it you came to tell me?"

"Since you have been at one of Temple's presentations, you already know that he asks for a personal token. People put them in the baskets along with their loving gifts. We use these to pray over and to help the individuals to rise to their proper level of success."

Wes noticed that Matthew had reverted to the party line. He decided not to interrupt him.

"We usually go through the baskets right after each event, count the contributions and put the tokens in secure boxes. Then we take the money to a night deposit and place the boxes of tokens in safes that are in several of our vans."

"Why do you put them in the safes? Aren't they just a collection of things – what we might call stuff?"

"Some are, Detective Wesley, but often there are items of value. People knew that Temple was going to work for them. They wanted to be sure that he knew they were true believers. Some of the most valuable items we have ever received were a one-caret diamond ring, an emerald bracelet and a Rolex watch."

"A Rolex watch? That's worth thousands of dollars!"

"That's right but it's a small investment in your own successful future. Wouldn't you give a Rolex if you knew you were going to be wealthy and powerful?"

Wes hesitated. He didn't want to say what he was thinking: that anyone who put a Rolex or diamond ring in one of Temple Carrollton's collection baskets was just plain nuts. Instead he asked, "What do you all do with the tokens?"

"It depends. Some are just stuff as you said. Many of those are discarded later in another town after Temple would bless them and ask that they always be a sign of success for the donor. Those of value are also blessed. Then those are sold to help support the crusade for all followers. Those sacrificial gifts by a few help many. Those givers have true charity in their hearts even though that may have not been their first intent. They're doubly blessed."

Wes again kept his thoughts to himself. It was obvious that he was not a true believer or would have ever been a Carrollton follower. He thought most of what Matthew Christian espoused was a bunch of crap.

The young man continued, "Because of what happened to Temple the night of his appearance, we hadn't finished counting the money or sorting the tokens. We'd put everything into the safes and got it all out again the next day. With more than three thousand followers in attendance, you can imagine that it's a tremendous task to sort everything. Of course, Augusta hovers over us waiting to hear the final tally. She's so careful about every dollar we bring in. Since she joined the staff, I don't think any of the lieutenants would dare try to take something. She would do them in! As they say, 'in a New York minute.'"

"Is she really that tough? She seems like a lovely young woman with an IQ of genius proportions." Wes wanted to hear more about someone who was considered tough and ready to do someone in.

"She's all that you say, but she doesn't fool around when the funds are being counted. I know my father was a millionaire many times. Some of that is credited to the way Augusta does her job. She was close to Temple because he felt the same as she did when it came to black ink. Remember he believed in the profits of his dedication. It worked for him, too."

"So is it something that was in one of the baskets that brought you here this morning?"

"Exactly." Matthew reached into the inside pocket of his jacket and handed Wes a Marriott envelope. "When I saw this card, I put it aside because it was so strange. Then when I thought about it more, I wondered if it might have something to do with what happened later. Where could something this old and this personal come from?"

Wes opened the envelope and extracted an ordinary driver's license. He was amazed. It was a Georgia driver's license for Temple Carrollton with an expiration date of more than fourteen years ago. The photo was definitely a younger version of the man who now lay in the morgue. Even with all the modern technology that can duplicate almost anything, Wes felt confident that this was the real thing.

The hair on the back of his neck quivered as often happened when he felt he'd just been handed an important piece of evidence. He looked again at the card and said, "Matthew, if we can connect this card with the person who put it into the basket, I think we'll have taken a huge leap toward finding the murderer of your father."

"I'm not a detective so I thought I might be overreacting, but when I saw this, I had an almost queasy feeling. I thought I might have even seen this person when we collected the tokens. You know, just like you and I had seen each other that night. I never thought I would see you again. I guess, really, I wish I never had."

"I understand what you're saying. Most families and friends of a victim wish they had never seen us until we can identify the person who stole a part of their lives. What's interesting about what you have here is that someone is sending us a clue. They either want us to discover something about them, about someone else or even about Temple Carrollton. Now we have to figure out what it means, but there's no doubt in my mind that it relates to the later event."

"Can I help?"

"What do you know about your father when he lived here in Atlanta? I know he was from Kentucky but was here for several years. That information has come up in our research. You call Birmingham your home. Is that where you were born?"

"Yes. My mother's family has always lived there. I'm nineteen years old so she was there before that." Matthew lowered his eyes and was in deep concentration. He looked up again at Wes, "There's something wrong here. My father always said he lived here in Atlanta with his family when he was going to college. He didn't talk about what years, you know, just his life.

"If that's true, then I was born long before he went to college. I remember living with my mom for quite a while. We didn't always seem to have money. That happened only when I got older; maybe like when I was around seven or eight. Then my father came and got me a couple of years later. I've been with his movement since then."

"Matt, all of what you're saying still could be the way it happened. You might have been born when your dad and mom were teenagers. Lots of families just sweep those events aside and go on. Your mom stayed in Birmingham, maybe to be near her family. Your dad may have been with his folks here and gone to college before becoming an evangelist."

Matthew Christian looked stricken. He felt like his whole life had been a farce. He'd heard what might be half-truths or even complete lies. Why would that be? Might he be Temple's bastard? Did his parents never marry? What about his brothers? Do they know more than he does? We're all close to the same age. Did his father begin his wonderful life of dedication to others with a secret of illegitimate sons? Does he want to know these answers? He worshiped his father. His mother always said he was her husband and a good man. He believed that. He didn't want Temple to slip off his pedestal. Whatever his father did, he must've had a good reason. The Lord would not have blessed his life as he did, if he'd been a bad person.

Wes saw the pain in Matthew's eyes. He wanted to comfort him, but he didn't know enough about the situation to say the right thing. He thought about how his own father and he had decided to tell his son, Jason, about the short marriage between Wes and his mother. They told him the simple truth. They told him that it had nothing to do with him. It was her way. Jason accepted his life. When he talked about the past, it was never with pain. Unfortunately, Temple Carrollton made another choice and now his son was feeling betrayed.

"Detective Wesley, if I can help you, let me know. Right now I have a lot of things to sort out. This morning has been terribly upsetting. I thought the license would be helpful to you. I didn't know it would be so painful for me. If it's OK with you, I'm going back to the hotel."

Chapter 27

Walter

As the day had progressed, the image of a cold beer at Manuel's became almost an obsession. Wes looked at the pile of notes on his desk. Constant telephone calls from every corner of Atlanta. Some of those callers insisted that they had the clue to finding who had shot Franklin Raub. Others wanted to harangue the whole police force for "allowing" the president of City Council to be shot. Many people were interested in whether the police were getting help from the 'saintly' staff of Temple Carrollton since they "obviously have a direct line to God." Then there were the few who were compelled to warn that Satan was present. He was going to wipe out all the leaders of Atlanta then move on to Dunwoody, one of the upscale suburban communities in the area.

There were even a few calls related to Ramblin' Randy suggesting that his murder was the first part of the conspiracy to create a whole new leadership team for the city. They couldn't explain how that fit. He had not been a business leader for years and seemed to have created his own destiny to destruction.

It was interesting to Wes that some of the callers had come to the same conclusion that he and Billy Joe had: that there had to be a connection among these killings. He was convinced that more and more people were paying serious attention to real crime television shows and books. The public was almost as preoccupied with criminals as the detectives were occupied with these lowlife characters.

Of course each call began as if the caller had important information. They wanted to get someone's attention. Wes wanted to tell them to go back to calling the local talk shows rather than take up his time. However, he had learned many times that a casual conversation could produce a worthwhile tip to follow. Since there still were no good, solid clues in any of the three murders, he was open to all suggestions. Unfortunately after hours of calls or messages left with staff, he did not see anything of great promise.

He had talked with Franklin Raub's secretary, Tomeika Jones, about the president's last day. Together they reviewed the man's business calendar for names that might create questions or voids of time that might suggest that he had something to hide. There appeared to be nothing obvious. Tomeika said that he had spent the day, like all days, running from meeting to meeting, listening to citizens' comments and reading the piles of paper that passed over his desk. She said he had mentioned that he was going to have to defend the new privatized water contract when he got to Manuel's that evening, but that was the best place to make a stand. Everyone who was somebody who had any interest in Atlanta sooner or later went to Manuel's.

Wes smiled when Tomeika had said that, since he knew that was where he too was headed in a few hours. Not that he considered himself 'somebody,' but he did know that it was the best place to hang out if you were going to see Atlanta's finest and not so fine. People who made the news and people who read the news all came to the grungy restaurant on Highland Avenue.

As he parked in Manuel's lot that covered an entire block, the detective was still thinking about his interviews with Tomeika Jones and several other staff members in Franklin Raub's office. Had he missed something important? Did anyone seem to be evasive? Was there an undercurrent of silence? He didn't think so. Everyone seemed genuinely distraught and baffled. "Why would someone do this?" He worked so hard for this city."

Wes knew that Walter would be waiting for him just inside the door at what was called "the police table." It had become a traditional spot now flanked by photographs and mementos of some of the more colorful members of the force. There was even a framed shirt of one of the deceased detectives who had appeared in several novels written about Atlanta and its seamier side. This was Wes' choice of where to chug a beer, eat a hot dog or meet your friends. Wes planned to do all three.

"Detective Wesley!" Walter's voice boomed over the early evening din. The noise would grow exponentially as more customers arrived to make their transition from work to play. Happy Hour lasted the whole evening here. It always seemed like one big party. Manuel's was not the place to go to hide away in a corner.

"Walter, you're amazing. You still haven't learned that in Atlanta the in thing is to be late. You're as dependable as my alarm clock." Wes slipped into a chair across the table from his friend and added, "How the hell are you? Damn, you look like one of those big executives at Coca-Cola."

Walter laughed, smoothed his hand over his new burnt orange, Oxford cloth shirt with a tiny polo player on the pocket, "Well, I do look a tad different than when we first met. Then I was wearin' cast off clothes from the Union Mission and shitty shoes I'd found in a dumpster. Whoever said they prefer the good old days, didn't have my good old days."

"Yeah, baby, you've come a long way. You've worked hard, Walter. Andy would've been proud of you. You've proven that no one ever is completely gone. Each person leaves his legacy. You're his. So what's going on in your life that I don't already know about?"

Walter talked about his job and that he had just upgraded his computer because he was planning to learn about designing web sites. He figured he could do some for people during the day when he wasn't at work. This was going to be a chance to learn more and maybe lead to a new direction in his life. "Of course, if it doesn't, I haven't lost anythin'. I know more and I still have my job and…."

Wes noticed the hesitation, "And?"

"Well, good bud, I got me a sweetie who thinks I'm fuckin'

fantastic."

"All right! You picked one smart enough to know a good man when she sees one. What does this wonderful lady do? Another computer whiz like you?"

"You got that right. We're both nerds. She works at CNN. She knows all 'bout computers as well as always knowin' the news. Sometimes I think she has a 'photo- mind.' You know, she seems to remember everythin' I ever said. I have to be damn careful that I don't promise stuff I really don't want to do, 'cause she remembers." Walter took a swig of his beer and added, "Don't get the wrong picture here. She got her a nice body too. Oh, yeah, man. My woman's got it all."

Wes hailed a waiter by name, ordered another beer for Walter, two for himself, four hot dogs and a double order of fries. He figured that would take care of them as they talked. He and Walter had developed a close friendship during the time Walter stayed with him while recuperating from a beating by the murder suspect in the shooting case of the Georgia Tech student.

In no time, the hot dogs and fries were gone. Two fresh beers sat between the two men when Walter said, "Oh, yeah, Ole Jasper said to say hi to you. He's been tellin' everyone that he got to talk to the best detective in Atlanta."

"Well, he won't say that for long if we don't soon pick up some clues to this week's three murders, including Ramblin' Randy's. These have really been tough. Maybe it's because we don't have you as our dep-u-ty."

"You knows I'm available. I would help you with anythin'. Just ask. Too bad, I wasn't sleepin' at the Mission that night. Maybe I would've seen somethin' like I did that night at Georgia Tech. You showed me how the littlest thin' can help you solve a crime. Ole Jasper keeps askin' me to retell how I was your dep-u-ty. He loves that story!"

"You were the turning point for us. Maybe we should hang that orange shirt up here with the police uniform shirt. We could label it: Another Colorful Atlantan."

"Hey, man, I can wait. Remember that this guy was gone at an early age. I want to enjoy what I got for awhile." Walter sent a hand salute toward the shirt, giving its owner his own style of respect.

"Funny 'bout Ole Jasper. He talks like he knew Ramblin' Randy better than the other guys. He's been tellin' little stories. I'm not sure if they're stories that are before or after the fact. Isn't that kinda detective talk?"

Wes laughed and nodded his head. Walter was always saying something that was amusing. "What're these stories? Maybe we can sort out the before or after the fact."

"He said Randy liked to talk about the past. I mean his were real good old days. When he lived in Buckhead. Had a helluva house. Big bucks in his pocket. Had his picture in the papers. Jasper once thought he made it up, but then decided that some of it might be true. Even when Randy was wasted, the basic facts never changed. It's a weird world."

"For sure. But back to the stories. Give me those facts, dep-u-ty. We need them for our case." Wes knew that Walter would like to know that his opinion was valued. There may be something in the tales.

Walter straightened up. His face took on a serious expression. He was transforming from friend to colleague. Wes was ready to respect his input. The former street person, who used to sleep wrapped in discarded plastic bags, began a litany of vignettes about Randall Robert E. Lee. Wes took a few notes to remind himself later. Much of what Walter was telling related closely enough to what was already known about the victim. There was a ring of truth in the stories. He listened intently. Suddenly he gave his full attention to the words.

"Ole Jasper, he says that Randy liked to brag about the important men that he knew and could always count on. They were as close as brothers, maybe closer because they shared secrets. Ole Jasper thought that was all a bunch of crap. Anyway, a few days before he was killed, Randy had been drinkin', saw

Jasper sittin' by himself in the yard and plopped down beside him. Those're Jasper's words, 'plopped down.' He said that Randy just couldn't wait to tell him that one of his special friends was comin' to Atlanta. That he was comin' just like Jesus rode into Jerusalem. People would be waitin' in line to see him and touch him and be blessed by him. Ole Jasper was laughin' and Randy got mad. He said he was too stupid of a son-of-a-bitch to know the truth when it was sittin' right beside him. Randy said, 'I'll show you. When he gets here, I'm gonna see him and get out of this place. My friend will take care of me. He has the power. We had special certificates that made us loyal and special.'

"Ole Jasper was still laughin' and Randy was getting' madder. He raised the Bible that he'd been holdin' and yelled, 'You'll see. I have proof right here. He'll save me.' Poor Jasper at the time thought he was talkin' about Jesus and that Randy was really losin' it. Then later when he heard about that preacher man, Carrollton, he wondered if that was who he meant."

Wes was fascinated. This story supported their conclusion that there is a relationship among these recently murdered men. It doesn't point to the shooter, but it does add strength to the task to dig deeper to find this tie. What he wondered now was whether they could discover the right connection before another man is killed.

Chapter 28

Janeen Newman Carson

Wes dropped off Walter at his place only a few blocks from both Manuel's and the police headquarters. He drove back to his office with only one thing on his mind: Randy's Bible. He believed that the reference that was made related to the little piece of parchment, not to Jesus. Of course, Randy may have thought that Jesus' help was for him, but it seemed more likely that his help was the tele-evangelist, Temple Carrollton. Ole Jasper was right-on when he made that connection. It seemed that people who live constantly on the edge of risk have sharpened perceptions.

He entered the building that never closed down or slept. He often wondered if the weariness of the building didn't transfer into the inhabitants' bones. Many times Wes felt fresh and ready to roll until he walked into the dreary surroundings called City Hall East. Years before when the Sears store closed down their operation and the building became a part of Atlanta's government, there was much said about this being a huge opportunity for the city. What it turned out to be was a huge expense for the city that was folded into the enormous debt that had been handed from one mayor to another.

He went to his office and took the Bible out of the Kinko's box. He flipped the pages and looked at the folded, worn parchment square.

"This is the key," Wes said out loud. "I know it is." He made a note to compare this scrap of paper and the certificate that was important to Temple Carrollton. That is if it ever materialized. Then he'd find a matching paper that belonged to Franklin Raub. His intuition told him it existed. The lab could tell him if they matched. He clapped himself on the side of the head and thought, "Stupid! Why didn't I ask Tomeika Jones about a special certificate? That's what I'll do first thing in the morning."

He looked at his watch. It was still early. He could give Janeen a call and stop there on the way home. Maybe not even go home. He thought of Walter and the thrill in his voice when he talked about his new lady friend. Life has a way of looking so much better when work is not the only focus. He picked up the telephone.

"Hey, wonderful woman, do you need the company of someone who worships and adores you?"

"Anyone I know? If you think I'm fishing to hear more beautiful words, you're right. You make my day with your sweet talkin'."

"You know him well, but what I had in mind was for you to get to know him even better. You just might have missed a secret place that's just waiting to be discovered. I'm ready to leave the office. I can be there in five minutes. I never had a girl before who lived right smack in the middle of town between my house and my office. The convenience is what has captivated my heart. I don't even have to worry about heavy traffic. Maybe some heavy breathing once I see you."

"Wes, you're just too much. But I'm willing to put up with you. Actually, I love having you around. Come on over. It'll be the best part of my day and I already had a great day."

Wes left a message on Billy Joe's voice mail to see him ASAP in the morning and headed for his car. Too bad he couldn't tear off his shirt and use a red and blue Superman cape like in the old comic books and movies. Then he could be standing at her door in the wink of an eye. He would just have to be patient because he was no Superman.

Every traffic light turned red as he approached. In the middle of one block, eight people straggled across the street. Wes had the choice of running over the last four or jamming on his brakes and keeping himself out of court. He chose his brakes and a tap on his horn. He immediately knew that had been a bad decision, since it encouraged the group to slow down rather than get out of the street. He wished he had been driving a patrol car. That would have moved along their well-padded butts.

• • • •

"Did you and Walter run out of conversation? I thought you two would close down Manuel's in the wee hours," Janeen was talking while she took two beers out of the freezer and opened a can of mixed nuts.

"No, we had plenty of conversation but....Well, you know that old song: wedding bells are breaking up that old gang of mine?'

"What? Walter's getting married? Wow!"

"No, I don't exactly mean marriage. Just that he's found himself a lady friend. I think he wanted to spend some time with her. It worked out, because I was thinking that I wanted to see you too. You know how I am about my Janeen fix. I think I'm hooked. I was never very tolerant about addictions. Now I have one too that I don't want to give up."

"Should I be pleased that I'm an addiction or should I help you look for a cure? Maybe AA could give you some direction. Twelve Steps? Or do you need thirteen?"

"No steps. I like this glow. If this is what uppers do, I'm all for them. Come over here and let's see how high I can go? You look mighty good tonight."

Wes reached for Janeen. She nestled into the curves of his body and they were silent and still for a moment. He kissed her lightly on the lips and was struck by the overwhelming force that turned the friendly kiss into one filled with passion and desire. She returned his kiss and held him as tightly as she could; wanting them to be one. She was shocked at the intensity of her feelings. She felt weak and strong at the same time. Her head seemed to be spinning while her body was throbbing. She wondered if those parts of her body were still connected.

Wes picked her up in his arms. He knew this magical moment

could have only one ending. He knew they were both in tune. There was no reason to turn back or take more time. He only needed enough time for him to take them both to her bedroom.

The room was almost dark. The hall light was on; spreading its soft glow into the bedroom, across the middle of the bed. When Wes saw the trail of light, he believed it was perfect for making love to the pretty woman he had in his arms. If he placed her carefully on the bed, the light would reflect on her breasts and down to her thighs. In his mind, he could already feel the silky skin that he would find under her clothes. He could feel the warmth of her body as he was removing her blouse and under garments. His excitement was full. He knew that tonight there would be no waiting, no tantalizing foreplay, no sweet words.

Janeen lay in the triangular shaped light pool. She had never felt so sexual. Fleetingly she wondered why tonight was so different. She thought, "I don't really care. I want every bit of Wes to be part of me and the time is now." She threw her head back, looked him in his eyes and said in a husky whisper, "Hurry. This is our time."

· · · ·

Wes opened one eye and saw that it was almost five o'clock. His mind was foggy but was clear enough to figure out that if it was dark, it might still be night. He felt Janeen move against the comfort of his body with her back against his chest. His one hand was still on her breast, which he remembered was the position he was in when he fell asleep. Earlier he had seen himself as Superman, but right now he felt he had used up all of Clark Kent's super power. He was beat. He needed more vitamins or less sex drive.

"Hey, are you awake?" Janeen asked sleepily.

"I think so. At least I see a clock that I would never allow in my dreams. Who wants to be pressed by time when he's living out some fantasy?"

"Hmmmm, a fantasy? Are you telling me that what I think we did, I really dreamed? Are you saying that this wonderful afterglow is simply a figment of my imagination? What a dirty trick. I protest!"

"No, we were for real. More than for real. We were damn unbelievable. Until I met you, I thought I was going to live to an old age like my dad, but, Sweetheart, you're sending me to an early grave. I should've met you when I was still young and horny. My intentions go way beyond my capabilities."

"No way. I can tell you that your capabilities are more than enough for this woman. Somewhere around three times, I stopped counting. I used to hear some of the students rave on about what they did the night before. I thought they were all making it up. I didn't even know such athletic love was possible. I'm going back to campus and apologize to those students.

"I guess if it's five o'clock, I might as well get up," Janeen stretched, turned to Wes and planted a kiss on his shoulder.

"Get it up? Are you kidding? I'd be lucky to sit up."

"That's not what I said. I think we need a rest. Maybe going to work is the only way to get it. I'm headed for the shower, in more ways than one."

In another minute Janeen had swung her slim legs over the edge of the bed and was headed into the bathroom. Wes lay there a short time listening to the shower water. Why not join her? There was enough room for him. He could whisper in her ear that he loved her and invite her to come back to bed with him. His thoughts wavered. He began to think about why he needed to talk to Billy Joe first thing. It would be a struggle, but he needed to get up and head for home.

Chapter 29

Billy Joe LaCrosse

"We've got to find another one of these damn certificates? We need to know who else might have one hung in his office or stuck in his desk. Billy Joe, what if Carrollton or Raub had similar certificates? We could be dealing with a serial killer. A very clever and lucky damn serial killer. We've got to make some progress before we have another body of someone we know. Atlanta is being targeted for some reason that we must identify. I think we have our own homeland terrorism. And I'm willing to bet that it's not some international conspiracy. This one is home grown. Just like Timothy McVey."

Billy Joe had walked into Wes' office within minutes of arriving at City Hall East. He knew from the message on his cell phone that Wes wanted immediate response. He looked at his partner. He thought he looked hung over. He and Walter must have tied on a good one at Manuel's. That's easy to do since often the conversation gets so heated and interesting between tables that the number of drinks being consumed is lost.

"I'm right with you, my man. We've been thinkin' this was our main clue. We just haven't been able to put it together with anythin'. Do we know if Raub has one?"

"No, but that's on my list for this morning. We need to see if Lee's widow can give us more information. We need to go back and talk to Raub's family. Also we need to find out about the one that we know Carrollton had. So let's get moving. If we find anything else, let's not miss it. We're running several paces behind our killer. This is going to happen again," Wes was talking fast but Billy Joe knew every thought was clear.

Billy Joe stood up. "I'll call Deanna Lee since she already

knows me. She knows that this paper existed. Hell, she's seen it. Maybe she can remember more about it. Then I'll go talk to the Raub's place."

"I'll start with Thomson Warrenton. If that doesn't work, I'll get to the Brothers Three. Kids like to sniff around their parents' treasures so maybe one of them will remember something. Let's contact each other as we finish with these guys. Once we get one of the awards or whatever they are, maybe we'll get some research done to learn more about what they mean or who else might have one."

· · · ·

Billy Joe went to his phone. Deanna Lee answered on the second ring and didn't seem at all surprised that it was the Homicide detective on the other end of the line. Her first question was about what progress had been made in finding the murderer of her ex-husband. Billy Joe explained that they didn't have a person of interest yet. There was some evidence that they believe would lead them to the perpetrator. He wasn't willing to tell her more because it might interfere with the case.

"I understand, Detective LaCrosse. Sometimes I wonder about all of the information that the media tells the public. The guilty person could be using those facts to help elude being caught. Freedom of the press has to be lead by prudence."

"We agree on that, Mrs. Lee. If we had time, we could pursue a whole discussion on the media versus justice, but I called for another reason. If you remember, we talked about the certificate that your husband hung on his office wall. Can you give me any details about that? Maybe some of the wording? A date? Maybe it was signed by someone you know?"

"Oh, Detective, I don't think I know anything. As I said, I thought it was rather childish to be paying attention to something like that," the woman hesitated as if trying to visualize the old memento, "I'm sorry that I didn't pay more attention. You do remind me that there was a silly signature on it. It was Phoenix Byrd."

"Phoenix Bird? Like on our Atlanta seal and on all of our

police shields?"

"Right, except this bird was spelled B-Y-R-D. I asked about it once when I was kidding Randy about his souvenir. He said very seriously, 'We're all going to rise above the others just as the Phoenix bird rose from the ashes.' I guess if he could have seen into his future; he would've known how wrong he was. That's it, Detective LaCrosse. I mostly remember that the stupid certificate was ordinary looking but carried a powerful message for Randy. If I think of anything else, I'll call you. Hope you'll call me as soon as you have some news."

Billy Joe assured her that he would do that, thanked Deanna and said that he would look forward to a call if she remembered more about the certificate. He added that many important clues came from outside the police department. He knew that he didn't have to say much else because the widow of Randy Lee was as anxious to solve the mystery of his death as he was.

• • • •

Billy Joe left the homicide office and drove across the city to the Raub home. He felt since Franklin Raub had been president of the City Council that it might be more politically correct to talk face to face. Maybe he'd make some points with the chief.

The street was empty, no neighbors standing around whispering about what had happened only a few hours earlier. He always marveled at how fast people could adjust and return to their normal routines. Murder was in the news often enough that it was no longer an event of great import except for the family that was left behind. This morning the only ripple in the otherwise serene street scene was the rippling yellow crime scene tape that still stretched along the perimeter of the Raub property.

The detective waited for a response to the door chime. He assumed that some of the family would be at home. He doubted that young Frankie had gone to school or to meet his friends as he would have done other mornings. Last night after finding his father's body, the young man was in shock. By this time, he would be feeling the enormity of what had just happened to

168

him and his mother. Their lives had reached a crossroad and an unknown person had determined their new direction.

He heard heavy footsteps approach and the door swung open. Frankie stood there looking like he just got out of bed. Eyes puffy, his long, thick hair was wild and he had on a rumpled t-shirt and a pair of gray sweat pants. He certainly wasn't expecting company and looked surprised to see him, "Ahh, hi, Detective. It seems like you just left here."

"You're right, Frankie. It was only a few hours ago. I've a couple questions on my mind and wanted a chance to talk to you and your mother."

"Mom's not here. She's meeting with our preacher. Making plans, I guess. There'll be so many people who'll want to be at the funeral. She wanted to keep it private but decided that my dad deserved a huge gang to say goodbye to him. He loved being out in front so why not keep him there for another day or so," While talking to Billy Joe, Frankie had motioned for him to come in. They headed toward the back of the house.

"I was making some breakfast so come on out to the kitchen. I can give you some coffee unless that's like accepting some kind of bribe. My dad was so hyper about that kind of thing. So if you can't accept coffee, I understand."

"No, Frankie, a cup of coffee is fine. The department doesn't consider that a bribe. Now, if you'd added a doughnut, I might have to decline." Billy Joe's big smile seemed to stretch from one side of his head to the other.

"Geez, I wish I had a doughnut. Mom says breakfast is supposed to be healthy food so she never gets stuff like that. Look at this: whole wheat bread, fake butter, bran cereal. Yuk. I stop at Krispy Krème on my way to school, but don't rat on me. She'd go ballistic."

"Your confession is safe with me. We police hear all kinds of secrets every day."

"Yeah, right. I bet they aren't about doughnuts," Frankie smiled for the first time. He was a handsome young man who had the interesting coloring of his mother and strong features of his dad.

Billy Joe accepted the mug of coffee from him and asked, "Frankie, we're interested if your dad belonged to any special clubs or maybe he was given a special award that he was really proud of. Can you think of somethin' like that?"

"Are you kidding? My dad had enough awards to paper the walls of this kitchen. You know how it is with pols. People are always trying to get favors so they give out some stupid award. I don't think he took any of them seriously. He knew the game. He just said, "Thanks, man, this is cool." Well, maybe he didn't say cool. He was too cool for that." Frankie smiled again at his own little joke.

"How 'bout somethin' that he had for years and years. Like long before he was in politics. Maybe when he was young."

"Oh, you must mean his Phoenix Byrd thing. Man, he thought that was better than being elected governor. I mean that. He would sometimes just stare at that silly piece of paper. He once told me that it cost him a lot but that everyone who belonged to the group paid the same. He also said that having it was like a lucky charm and that he wouldn't be president of the City Council without it."

"That's a very strong feelin'. Did he give you an amount of what it cost him?"

"No. I asked him the same question and he said, 'A lot. But I did it.' Don't you think that's kinda a funny answer?"

"Well, Frankie, you know how parents are. Sometimes they never explain. I know my kids say I expected them to have been born already understandin' what it took me a hundred years to learn."

"Damn, Detective, you don't look a hundred, but I guess your kids know. Besides they're right. Parents do act weird. I think that's documented right in the Bible. Well, OK. Maybe not the Bible, but we can see the strange things that our parents do. We're not stupid. What else did you want to ask?" Frankie was relaxing a bit as they talked. He ate toast piled high with sugar-free strawberry jam.

"Do you know where this Phoenix Byrd certificate is now? Could you show it to me?"

"Maybe. My dad always kept it in his desk. I'll go look," the boy said as he started out of the room. He stopped and turned, "Do you think this old piece of crap had something to do with my dad being shot?"

"We're not sure yet, Frankie, but we think that it's the best clue we have so far."

After putting the certificate into his briefcase, Billy Joe drained his coffee mug and Frankie walked him to the door. He walked directly to his car and was opening the door when he heard his name, "Detective LaCrosse, wait. Hey, don't take off yet."

He turned and saw Franklin Raub's sister-in-law jogging toward him. She looked healthy and strong. Her skin glistened from the effort. She didn't look all miserable and exhausted like so many runners on the streets. Her hair was pulled back into a thick pony tail that bobbed lightly with each stride. Billy Joe decided that Franklin Raub certainly had been surrounded by beautiful women.

"Wow, I almost missed you. Didn't know you were going to be back to visit so soon. What's up? Have you found the killer?" Laurel Plitz sounded both hopeful and challenging.

"No, Ma'm, but we're closer than we were yesterday. The leads are slim. This killer has been very lucky."

"Maybe the person has been very good. This isn't just a casual, everyday shooting that we've become accustomed to. Detective, it looks like this person is already way ahead of you guys. It looks like you have three corpses that could somehow relate. My roommates say that those three men really pissed off someone. What do you think of that?"

Homicide never lacks for amateur sleuths. Everyone has a theory. When he was first transferred to Homicide, these theories would get to him, but he soon learned that often this guesswork provided a new idea that turned out to be of value

"Very interestin'. Can you think of someone your brother-in-law ticked off?"

"That could be a very long list, Detective. You may never get through that group of suspects. It might be easier to start with that Preacher Man. Surely, Reverend Holier than Thou, had only legions of fawning friends. But maybe there was one time when he might not have 'turned the other cheek.'"

"Ms. Plitz, do you know if Franklin Raub knew Temple Carrollton?" Billy Joe thought the question was worth asking.

Laurel thought about that for a moment. She had never heard Franklin say the name Temple Carrollton but... "You know, Detective, I can't say yes or no. I can tell you this: Franklin paid attention to that man when he was in the paper or on the TV. He just seemed to give a little extra attention to that big phony. Maybe he was simply intrigued. Maybe he wished he had that much power. Just last week, when there was a big Carrollton ad in the paper, he pointed it out and said, 'Now there's a man who's a big success. He knows the system.'" She crossed her arms over her breasts giving Billy Joe the feeling that she had punctuated the comment with a huge exclamation mark. Was she purposely sending a message to him or innocently repeating the conversation?

"You called him a phony. Why? Did you know Reverend Carrollton?"

"No, but anyone who trades money for promises of guaranteed success and then targets mostly the young whose judgment is still in its infancy is not sincere nor real. That man was a charlatan. He was also a womanizer. No, I can't give you chapter and verse to prove that statement, but I've heard lots of gossip. He was seen in many nightspots in Atlanta. Always with a different, very young, attractive woman. The gossip is based on that kind of 'churchly' behavior."

Billy Joe was amazed. He came here to hopefully learn

about the Phoenix Byrd certificate and he got an unexpected earful. Laurel Plitz was a relaxed conversationalist. She probably enjoyed knowing something that she assumed might be news to him.

"Well, your brother-in-law was also a very successful man. I'm sure many people would say that he, too, knew the system."

"You bet he did! That's probably why he was intrigued with the good reverend. They were rather alike in some ways." She looked at her watch and let out a little girl screech, "Damn! I'm going to be late. Gotta run. Good to see you. Stop in again when you're in the neighborhood. We need some interesting and good-looking men to grace this street. Can you believe out of the seven houses on this block, the population is 21 females and six males? As we often ask, what is wrong with this picture? So long, Detective. Have a lucky day."

Chapter 30

Wes T. Wesley

In case Wes got back before he did, Billy Joe used his cell phone to leave a message, "Hey, Wes, I got a certificate. Frankie Raub knew right where it was. I have it with me, but I'll be damned. I don't see how it's gonna help. All it probably proves is that these guys knew each other for a lot of years. But, I also got an earful from Franklin Raub's sister-in-law. She's full of theories and little stories. You'll get 'em all when I see you.

. . . .

Wes was still pursuing the illusive certificate in another part of town. He had gone to the Marriott, couldn't find Thomson Warrenton so he tried Augusta Martinez's room. Although she didn't sound happy to hear from him, she said she would come down and meet him in the lobby.

The detective waited at the bank of jauntily lit elevators and thought there was a circus atmosphere in this part of the lobby. The shape of the elevator cars, the sparkling glass panels and the twinkling lights reminded him of the fancy tents and cages that were his recollection of the circus from when Jason, his dad and he would go as a special treat. He could feel lightness in his body as he remembered those wonderful days. His mood was broken when he heard his name.

"Detective Wesley, I think I caught you daydreaming," Augusta Martinez was standing close to him, again looking like a teenager. She had on low-slung jeans and a short crop top with a picture of Temple Carrollton on the front. After thinking that it was too late to advertise, Wes wondered what was on the back. Maybe a basket overflowing with dollars and trinkets?

"You did, indeed. I was having a short walk down Memory

Lane. Not exactly a senior moment but getting close," Wes admitted, "Thank you for agreeing to see me. I have a couple questions. Then I'll get out of your way."

"It's OK. Why don't we sit over there where the hotel has conveniently created a place for us to talk? We'll help make the place look like it still has some guests. I understand that the census is down almost 40 percent. The manager would like you to announce that the killer is behind bars and will never enter the Marriott again. Can you do that, Detective?"

Wes heard a real edge in her voice as she threw out the question. If he knew her better he might ask if she was mad at him. He tried to remember how they had parted yesterday after he interviewed her. He couldn't think of anything in particular.

"Not right now. Our shooter is very careful. Seems to have a precise plan. Wants to keep us working overtime."

"What do you mean plan? The guy comes in, shoots and walks. That's a plan?"

"Yes, but we're theorizing that the murderer has repeated that sequence more than once so we're looking for a tie to other cases, which, Ms. Martinez, is why I'm here."

Augusta looked at him coolly and said, "Interesting. What is it you want to ask? I really need to get back to my job. Nothing is being accomplished. I have had to take care of canceling our engagements and making plans for a funeral when your very slow medical examiner finally releases Temple's body. We're going to need a huge place to accommodate all the followers who want one last blessing from their savior."

"Savior? Isn't that a bit strong?"

"No, it is not. He was that to many. That's why Temple flourished. Now, what do you have on your mind?"

"What I wanted to ask someone who was close to Carrollton was whether he had an award of some kind that he was particularly attached to. Maybe a certificate that was special."

Augusta Martinez appeared to be thinking about her response.

"Why would an old certificate be important?"

"What makes you think that what I'm looking for is old, Ms. Martinez?

Augusta was furious with herself again. What was it about this man that made her say things she didn't want to say? She wished she hadn't answered her telephone. She wished he'd get out of her life. She had things to do and he slowed her down. She had her own plan to follow.

"I didn't mean that what you were looking for was old. It's just an expression. Like that old thing. I'm sure you know what I mean."

"Sure, gotcha. Just an expression. So do you know about an old certificate that your boss kept?"

"He had lots of stuff that he insisted bringing along from place to place. He had lots of things people would give him. For someone who lived most of the year in hotel rooms, he was a regular pack rat. He thought lots of things were worth keeping."

Augusta was sure she knew what the detective was looking for, but she wasn't sure she should mention it. For some reason this certificate had always been a thing of mystery and intrigue. When she had seen it, she had a very emotional reaction to it. Like maybe some of Temple's energy was spread across that paper. She was also sure that Thomson knew more about it. It seemed strange that one day she had seen the two of them put it into the trash along with a pile of other items that were filling up their trunks. Temple had reached for it once, but Thomson laid his hand on his shoulder and said something in a whisper.

She had worked out her own meaning for the simple parchment document but had never spoken about it to either man. She didn't need their opinions. She had gathered enough clues by herself, and they did not add to the saintly façade that usually surrounded her boss. She was sure the certificate related to another unknown place in Temple's history that he wouldn't want to have explored by the media.

She knew that what Temple Carrollton appeared to be to the

public was not the person who resided within the aura. If they were going to keep this cash cow going, it was critical that they all work at keeping the legend alive. The body may be gone but the myth must linger on. That was the promise she had made to Thomson. He'd said that he didn't care if they never found who did it, if it meant that the Carrollton Enterprises was killed in the process. She agreed completely.

"What kinds of things did he save? Maybe in all of those piles of stuff, there is this old certificate. Do you remember seeing anything that might be it?"

"Someone would have to go through hundreds of poems, honors, proclamations, letters etc., etc. and another etc. You have no idea how much we've been loading and unloading in cities all across the country. I wouldn't see any of them more special than another. I just don't think I can help you. But, I can ask Thomson, Matthew, Mark, Luke and even my roommate, Annie. Someone else may have seen what you're looking for. Or do you want to ask them all yourself."

"Yes, I will get to each of them soon. But you've been helpful. When do you think Thomson will be available? I would like to talk with him again."

"He thought he'd be back from his meeting about a funeral location in a few hours. I'll ask him to call you, if that would be helpful."

"You can mention I was here, but I'll be trying to contact him too. Thank you for meeting with me, Ms. Martinez."

Wes waited until he saw Augusta step into the elevator and the doors silently close behind her. He knew she was hiding something, but that at the moment she wasn't going to tell him. What is it about these parchment remembrances that seem to raise emotional responses?

The detective turned and headed for the door. He wanted to get back to talk with Billy Joe. They weren't moving this case along fast enough. Every time he picked up his voice mail, e-mail or took a call it was someone screaming about murderers running wild through the streets of Atlanta. If they didn't put these clues together faster, his instincts also screamed that they were soon going to be investigating another shooting.

"Detective Wesley, hey. I hope you're not here about another problem in this hotel. The place is almost empty as it is."

Matthew Christian was stepping off the escalator. Wes had almost walked into the young man as he was hurrying toward the front entrance. Did he believe in coincidence? Hardly ever. So he felt confident that this encounter was meant to be.

"Matthew, I was going to call you. Instead, here you are. I can ask you a question. I think it's important to finding your father's murderer."

"Ask me. I'd like to help you get that scumbag."

"I'm trying to track down a certificate that your dad had for many years. One that was very important to him. We think it's a clue. Since they're both old, it could even relate to the old driver's license."

"Oh, I know exactly what you're talking about. When my brothers and I found it in a box of souvenirs, we thought it was what inspired our dad to get into this business. It said that Temple Carrollton belonged to a special group called the Good Ol' Boys and that his success would come because of his earning this award. Hey, I don't mean those were the exact words but, you know, it was what it meant."

"Yep, that sounds like the one. Do you know where it is?"

"Haven't a clue. We found it maybe two years ago when we were in Denver. I haven't seen it since. He always had it in this same box in a cardboard folder, like you put photos in. Maybe a year ago, when we were back in Denver, we got talking about that thing and looked for it. It wasn't in the box anymore. Haven't thought about it again until you asked. What does it mean?"

"Maybe nothing but we believe that it can help us identify the perpetrator. Thanks for having a great memory. Your information is going to help, Matt."

"Good. I'd like that."

"Me, too. Right now, I gotta get back to the office. I'm glad we ran into each other." Wes shook Matthew's hand and then impulsively patted him on the shoulder, "Matt, we're going to find this person. It won't be long now."

Chapter 31

Wes T. Wesley

As he left Krispy Kreme, Billy Joe tried reaching his partner again. This time Wes answered on the first ring. Billy Joe told him that he had a certificate in his hands that had belonged to Franklin Raub.

"You're one step ahead of me..."

Then Billy Joe interrupted, "Always. But do go on."

"I will, thank you. I ran into Matt and he confirmed that there was such a document. He added that he hadn't seen it for a couple of years. I'm going to try Warrenton later. I think he'll know more and we'll see if he wants to keep it a secret. I didn't see him because he was out trying to rent the Georgia World Congress Center for the funeral."

"You're shittin' me. Is that the truth?"

"No, but it's close. Billy Joe, think about just the regular turnout for these guys' funerals, let alone the curious public. They'll need huge auditoriums. Maybe they could include some room for Ramblin' Randy. He'll probably need a few extra mourners."

"I'm headed to pick up some Johnny's pizza for lunch. I'll get you some too unless the Carrollton gang invited you for a fancy Marriott lunch."

"You sound like you already have your mouth full. Are you eating our pizza?"

"No way, pardner. I'm eatin' a doughnut from your own personal shop. By the way, the girls say hello."

It was too late for doughnuts, but Wes could almost smell the pungent aroma of the spicy, tomato sauce made, according to Johnny himself, 'lovingly by the hands of the Mafia.' Wes wasn't enamored with many foods from the north but he knew that Southern pizza had a slight resemblance to hard grits topped with Campbell's tomato soup. Johnny's was the real thing.

"Great idea. I'm going to try and reach Thomson Warrenton when I hit the office. I'll be right there waiting for you and the pizza."

"I'll be there. Then I can also tell you about my conversation with Ms. Laurel Plitz. If Eve is in, I'll ask if her love affair with research and technology can find somethin' for us. Maybe run the name Phoenix Byrd. Sounds like a joke but it isn't a joke today."

. . . .

Wes sat with the telephone receiver propped on his shoulder. He counted the rings thinking that Canton Roswell would not approve that he was already at five, six...

"Thank you for calling the Atlanta Marriott Marquis. How may I direct your call?"

"Thomson Warrenton. He's a guest."

"My pleasure, one moment please."

"Thomson Warrenton."

"Mr. Warrenton, this is Detective Wesley. I missed you earlier today when I was in the hotel."

"I was meeting with the undertaker about the funeral location. It cannot be at his establishment, but we have everything in order, Detective Wesley, except you still haven't told us when we can claim Temple's body. That is critical. Wouldn't you agree?" His closing question was coated with sarcasm.

"Yes, I would agree. I'll check again with the medical examiner and get back to you today. We don't want to inconvenience you, sir. By the way, why did you decide to have the funeral here? Wasn't Carrollton from Kentucky?"

"Oh, yes, but it's a small town. Atlanta is a major city. This is so much better for visibility."

Wes was only momentarily surprised at what seemed a callous response. His second thought was, 'Of course, maybe the mourners will drop more mementos and money.' He put his cynicism aside and said, "In the meantime, I have a question to ask Do you have the parchment document that Reverend Carrollton carried with him for years that he felt was important enough to take all over the country?" Wes decided he would present the question as if he already knew a lot about it.

There was a brief hesitation. A less trained person may not have noticed, but to Wes it was not a moment of silence but rather like a long, warning blast of a truck horn blaring in his ear.

"What document? I don't believe that I know what you have in mind."

"The one signed by Phoenix Byrd. That document, Mr. Warrenton."

"Sounds very Atlanta to me. Don't you folks use the Phoenix bird as a symbol for the city? Did I not hear that this is the symbol of the rebirth of Atlanta after General Sherman torched everything in sight?" Thomson Warrenton was stalling for time.

"Yes, you have your history right but let's talk about Phoenix B-Y-R-D. Where is that certificate? I have already heard from several people that it exists."

Warrenton felt defeated. He didn't want to have to rehash the past. It didn't do Temple any good then and it certainly wasn't going to help the Carrollton Enterprises now. His next thought he spoke aloud, "Now who told you something like that?"

"It makes no difference. I'm asking you now but maybe we should have you come over here. We can talk about it in my office. I thought you would have no trouble remembering an item that seemed so important to your boss. You have implied that you two were very close."

"Yes, we were very best friends. It's just that you seem to be talking about something that relates to many years ago. How could ancient history have a bearing on this brutal murder?"

Wes was tired of his avoidance. He wanted some hard facts. He didn't care if it was ancient history or a vision into the future, "Mr. Warrenton, you've just reminded yourself that this is a murder investigation of your very best friend, Temple Carrollton. Because of that, let's cut the crap. Tell me about the document now or come down here. We'll work on the facts and your problems with the facts." Wes waited   impatiently for a response. He wasn't in the mood to play games. He was still sure that these shootings were going to continue.

"I'll catch a cab as soon as I report to the others about funeral arrangements. I know I'm not too far from your office."

· · · ·

Eve's car was parked on the top deck. Even with the bright sunlight, it still was dull and dusty looking. Billy Joe doubted that the girl had ever waxed it. She probably never washed it either. Females definitely do not take their transportation as seriously as males. He would never go through more than a few weeks without polishing that fantastic purple paint job on his car. He laughed because his wife said that she was sure he was often mistaken for a pimp when he was driving on Metropolitan Avenue. He didn't mind the jokes because that car was the fifth member of his family.

Eve was walking toward her car as Billy Joe had finished writing on the hood, 'A clean car is a happy car.'

"Hey! You're trespassing, mister. I may call the police. I understand they hang around this parking deck a lot."

"Hell, Eve, they would probably give you a ticket for pollutin' the environment. Never should that car be seen in public. I'm surprised the chief hasn't told you to take a bus."

"Funnyman. Funnyman. Enough of your sarcasm. While you've been concentrating on whose car is the shiniest, I've been helping you do your job. Not only did I answer a half a dozen calls about a murderer running amuck in the streets, I also have found another possible tie between Lee and Carrollton.

"Remember the cigarette butt in the hotel room? You said I could send it to the lab for tests,"

Billy Joe interrupted, "Sure, we said go for it because we

know you're lookin' for material for your thesis. So…"

"For one thing, I noticed that it was the same brand as the pack that was in Lee's box of stuff. So I took some hairs from his comb and sent them and the cigarette butt to be tested for DNA."

"Why do that? That doesn't make any sense. Randy Lee was dead before we ever found the butt in Carrollton's room."

"Might not make sense, but the brand matches so let's wait and see. I gotta run. I'm going over to have a quick visit with my mom. See what ways she has devised to make me wish I had stayed away." Eve unlocked her car door and slipped behind the steering wheel.

Billy Joe watched her as she zoomed out of her parking spot and headed for the exit. There was no doubt in her smug attitude that she was daring them to find something better than she had. He agreed that this could be an odd turn. Could Ramblin' Randy have been with Temple Carrollton before he was shot behind the Union Mission? How else could that cigarette butt get in the preacher's room?

Chapter 32

Thomson Warrenton

The elevator creaked to a stop. Thomson Warrenton had closed his eyes to save himself from having to relate to this unappealing building and his current mission. Since Wesley already knew about Temple's precious certificate, he had to concoct a story that might fit without touching on the true history. He thought he had gotten rid of the real thing forever when he finally convinced Temple that the memory of the club and its members was better buried in a trash container.

He got off the elevator. The environment did not improve. He did not like what he saw, smelled and heard. He hoped that this could be a short and not too painful meeting.

"Mr. Warrenton, thank you for coming. Let's go sit in the interview room. It's not the greatest, but it's better than my cramped office," Wes greeted his visitor.

They each took a chair and pulled them up to the table. Wes took out his recorder and his small note pad. He was looking forward to adding some valuable information to what little they had.

"OK. You know what I'm interested in knowing, so let's hear it. What's the story behind the certificate?"

"It's like so many of the mementos that Temple felt were important. He was a collector. If he had had a family homestead, it would have been full of antiques and stuff that told a story of the past. As for the certificate to which I think you are referring, it was just a rather immature attachment to a little club of friends when he was a young man; like being in a Boy Scout troop."

"Are you talking about a child, a teenager a young adult? Where was this club? Who belonged?" Wes was hoping to hear

Lee or Raub mentioned.

"Probably late teens or a little after. I'm not all that sure. It wasn't something that we talked about, Detective. Let's put it in perspective. It was close to fifteen years ago. Who pays attention to those years once we have passed them and realize the best is yet to come?"

Wes agreed, "We know that's the truth. Who would want to go back to those teen years?"

"Exactly my point. I see that you understand how insignificant something like an old certificate could be," Thomson Warrenton sighed. He relaxed; leaning forward on his elbows.

'Old certificate.' The same words that Augusta Martinez used. Did that imply that the two of them had already discussed the questionable document?

"I would agree that most of us would look at an old club membership as being unimportant to us as adults, but, Mr. Warrenton, all the signs so far are that this was important to your boss and friend. Tell me about the club and, oh, yes, who were some of the members?"

"I just don't know much, Detective. Boys will be boys. That's how I always felt about it. They went hunting together, out drinking, took some weekends at the beach, probably loaned each other some money. You know, always together because they felt secure in gangs at that age. I also got the impression that some of the loans were paid off years later when they each became successful."

"And, did they all become successful? Just like Temple?"

"Well, maybe not that successful, but he always talked like they had done well."

"And who were these men who had done well? Who paid off some of the loans later?"

Warrenton did not want to mention any names that were too well known in Atlanta. He decided to take a chance and name one man who had moved to Miami and started a chain of restaurants. "I remember one name that Temple mentioned a few times. I don't know where he is or what he does now. His name is Gregory Larkin. I really think that's all the help I can be."

"Let's see what we have here. A club that was important to Temple Carrollton, a certificate that was of enough value that he carried it around for years but never talked about what it meant, and exactly the same pattern in the life of another man, Randall Lee, who, by the way, Mr. Warrenton, was also murdered this week. Now do we see a connection? What do you think, sir?" Wes looked directly into the man's eyes and held the stare until Warrenton had to look away.

"I don't think I know or ever heard of the name, Detective. Should I know him?" Did he sound convincing? Can he plead that he doesn't read the Atlanta newspapers or watch television news? Of course he can.

"You may have missed the report in the news because it happened just the day before your own tragedy. But let me fill you in. Randall Lee was about the same age as Carrollton, at one time a very successful businessman, was shot in the night, close range shots with no struggle, no obvious evidence....."

"I don't see where this has anything to do with Temple's murder," Thomson broke in.

"You didn't wait for the clincher, Mr. Warrenton. What I was about to say was that both men had a certificate that was signed by Phoenix Byrd."

Thomson looked amazed. Perhaps because he knew that name so well or because he was shocked that the detective knew it. He wasn't sure what to do. Stay quiet or respond. He chose to respond, "What a coincidence. I know that I never heard Temple mention this man. And wouldn't you think they would plan to get together when Temple was in Atlanta?"

"We think they did. A cigarette butt left in Carrollton's hotel room appears to have been Randall Lee's." Detectives always had the leeway to skirt the absolute truth.

Thomson Warrenton now understood that he was going to have to work extra hard to keep the Carrollton Enterprises alive, well and unscathed. That's what mattered to him and that's what he is dedicated to doing.

"Detective Wesley, even if your conclusion proves a long ago relationship between this Lee man and Temple, how could there be any advantage to trying to put together an ancient history hypothesis? Should you not be concentrating on what has happened now, this week?"

"That's what we're doing. By doing that, we're led over and over again to this Phoenix Byrd certificate. We can't put it aside. We believe that these killings relate directly to the members of this Good Ol' Boys Club. Now, what else can you tell me about other members of this group? What more can you tell me about Gregory Larkin?"

"The answer to both questions is 'nothing.' Temple and I had a huge enterprise to run. We did not sit around talking about what he did as a young man."

"I remember how you first met your boss: the time in the church when he was extremely upset about something. What was bothering him? Did it relate to this club?"

"Absolutely not! I don't know why you would jump to that conclusion. He was struggling with…," He hesitated. He decided that making one big confession was best at this point "…with the fact of having fathered three sons without the sanctity of marriage. He did the right thing and continued to take care of them. He also took care of the mothers, and we will continue to do so as long as Carrollton Enterprises prospers. This relates not one bit to the other subject."

"Let's change the direction again, Mr. Warrenton. I'm interested in the names of other members of the Good Ol' Boys Club. Let's start with another name in addition to Larkin." Wes' voice was no longer conversational. His voice had hardened. He stood up, looming over Warrenton.

"I simply do not know anyone. Larkin was in my mind because Temple had mentioned once that he had received a check from him for a debt. He added, 'See, my old buddies come through.' I

188

remembered that he was in Miami because we were there at the time."

"Mr. Warrenton, might you be able to add the name Franklin Raub to the club roster? Did your boss ever mention being a buddy with the Atlanta City Council President?"

Thomson felt pressure in his chest and up through his shoulders, "Franklin Raub? Wasn't he murdered this week too? What are you suggesting, Detective?"

"I'm not suggesting anything. I'm asking you questions. I'm talking about three men who all carry certificates signed by Phoenix Byrd who were killed all in the same week. We're trying to find a serial killer. We're trying to find who might be next on this guy's list."

Thomson Warrenton was afraid he would faint. Something was happening here that could ruin his whole life. It could end the Carrollton Enterprises.

"I don't believe I ever heard Temple speak of this Raub person. I cannot help you."

"Mr. Warrenton, I would suggest that you go back to the hotel and start looking for some information; perhaps names, dates, companies, etc. and get back to me. You want to also think about something that's in our justice system called withholding evidence. I suggest that because we're convinced that there will be more murders that relate to these three. I'm sure you don't want to be standing before a judge trying to explain how you had access to information about dead man number four, five or six. Well, you get the picture, I'm sure."

Chapter 33

Vance Bowman

After walking Thomson Warrenton to the elevator, Wes returned to his office. He reached his desk just as the telephone rang. He slipped into his desk chair, reached for the receiver and leaned back with the phone cradled on his shoulder, "Homicide. Wesley speaking."

"Ah, yes. Umm, are you a detective?"

"Yes, sir. Detective Wesley, Atlanta Homicide. Who were you calling?"

"I was calling you, I guess. I asked for the person who was investigating the Temple Carrollton murder. This is a terrible thing to happen. How're you doing? Have you found the killer yet?" The voice on the other end of the strange conversation was male, educated, not too old and very hesitant.

Wes walked to the doorway and got the attention of another detective as she walked by. He looked at his caller ID, wrote the number on a piece of scrap paper and added: trace this number. The woman gave him a wave that said OK and kept moving.

"No, sir, this is a very complicated case. Who is this?" Wes hoped that a direct question would produce a direct answer.

"Just an interested citizen. It seems scary that this could happen in one of our premier hotels that has its own security force. Not the same situation like a homeless man being shot near the Union Mission, right?"

"Who do you mean, Mr. ....?" Maybe he would fill in his name.

"That Lee guy. The paper said that he was a Georgia Tech alum. Probably lots of people knew him. Wouldn't you agree?"

Wes concentrated on the voice. There was a slight, soft

Southern accent, but it was almost unnoticeable. The man seemed a bit out of breath. Could be from exertion? Excited? Stressed?

"Did you know him, sir?" Wes was sure he already knew the answer.

"This is awful, Detective. This couldn't be worse," the man choked on the last word. Then there was a long pause, "I can't believe this has happened. What does this mean? What do you think is going to happen next? Do you have any clues about the murderer?"

Wes heard all the sounds of hysteria. The man's voice was rising. He was talking faster, hyperventilating. Wes recognized fear.

"Sir, try to calm down. Maybe we could get together. Could we meet somewhere that would be convenient for you? We can choose a place where no one will see us or overhear our conversation. I think I can help you."

"I don't know. It's just that I'm so nervous. I knew all three of the men who were shot this week." Again the man choked. Wes heard his heavy, erratic breathing. Then he seemed to grab hold of his emotions and added, "I guess lots of people knew them. They were all well-known in Atlanta, but I knew them since we were young."

Wes' pulse quickened. He was betting that this was another member of the Phoenix Byrd gang. This may be the break he'd been hoping for.

"Can I meet you somewhere, sir? I can leave now. I can be almost anywhere in the city in less than twenty minutes."

"No, I don't want to meet you! I just want to know how close you are to finding the motherfucker. How can you let this son-of-a-bitch run loose? You're putting many men in Atlanta in jeopardy. Why aren't you as willing to go out and find this murderer as you are to meeting me? If you were doing your damn job, I'd be able to sleep at night. I can't go anywhere now without watching over my shoulder. But I don't even know what the fuck I'm looking for." The man's voice was becoming shrill.

"We're looking at a lot of clues, sir. We're especially looking at who all three victims knew. Who maybe all three established an adversarial relationship. Where they may all have been together or even at the same place at different times. Do you have a theory on that?"

"No, except that all of them probably went to many of the same places. They were successful men who had high profiles. Do you think that is why they were chosen?"

"Could be. We just don't know at this point. If there's a connection with them and perhaps others---," Wes paused to be sure the man would hear his next words, "---even you, sir, we haven't found it yet. If we knew for sure, we could consider police surveillance. We don't want another murder this week of one of the city's leaders. Right now, we believe this could happen. We could help you, sir, if you're nervous about who's out there on the streets."

"No, I'm OK. You can see why I'm nervous. Most people don't know one murder victim in a lifetime. I know three in one week. It's been a shock. But, no, I'm OK."

"Have you spoken with anyone else who's nervous about these shootings? Anyone else who feels this could be a threat to his own life?" This man was not cooperating. He hadn't mentioned his name, any other names, places or why he felt connected.

Detective Wesley looked up as his colleague placed a slip of paper in the middle of his desk. The number was listed for Vance Bowman on Northside Drive. The name sounded vaguely familiar, but he couldn't place it. He looked at the other detective and whispered, "Who?" The woman took the paper back and wrote: Editor of the Atlanta Economic Review.

Wes made another attempt to get some concrete information, "I think it would be good for us to meet. You may be able to help us prevent a fourth murder. We can talk about others who you believe could be in danger. Your opinions may break this case, sir. You could be responsible for bringing down this madman."

"I think maybe I overreacted. Thanks for talking to me. I have to believe that you're doing the best you can. This all has to be a damn coincidence. I'm sure that's what it is." The man's voice lowered. He then added, "If I think of anything for you, I'll call you back." The dial tone buzzed in Wes' ear.

He picked up the scrap of paper. It wouldn't be hard to find Mr. Vance Bowman. Perhaps if they faced off across his desk, the gentleman may become more talkative. He may also realize how easy it is to find someone in Atlanta and he may not like that thought one bit.

The detective's phone rang again. He picked it up hoping it was Bowman calling back.

"Homicide, Wesley speaking."

"Hey, Wes, it's Dino from the Marriott. How's it going? You're not having a good week, I hear."

"You're right."

"That's why I'm calling. I've spent hours going over the hotel security tapes. I checked several hours before the murder and several hours after. It felt good to be doing some real investigative work. I also had an interesting conversation with Janet Orr, one of the female staff. She talked to Carrollton when he first returned to the hotel from the Georgia Tech event. She said that the preacher was almost purring about the great evening. How it was just going to get better because a 'lovely lady,' her quote, was coming to visit him. Janet couldn't decide what was making him purr more, the memory of his performance or the anticipation of his visitor. Temple Carrollton was a fuckin' paradox. I guess when you get that rich and famous, you start to write your own rules, right?"

"Some people don't even wait till they've got the bucks. So what about the tapes?"

"You know how when you're on the penthouse floor, you can only get there by using your room key. That means that whoever would come to see Carrollton would need him to use the key. I have on tape him meeting a woman at the elevator and escorting her to his room."

"Damn good, Dino. What can you tell about this person?"

"Almost nothing! Ain't that a bitch? I'm gonna get these to you but I wanted to tell you about them. What I see, and you may see it differently, is what certainly appears to be a female but she is very careful not to be taped. Everywhere there was a camera, from her approaching the elevator to when they enter his room, she is videoed from behind. No face, no profile, nondescript but rather suggestive clothes and a huge head of hair."

"Sounds like the typical hooker to me. They have cased the hotels so many times that they know every inch to avoid. You know, Dino, they're professional about keeping their jobs as well as doing their jobs."

"Could be, but the way he greeted her and gently guided her to and from the elevator didn't look like how a man like that would treat a hooker. Besides, why would he even mess with a prostie? He can get a thousand young women and girls just by projecting his heavenly aura. Nope, my instinct says it wasn't a hooker. I checked out the tapes after they went into his room. Nothing for about 45 minutes. Then here she comes. Right out of the same door and just as careful about not being seen. I'd say really cool. I stayed with the tapes for about another hour. Didn't see anyone else enter that room. There were a couple housekeeping people that showed up. None at that point went to that door."

"If you can't see a face or anything else that gives us a clue to what she looked like, did you consider that it could be a man disguised as a woman to get easy entrée to the suite?"

"Yep, Wes, that's gone through my mind a lot. It opens another messy avenue. If it wasn't a woman, then the guy has to be gay. He moves in a feminine way. You'll see it when I get the tapes to you." Dino remarked.

Wes thought about the new possibility. Carrollton didn't have a pristine track record. Here was a man who had at least three illegitimate sons, kept them under strict discipline and seemed to be enamored by a long list of young women.

"Dino, I wonder about this elusive club or group that all three of these guys belonged to. Maybe it was about sex. Could it have been about being gay? They were young, they were unsure of themselves. They kept the memory alive. Maybe it was about something that they wanted to hide."

"All good conclusions, Wes. Just need to find something to get it all to hang together;, have it lead to the right person. I've seen all those pretty Carrollton lieutenants around the hotel. It does make one wonder why the preacher man chose the same type over and over again. Let's think about it. I'll see you later. I'll get the tapes over there whenever it's good for you."

They made a time late enough so Wes could make his surprise visit on Editor Bowman. He would ask Billy Joe to meet Dino and him back here later.

Chapter 34

Vance Bowman

"Detective Wes Wesley to see Mr. Vance Bowman."

Wes was standing before the receptionist's desk and offered his card as he spoke. The beautiful, young woman who was smiling back at him should have been in the Miss America Pageant. Long honey colored hair, sapphire blue eyes and a body that made her clothes look like they cost thousands of dollars. The Atlanta Economic Review hired the right person to make a fantastic first impression

Wes wasn't surprised that her voice was as honeyed as her hair, "Detective Wesley, do you have an appointment? I don't have you in my book."

"Too bad," Wes thought, "I'd like to be in your book. Then I would send the book to my son Jason and say, here's the one for you."

Instead he said, "No, Miss…" his eyes dropped to the name on her desk, "Angie Mason. I have no appointment. I believe that if you tell Mr. Bowman that I'm here, he'll find time for me. I'm following up on a recent conversation he and I had. I was interested that he and I have several acquaintances in common."

"That would be easy in this city, Detective Wesley. Mr. Bowman knows just about everybody in Atlanta. Let me see if I can find him. I know that he's in the building but not in his office." She presented him another gift of her captivating smile.

Angie Mason left her desk and disappeared through huge, polished brass double doors. He looked at the rest of the large reception area and decided that every bit of it shouted: we are successful and you want to be a part of our world. The walls were covered with photos of well-known people, framed articles and awards. Wes found that he was scanning the collection for the Phoenix Byrd certificate. It wasn't among the items. What a coup that would have been to find it so easily.

The beautiful woman returned and carefully omitted the title detective, "Mr. Wesley, Mr. Bowman said that he's very busy and is just going into an editorial meeting. He appreciates that you stopped by." The way Ms. Mason delivered the rejection reminded Wes of Janeen and how well she does the same thing for her boss. They were so sweet about the words that no one can take offense. He would not take offense but he was going to stand his ground.

He unbuttoned his jacket and casually put his hand in his pants pocket. He knew very well what effect the sight of a gun had on regular, law biding citizens. He saw the moment of shock on Angie Mason's face.

"I'd like to see him now but if I must, I'll wait until he's out of his meeting. You won't mind if I get caught up on some department calls while I'm waiting. I have some detectives who I need to speak with and I must talk with the chief about the shooting of our City Council president. I can do it right here while I wait. You know, until Mr. Bowman's editorial meeting is finished." Wes' demeanor was as innocent as Ms. Mason's was sweet. He knew the other people waiting for their appointments were following every word of this conversation.

"Of course, that will be fine, Mr. Wesley, but I'll ask Mr. Bowman how long he thinks he will be. You could always leave and come back. That might be more practical for you."

"Don't worry about me, Ms. Mason. I can do my job almost anywhere."

This time, the woman scurried through the impressive brass doors. She seemed to have lost some of her languid grace. He was sure that her boss was going to hear the whole story.

Wes sat down and took out his notebook and recorder. He may not even need these props. The hasty retreat of the receptionist was a clue that he would get more attention this time.

Within three minutes Angie was back. She looked at how he had set up his little office and the holstered gun that was still darkly sitting on his hip. She almost tripped over her three-inch heels.

"Mr. Wesley, Mr. Bowman said he will postpone his meeting a few minutes and greet you in his office. He didn't want you to have to wait for maybe an hour."

'I bet he didn't,' Wes thought but said instead, "That's so thoughtful, Ms. Mason. Thank you for your help. I know you were instrumental in getting him to change his mind." His innocent act was still in place. Now it was his turn to go through the shiny, brass doors.

. . . .

"Ms. Mason says you're a detective. Your card says that you're in the Homicide. I don't remember meeting you somewhere, as she said. I guess I'm asking, why you're here."

Vance Bowman stood behind his desk with both hands tightly holding the edge of the highly polished wood. He had thinning blond hair and dark brown eyes that were glaring at Wes through small wire rimmed glasses. He was of medium height, which made the extra pounds he had acquired over the years cluster around his ample waist. His tie was loose and hung below his opened collar. Not an imposing man in appearance, but what he had accomplished with this revered publication was impressive.

"I came to finish our telephone conversation, Mr. Bowman. I believe we have more to talk about. I truly appreciate your call and understand why the murder of your friends would be so upsetting."

"My friends? If you're referring to the recent shootings, you could call these men practically the friends of most business people in the city. Why target me or are you calling on all leaders in Atlanta?"

"Mr. Bowman. Unless you have people stopping in to use the telephone in your home; you made a call to me within the last hour.

We have no problem identifying calls that come into our office. The fact you made that call and the content of our conversation adds up to me wanting to ask you more questions."

Vance Bowman felt exhausted. He could continue to act like he had no idea why this man was in his office, but after a sleepless night and a nerve-wracking day, he was too stressed out to work at it. He didn't want to ever talk about the Club, but he didn't want to be the target of some crazy killer more. He was sure that there was a relationship to the events of the week and the group that he had always admired and protected. They had their story and he would replay it if necessary.

"OK, Detective Wesley, I did call you. I told you why. Other than seeing someone striking down other leaders in Atlanta, I have nothing else to tell you. Because of my position at the Review, I am very visible and therefore feel vulnerable."

"Mr. Bowman, I can understand your misgivings. I'm sure many share your feelings. That's why it's so important that we gather as much information fast before another man is struck down." Wes had hoped to raise the fear factor with this man by having him think of himself as the next victim. He watched Bowman's face and saw that his words were taken seriously.

"I can't just hide. I don't want to be a headline in my own paper. I can't talk to anyone. When my wife asked me why I was up most of the night, I lied and told her I was working on a big financing deal. I don't know if I can talk to you in confidence. Can I buy protection from the police? Should I go to a private detective agency?" The man said the last few words into his hands that were holding his head as he dropped into his desk chair and lowered his head.

"Mr. Bowman, we want to prevent more shootings that seem to be targeted at our successful business leaders. We don't think they're random shots. We're sure they relate to the group that we call the Phoenix Byrd Club. We think we should be talking to these members and cautioning them to be careful. We cannot protect them from someone who's still unknown to us. Who could this be?"

"I really don't know. I'm afraid the relationship of these men somehow connects to a group that ran around together about fifteen years ago. Randy, Temple and Franklin were all my closest friends then. We all belonged to the Good Ol' Boys Club. I know that sounds really hokey, but we thought it was clever." Bowman looked devastated. Wes thought the man might cry. His hands shook and his eyes darted around the room before settling on the detective.

"How many others belonged to the club?"

"It was a small group. There were only thirteen. That's why we considered ourselves so exclusive. We could talk about this elite group and know that so many other guys wanted to belong. We thought choosing thirteen was also clever. We were smart enough that an unlucky number was beneath us. We laughingly bragged about our small membership, 'The only way you can be a member is for one of us to die.' That's not so funny anymore now that there are three of us dead in one week."

Vance Bowman choked on those last four words and finally lost all control. Tears ran down his cheeks. He gulped several times trying to stop crying and finally whispered, "I don't want to die."

"Mr. Bowman, we can't do anything for the three who are gone, but you may be able to help the others. It seems that Atlanta is the area being targeted. How many of your club members are still in Atlanta?"

"Actually there are only eight. That means now there are only five of us. Temple was the originator. Just like with his ministry, he knew how to put an organization together. He showed us how being loyal to one another would have a big payoff. We would be stronger together than alone. We would always be there for one another with whatever support was needed at the time."

"That didn't seem to work with Randy Lee. What happened there?"

"Oh, we tried, Detective, we tried. We finally decided, after even his wife gave up on him, he was doing what he wanted. Some people just want to drink. You know, it's their choice. Randy could have had all the help he wanted from us, but he told us to get off his back. So, we did. It was his choice."

So much for loyalty forever and all that shit. How about loyalty when it isn't too much effort? Yeah, that works for the Good Ol' Boys Club.

"Do you still have your Phoenix Byrd certificate, Mr. Bowman?"

"Oh, yes. I keep it tucked away. That was always one of the questions we would ask each other. Everyone kept it. Even when Randy was still talking to us, he said that he never was without it."

"What was it that kept you so close? These kinds of groups usually have a limited lifespan. They're important at the moment. Then they fade away just as many of our other relationships. Like old girlfriends that now we don't even remember their names."

"Not our group. We're still close. We'll continue to be close. We're close in spirit. Unless someone has a need, our promise to the club is that we never get together. We don't socialize. That's what makes it tighter than an old girlfriend or even family. Our connection is beyond the human contact. It's at a higher level. We sealed that by becoming blood brothers, if you know what I mean." The man gave Wes a knowing look that went with those words.

"I guess you mean that you did the symbolic exchanging of blood and probably have the scars to prove it." Wes watched as Vance Bowman nodded his head vigorously. It was the only vigorous motion that he had made since Wes entered the room. He also had some color back in his face. Wes decided that the remembrances had helped him forget about his Problem of the Week. It was time to get back to that.

"I need the names of your other Blood Brothers, the Good Ol' Boys. We should see what's happening with them. Have you talked with any of them about what appears to be a pattern? Has anyone called you? What might be happening in other cities where some live?"

"We've spoken. We agreed that this was a time when we needed to be in touch. That doesn't make our higher connection weaker. It's more like when Randy needed help. We do the right thing. No one talked until after Franklin's murder. The other two, we really thought could be a coincidence. With the life Randy led, sudden death wasn't unusual and Temple could be hit simply because he was so important. People might get mad at him because they wanted more or something different. Do you really think there'll be more shootings, Detective?"

"Yes, I do. I don't know why you all have been chosen, but someone knows about your Good Ol' Boys Club and has decided to reduce its membership. If we're still talking about immature kids, who you were back then, we could joke that someone else wants to become a member. But, you're all grown up so that doesn't work."

Chapter 35

Danielle Jarvis Swain

Four Atlanta Homicide detectives were gathered in the interrogation room. Wes and Billy Joe were glad that Golly Grand and Mike Fisher had been assigned to this case.

Golly, short for Goliath, had eight years experience in Homicide. He came from Philadelphia seeking better weather and a higher salary. He found half of his goal. He justified the lesser salary with the fact that the cost of living was lower in the south. He liked living in Atlanta. For relaxation and to keep in shape, Golly took his 6 foot 6 inch frame to a public park three times a week and played basketball. The teenagers, who made up most of both teams, were pleased to have a policeman on the court. Goliath Grand was happy to have a chance to interact with kids who needed an adult friend and a role model.

Mike Fisher was the youngster on the Homicide team. He had been there less than a year but had been in the Commercial Robbery Unit for three years. He was familiar with crime and how one action can lead to another. His baby face, framed in blond wavy hair just like the Carrollton lieutenants, gave suspects in a murder case the feeling that he was soft and easy to fool. Many learned the hard way that first impressions were often wrong.

They all looked over the short list of men, that Wes got from Vance Bowman, who were all members of the Good Ol' Boys Club. Wes ticked off the Atlanta men in his mind: three of the men were gone, he had met Vance Bowman, one was the mayor, there were names he had heard of and one he did not know. He was amazed that he knew one of the names of a man who lived in Charlotte. He was the owner of the Panthers, the professional football team. Easy to see he had been successful. Another man had died when he was quite young. The last three were all in Miami. The good old boys had all kept their Southern roots planted in Southern soil.

Wes looked at the other detectives, "What do you think? Know any of these guys?"

"Damn, who would have thought we were gonna find the mayor himself on the list? The others in Atlanta I've heard of, Wes. Read about them from time to time in the newspaper. That doesn't mean I know them," Billy Joe said and the others mumbled their agreement. "Whatever there was about this group, the truth is that when it comes to success, they made it. I bet that's where Carrollton got his idea for his ministry? Maybe this club was his experiment. Then he wrote a business plan and figured out how to create an obscene bottom line. It worked for him."

Wes went back to their problem. "It looks like we have five men at immediate risk. All should be contacted. Eve's quick stats have enough information that we should be able to get in touch with the local men right away. We're lucky to have an intern who really likes to do this work. Sometimes she gets me what I request so fast that I believe she was just waiting for me to ask.

"I don't think we should call these guys in Atlanta and say, 'Hey, check your back. You may be next,' so let's each take a name, call for an appointment and go see that man. Open a conversation that isn't going to make him have a heart attack. We don't want to add to the demise of the Club. See what information any of them can give you. Then let's compare notes. We might want to consider assigning a couple officers to check them out regularly. We want to be as low key as possible to keep down the media leaks down. I guess if we can't reach each guy, we need to leave a serious message so he will call back.

"We want to do more than warn them to be damn careful. We want to see what we can learn that might help find the motherfucker. Have they had anyone following them? Funny telephone calls? Letters that seem to threaten? Could this be an old boys-will-be-boys grudge or have they all pissed off someone in the past few weeks? Do they all have the same mistress? Is she on the warpath?

"I'm going to call the major and tell her what we're doing. Let her know that the mayor has been identified as belonging to the group. She may have some inspired ideas of how to handle that bomb. If not, I'll take that one. Some of these men are going to raise some very big flags. And when contacted, they're going to raise some shit. I can't imagine what's going to come down when we walk into the mayor's office. He was so concerned when Raub got it. I wonder if he thinks he's a possible target."

As they divided the names, a loud voice was heard from outside the door. "Hey, Wesley, telephone. It's your cute little anchor-girl. If you're too busy, I'll be happy to go talk to her."

Wes grabbed the telephone.

"Dani, what's up?"

"I got another call, Wes. You know, about the shootings. The voice is still disguised, but I'm sure that it's the same person."

"We'll soon have to put you on the city payroll. You're doing some overtime for us. What's the message this time?"

"That this has been a long week for a certain group of men in Atlanta, but the week may just get longer. The person said that clues were hard to find, but soon they'll all come together. Unfortunately, this murderer will not be available to be caught. What do you think that means, Wes? Not available. Like the killer is just going to disappear?"

"I wish I knew, Dani. Whoever's calling you is right that there are few clues. It still sounds like someone who's daring us to find him. I think we have a sicko."

"Wes, you said him. I'm still not sure if it's a man or a woman. I do find it interesting that they call me instead of you."

"Probably thinks it's safer. We might trace the call or hear something like background sounds or voice traits that could give us a solid lead." He was thinking about Bowman's call and how it led him directly to the editor's front office. "Or maybe it's a crazy admirer who just wants an excuse to talk to you. I have a

couple guys here who would walk from here to your place just to
get one of your beautiful smiles."

"Oh, right. You sweet talker! Thanks for the flattery. Got to
run. We're going to do a BreakIn! on this call. Let the public
know that Channel 22 has news that no one else has."

"Hey, Dani, don't hang up! If you're doing a BreakIn!, how
about asking your public to call if they have any information that
might help find the perp? Suggest that maybe there's a connection
to these three murders and that new information may help prevent
number four. Just say that this is one possible theory. You don't
have to mention where that theory came from." Wes wanted the
other Good Ol' Boys Club members to be as nervous as Vance
Bowman and taking their mortality seriously.

"Give me a call if something happens. Oh, no. With the way
this week's been, it sounds like I'm waiting to hear that we've
lost another big deal Atlanta man. Not what I meant. Sorry. See
ya'." Dani was gone.

Chapter 36

Mayor Erich Regis Maxwell

Dani talked with her boss about adding the request to the public to the BreakIn! segment. He said to be sure that in the message it was evident that Channel 22 was out in front with the freshest news. He hoped that the switchboard would light up indicating that the public watched WPTR.

Within minutes of the broadcast, his hopes were answered. Calls continued for more than an hour. Before time for the next newscast, several names had been suggested as potential targets, and the name Good Ol' Boys Club was mentioned several times. These men, they were all male voices, were willing to tell Dani that this was a group that had been established many years ago. The callers, who claimed to know about the Good Ol' Boys Club, were not willing to give their names. One added that he wasn't surprised that they were being "bumped off" because they used to be so impressed with themselves that they made everybody mad. The ending sentence for all calls was that no one had a clue as to who might be the murderer

Dani left a message for Wes when she was told that he was out of the office. She didn't know if her information could be critical, but she knew the Homicide team would use what they could.

· · · ·

Billy Joe, Golly Grand and Mike Fisher had gathered in the unit at the end of the day. Only one had reached his local 'good old boy.' Houston Montrose, president of the Montrose and Byrd Group Inc. and Norman Park, chairman of the power company, were both out of city. Montrose was out of his office for the day, due back later tonight. Park's secretary said that he was in southern Georgia at his hunting plantation. Detective Golly Grand had made telephone calls to the men in Miami and Charlotte and found that they were in their offices, but were not cooperative.

"Beats the hell out of me! " Golly exclaimed. "If I was being seriously considered for target practice by a serial killer who probably had me in his sights, I would want to talk to the police. These guys all took the attitude that they did not live in Atlanta and their little club years ago had long been forgotten. One even pretended that he had no idea what the Good Ol' Boys club referred to. He joked, 'Anything named the Good Ol' Boys Club deserves to end. How tacky.'"

Billy Joe had talked with Irwin Fitzgerald, a successful real estate developer in the Southeast. "It took some persuadin' but good old Irwin finally said he knew about each shootin', had wondered about the ties to his friends and had talked with Vance Bowman. Fitzgerald was concerned but felt sure that we, the Atlanta police, would have the suspect any moment now. He'd call if he noticed anythin' strange or thought of somethin' that we should know. I would categorize him as cool.

"I left his office, waited about a minute and opened the door again as if I forgot somethin'. Sho'nuf, guys, he was already on the phone. I waved and said, 'Don't lose my card.'"

"Well, even if we didn't learn anything, they have all been warned. We did our community service for this day," Mike Fisher observed, "What we need is a report from our fearless leader and his encounter with the mayor and the major. Damn, he can have that contact. Let me be far, far away."

"Far, far away from what?" Wes asked as he approached his team from the elevator lobby.

"From you and the major as you called on the mayor to say, 'We think you're in the sights of the Good Ol' Boys killer.'"

"Not a bad idea. It wasn't the most fun thing I've done this week, or maybe even this year. Tell me how ya'll made out. Then I'll add to the mess."

It took only a few minutes to bring Wes up to date. Even with questions and comments from the group, he was soon again in the spotlight.

"OK. Here it is. I called Brassy to get some time with Dagmar. He chewed out my ass for putting the major in a bad light because we hadn't found the shooter yet. Then her well-starched highness took over where he left off. When I got to tell her why I was calling, she exploded with a few un-carefully chosen words. Then she sputtered and said how would we tell the mayor that he might be shot any moment because our detectives hadn't found the killer? She went on to let me know that she considers us completely incompetent; that we'd all be reviewed when this case is closed.

"She said she wasn't any part of our 'slovenly behavior,' a quote, and that I could just take my ass downtown and call her later. She was having dinner with friends. I had no idea that the woman had friends, but she claims she does. She had Brassy call the mayor's office to say I needed some time to bring him up to date on the case."

Wes hesitated, reached for the Coca Cola can he had left on the desk earlier in the day and proceeded, "I was welcomed with a smile and a hearty clap on the shoulder. He was so glad to see me. Our police department was the best. We're all on the same team. You know all the political bullshit. Then I dropped the other shoe and he was no longer on my team. He really didn't want to talk about the 'situation,' his word. It was our job to find the killer. Do it now! He couldn't waste his time doing our job. I listened and let him rave on. It was a shock and he needed to leave off steam. Then I suggested we had to talk to save his life. Funny how that caught his attention."

Wes took another swig of his flat Coke before resuming. "I told him what we know, how there is this club thing among all the victims and he has been identified as a member. Of course, he gave me a hundred reasons why that wasn'tt true. I got talking again about being shot and the bodies that are already lying in the morgue. He climbed down a bit from his very high horse. He finally said that he had belonged to the group for 'a very short time.'"

"Yeah, right," Mike and Golly said in unison.

"He reluctantly said that he felt in danger and had increased the detail around his house and in his car. I asked about his family. He said he didn't think they were in jeopardy and his wife knew nothing about the group. He warned that he wanted it to stay that way...."

"Fat, fucking chance." Another chorus by the two detectives. Billy Joe simply nodded his head in agreement.

"He wanted to know who we had already spoken to. Who we planned to contact. He seemed nervous about our talking to the others. I didn't tell him that so far we hadn't learned anything from his buddies. Let him worry about that 'till he talks to them. When I asked about the Phoenix Byrd certificate, he claimed that many years ago it had gone to the dump with all his other teenage trophies. Hmmm, wonder what those trophies were? That short, round, roly-poly body doesn't advertise being an athlete. We left it that he should go nowhere without adequate protection and we would keep him posted several times a day. He then added, 'I want to know whatever you're doing before you report to your major or the chief. This is not going to mess up my political plans.' I do believe our mayor has a secret. All we have to do is find out what it is."

Billy Joe sat up in his chair and leaned on the table, "When you find this many men all protectin' what appears to be the same thin', it's usually somethin' really unethical. Because they all have such diverse businesses, it doesn't look like money. Because they don't seem to keep in touch regularly, it doesn't look like politics. I would hope we can rule out murder. At this point, I would say this secret they all share is....."

The chorus now included Wes, "....sex."

Billy Joe added before the others spoke again, "Somethin' that happened back in their good old, bad old boys' days. We need to be lookin' in that direction."

Warming up to having a definite direction, all four men started talking at once but were quickly silenced by another voice.

"Hey, Wes, it's the mayor. He's on line one for you."

Wes looked at the telephone like it had just lit up like a terrorist bomb. After his uncomfortable meeting with Mayor Maxwell earlier in the afternoon, he did not look forward to being in his sights again.

The other detectives leaned closer and Golly said, "We could claim you just took off for Iraq because you felt it was safer than Atlanta. Think he'd appreciate that thought?"

Billy Joe laughed, "Don't worry, Wes. We're all ready to take your job. We won't even miss a beat."

"OK, OK. Thanks for the damn support. You guys are just the fuckin' best." Wes was already reaching for the telephone.

"Wesley here."

"Detective, I want to apologize for being rather inhospitable when you were here. This week has been a terrible strain. We need to work closely together and be sure that our city leaders are protected. This madman has got to be stopped. In the meantime, we need to address safety for all.

"You have theorized that there is some tie between these murders and long ago friendships. I believe you're wrong. I believe you're heading in the wrong direction. I want you to widen your scope. Look at other civic leaders and see who of them also should be considered either future victims or even suspects."

Wes raised his eyebrows and rolled his eyes.

"Now, Detective, I want you to pay more attention to the present rather than the past. Who in our current leadership might covet another's position? Who might be looking ahead to an important political position that could be lost because of a competitor? I don't want you to limit your investigation simply because these men knew each other. Of course, they knew each other. They were known by most of the people in the Atlanta business world. I want a report back to me within 24 hours about who you want to place on these two lists: possible victims and possible suspects. Have I made myself clear?"

Wes was silent for a few moments. He was envisioning the short, rotund mayor - wearing his habitual gray suit and blue, Oxford cloth, button down shirt with his sandy hair that curled behind his ears - sitting at his large, highly polished, completely clean, mahogany desk. If the mayor was meeting with a staff person or a constituent, there was never a paper left on the desk. Everything about Mayor Erich Regis Maxwell announced that he was conservative and in control. Even his campaign slogan "No More Mistakes" gave Atlantans a feeling of security and, on Election Day, brought out the largest number of voters in over forty years

"Mayor Maxwell, thank you for calling. I understand the tension that you feel for your city and yourself but..."

"Detective Wesley, this has nothing to do with me except as the mayor."

"Yes, of course, sir. That's exactly what I was saying," Wes again rolled his eyes for his colleagues. He put his hand over the receiver, smiled and whispered, "It's the political line."

Wes then returned his thoughts to the conversation, "Yes, sir, we have the same objective: to not allow more of these killings. We've put extra detectives on the case and have talked with many people. Our best information says that we must hone in on the group that has been close for over 15 years. We cannot spread ourselves so thinly that the other Good Old Boys Club members are in harm's way."

The mayor immediately responded, "I don't want you using that term in relationship to this case. Is that understood? You will give the impression that there is some conspiracy operating in this city. That is unacceptable with this office! Of course, you are to protect the leaders of Atlanta, but I will be putting out the word with the Chief that your investigation is too narrow. Now, Detective, go do your job. Do not make trouble for those who have helped this city flourish. I will expect to get regular, personally delivered, progress reports until this case is closed. And, I expect that will be very soon! Goodbye, Detective Wesley."

Wes replaced the receiver and shook his head. Three sets of eyes and ears were waiting anxiously for Wes' reaction. It was easy to see that the mayor had delivered some ultimatum. What was it?

"We are in deep shit!"

"What's up, Wes?" Billy Joe asked.

"Without doing anything extraordinary, just doing our jobs, we have stumbled on something that has the mayor really scared. I think we're creeping up on a story that could ruin his career and maybe those of our other Bad Boys. We're going to have to tread as carefully as possible, but I want you to know right now, we're also going to do our jobs. We're moving in the right direction and we're not stopping." Wes then repeated what Mayor Maxwell had said to him.

Golly was the first to respond, "So the mayor's ready to sacrifice his buddies to make this case look like something else. Now that's loyalty."

"We will add a couple names of other civic or business leaders so that we aren't fired before we can get this killer, but we're going to continue to learn more about our star players. Mr. Phoenix Byrd got them together and we're going to keep them there."

Chapter 37

Irwin Fitzgerald

Wes was beat. Driving away from City Hall East headed for a quick dinner, he could not shake the feeling that there was another murder just around the corner. He looked at the sky and noticed that it was already dark. All the shootings had occurred at night. Was that because it was easier to hide or perhaps simply that the murderer has a job? Is the guy moonlighting? Wes smiled and said out loud, "Just like all the cops in Atlanta. This menace has his day job and his night job. Atlanta police do it for money. I wonder why the Bad Ol' Boys' killer does it."

He pulled up to a red light and while waiting for it to change to green, he shuddered. Yes, it was night and these men were in jeopardy. He made a quick decision, made a u-turn on the green and headed back to his office.

. . . . .

Wes sat down at his desk still adorned with worn-out Styrofoam coffee cups. He flicked through the top papers on his desk left there by Golly, Mike and Billy Joe. The telephone numbers of the businessmen were on the information sheets. Numbers for offices and homes carefully copied by Eve in her precise handwriting and signed, "For you from me."

They might think he's crazy, but he was going to call them. Warn them to go nowhere tonight alone and watch people who seemed to be interested in them.

He would leave his cell phone number with each of them. Tell them to call at any time. He would probably be considered an alarmist, but he was willing to take that chance. He did not like the feeling that had come over him in the car.

He reached Vance Bowman, told him why he was calling

214

and expected to get a very cool response. Surprisingly, he was not only polite but almost talkative.

"Thank you, Detective. I appreciate your thoughtfulness. I can see by the time that you're already way past regular working hours. I know you can imagine that it's been a stressful day. My only intent is to have dinner with my wife, share a special bottle of wine and hit the rack. I will not be out running the streets."

"Sounds like a great way to spend the evening, sir. I might just do the same as soon as I leave here. Unfortunately, I have neither a wife nor a special bottle of wine. Do be careful. Call me if you see anything suspicious."

Wes placed the other calls. He spoke with Houston Montrose, left a message with Norman Park's daughter and left a message on Irwin Fitzgerald's voice mail. He did not call Mayor Maxwell. He knew that extra security had already been deployed. Too bad the mayor didn't do the same for all of the Good Ol' Boys Club members.

Detective Wesley picked up the receiver one more time and dialed. He waited to hear Janeen's voice, either electronic or the real thing. On the fourth ring, he heard the recording and left a different message than he had for the men, "Hey, sweet lady. Was hoping you would be there so I could come and have you erase a very ugly day. Since you are not, I'm going to go home, climb into my bed and fall asleep dreaming about you. Talk to you tomorrow. Love ya'."

Mary Mac's to Go sounded like as much as Wes was up to. Comfort food in the Southern style was perfect for how he felt, especially since there wasn't any other warm and luscious comfort just down the street where Janeen Carson lived.

· · · ·

Wes was finishing up Mary Mac's collard greens and watching CNN News, when the telephone rang. His next reaction was to cross his fingers and whisper, "No, not tonight."

"Wesley here."

Billy Joe's voice was without any emotion. "Hey, Wes, we

got another one that looks mighty suspicious. It's suspicious because the name of the victim is Irwin Fitzgerald. I just picked up a call on the radio from Zone 5."

"Damn, damn, damn. I couldn't reach him tonight. The others I felt OK about, but he was a worry. Damn!"

"What're you ravin' about? What do you mean you couldn't reach him?"

Wes quickly explained about going back to the office. "We'll never hear the end of it; that we can't protect even five men in Atlanta. Shit! Where did it happen? Where am I going to meet you, Billy Joe?"

"This is really weird. Remember that big development we saw when we went to Roman Lily's to eat with Eve? That project was bein' developed by Irwin Fizgerald's company. They found the body in back of the leasin' office. That's where I'm headed. I'm closer than you are so I'll start askin' questions until you get there. You know, Wes? I might just stop listenin' to the police radio. Cleo says that it's time I get a life. After this week, I agree with her. When we get over this case, let's us take off for a sunny beach."

"I don't think you and I going to a beach is what Cleo had in mind."

"Oh, we'll take her too. She likes you. She would like Janeen, too, so we can take her along too."

"Now you're talking" Wes responded enthusiastically, "See you in about fifteen minutes."

Wes groaned and clicked off the television. He felt, old, tired and defeated. Something was happening around him that he felt was changing his life, changing his opinion of people. He hadn't known most of these dead men, but they were important to Atlanta. Yet there was a sinister undercurrent that had to do with their relationships. It started with that damn club. He was going to find out what this all meant, even if they didn't want him to. And that included the mayor.

The Mayor! Shit. He better call him before he did another

thing. Even though Erich Maxwell probably knew what had happened, Wes wasn't taking any chances.

Detective Wesley hung up the telephone feeling older, more tired and more defeated. Mayor Maxwell was just leaving his home to head for the murder scene. He curtly told Wes that he would see him there. Then he hung up.

· · · ·

The street was awash with red and blue lights. The scene was the same as the Raub neighborhood only hours ago. Streaks from the strobe lights swept across the cozy, little restaurant, Roman Lily, and over the ice cream parlor in the same block. Wes thought about what a different picture this was than when Billy Joe, Eve and he were there. He thought it would be wonderful to return to last week when all he had on his docket were two drug-related shootings and a domestic murder/suicide. Ah, yes, give me that peaceful life.

He saw the mayor's car out of the corner of his eye and decided to avoid the man. He would have plenty of time to get blasted by him. Right now he would find out exactly what had happened.

Billy Joe waved. The two of them walked behind the leasing office. The body of Irwin Fitzgerald was covered and the Grady Hospital medical personnel were standing nearby. They were ready to transport the body, but first the detectives had to finish their preliminary investigation. The two detectives spoke to the two emergency techs as they approached the scene. They weren't close friends, but they had shared many of these situations together.

Just as Billy Joe was pulling back the covering, Golly Grand and Mike Fisher rushed up. Both were panting like they had run a mile.

"We couldn't get close because of all the cars. We heard this just as we got in the car outside of Manuel's. Can you believe it? We were just talking about this a few hours ago. We tried to warn them all. This shooter is beginning to act like he's on a regular schedule," Golly stopped to catch his breath.

"I know. I feel like this is deja vu," Wes said to no one in particular.

Irwin Fitzgerald's body was lying face up. There were several places where blood had collected: seeping into his yellow, golf shirt with a small Ralph Lauren logo on the sleeve, spreading down below his belt into the material of his trousers and another spot that was dripping blood onto the ground from just below his chin. Looked like two shots. Clean. No struggle. Almost the same as Lee, Carrollton and Raub. The murderer was doing a better job at killing without leaving a clue than the detectives were figuring out the answer from the others they had collected.

"Anything found around the immediate area?" Wes had turned to ask the security guard who was standing nearby.

The woman in the brown uniform with a visible shoulder patch that was embroidered: Bell's Security Troop, Inc. stepped forward, "My name is Frances Rice. Been with Bell's for almost four years. I found Mr. Fitzgerald. I knew him well. He'd often drop by in the evenin' to see how things were. He din't mind takin' time to check out the development, even at night. He was pretty well known in the neighborhood, too." She smiled at a recollection, "He sure did like his ice cream!" Her eyes went to the ice cream parlor across the street.

"No, Detective, I din't see nothin'. Din't hear nothin' neither. This's a big development, as you can see. Gonna be nice. I was all the way at the other end makin' my rounds. Came up here, checked out that the buildin' was locked. Then walked to the back as I was ready to start the track again. There was Mr. Fitzgerald. Just like you sees him now. I called 911 quick. Then I looked around for anythin' that seemed out of place and waited for you guys to show up. Then all hell broke loose. Police, Grady ambulance, a major and finally the mayor with his gang. He's really pissed. You'd think this was an attack on him personally from all the things he's been sayin' to the people with him."

All four detectives shuddered. They knew this wasn't good

218

news for them. They knew that no one wins all the time, and this week seemed confirmation on that old adage. Yes, this was an attack on Mayor Erich Maxwell as well as on Irwin Fitzgerald. It was, indeed, very personal. If some story, whatever it is, gets out, he feels that it's going to be a problem that will travel directly to the office of the mayor. And from there, unfortunately, directly back to Homicide.

"Did you check the body, Ms. Rice?" Wes asked.

"No, sir, I din't touch no body. I knows you guys frown on that. Felt his pulse is all"

Wes pulled on latex gloves, patted down Irwin Fitzgerald wondering if he had a gun. It wouldn't be strange since he roamed around here at night. Who else knew his habits to check on the development and say hello to the security guard?

He found no weapon of any kind. He found a wallet with a wad of bills in it. Not robbery. Credit cards, driver's license. All the usual things. It was looking more like their Bad Boys killer, but Wes kept hoping that it was something else. Couldn't Irwin accommodate them by having a jealous wife or a partner with whom he had a fatal fight?

He found a small, folded piece of paper. He immediately thought about the Phoenix Byrd certificate. The hair on the back of his neck bristled. He unfolded the paper. It was torn off some cheap tablet that you could buy in any drug store. Not much of a clue there. Written in pencil, 'I'm getting tired of this. Aren't you?' Could this mean that there was a mistress or a confrontation with someone? Wes wanted this to be true. He'd like to build a whole case that said just that, but he knew from his experience that this just wasn't going to be true. Yet, he said to himself, "Maybe...."

"What does it say?" asked Billy Joe, "Do we have a warm clue?"

"Who knows? It says, 'I'm tired of this. Aren't you?' Hell, it may not relate to his death at all. He might have just had it in his pocket from earlier in the day. He turned to the security guard,

"Maybe it refers to the flavor of ice cream since he obviously ate often enough that you noticed."

"I sure did since he would bring me a cone now and then. We would chat while we polished them off. Mr. Fitzgerald always had chocolate, so I don't think the message was about ice cream," Ms. Rice said with a touch of pride in her voice because Mr. Fitzgerald bothered to give her a thought, and she knew a little bit about him. Then she was sober again. The man was gone. This was murder.

"Hey, Wesley, the major and the mayor want a word with you." Brassy had quietly walked up to where the detectives were assembled. "This just isn't your week, Mr. Big Detective."

Wes dropped the paper in his pocket, stripped off his gloves and followed behind Brassy toward a group of people standing beside the mayor's car. Life's little bumps. Just a blip on the radar screen. It's only one case and then life will go on. He thought all these things to himself as he got closer to the group.

"Well, Detective Wesley, I didn't know we were going to get to visit so soon again. Just a few hours ago I thought we had finished our business. Here I am again hanging around another murder scene that is your responsibility. Surprised? Maybe not. It seems you and your colleagues just cannot get it together." Mayor Maxwell paused.

"Yes, sir, we have a tough one this time. We spoke with all the men or left messages for them; whoever we thought was at risk. We…."

One of Erich Maxwell's entourage spoke up, "What do you mean? Do you have some list of people who might be next? How…."

The mayor cut him off, "Detective, I think you should talk less and act more. What's your next step?"

"We'll investigate this murder the same as we do all murders in Atlanta, sir. Some just take longer than others. Actually some are easier because there are known suspects and often they kill with witnesses, or later people want to rat on them. This isn't one of those. Fitzgerald is a man who probably half the city knew his name. The other half knew him personally. He has no record. He seems to be respected. Now the questions are, with all of these positives, who didn't like Mr. Irwin Fitzgerald and why?"

"And that, Detective, is exactly what I want to know and I want to know damn soon? I'll be looking for the information and reports that I asked of you this afternoon. Good night." Mayor Erich Regis Maxwell turned and got into his car. Wes noticed that the man's hand was shaking as he opened the door.

Chapter 38

Eve Zachary

It was a gray day and that always made the Homicide offices in City Hall East particularly dreary. The old building never was a pleasant place, but the lack of sunlight filtering in through the large, streaked warehouse-style windows only added to a feeling of gloom. The Bad Ol' Boys Club team of detectives had gathered early, complete with warm Krispy Kreme doughnuts and lots of hot coffee. It had been a short night. All agreed that strong fortifications were mandatory.

"Where's Eve? She's usually here before the rest of us on her way to class," Billy Joe asked.

"She called to say she had been in early, but had to drop off a paper at school and then she would be back," Golly answered rolling all of the words around the sugary doughnut that he was eating, "She better hurry or there will be no doughnuts left for the kid."

"Let's start looking at all of our information and see what we can hang together. Don't leave out anything. It may seem small or pointless, but we need every damn thing. We don't know where we're going yet and it's already four days since the first murder. We could make a case that the trail is getting cold except the killer is keeping it hot, that's for sure." Wes was letting everyone know that the meeting had started.

All the detectives gave opinions, added facts, laid out what they had done, looked again at photos taken at the crime scenes, studied every word on the Phoenix Byrd certificate, and argued about some conclusions. It was a normal day at the office.

"Where is the research that Eve got us on the Bad Boys? We had it yesterday." Wes was looking through the piles of paper on his desk.

"I don't see it. Maybe it's back on her desk since she came in early. I can look for it," Billy Joe offered, "She and I have created almost enough paper to cover all of these sad ass walls."

"OK. Take a look. Then I want ya'll to see the video that Dino brought," Dino had made his conclusions, but how will the others see it?

They all could hear Billy Joe shuffling papers in the cubicle nearby. He probably was right about how much paper was accumulating in these cases. The Atlanta Homicide Unit had never investigated a series of killings like these: all prominent men.

Billy Joe soon returned. "I found a folder marked Suspect Information. It's very impressive. That gal surely does work hard. She has gotten more than just the telephone numbers, locations etc."

"Suspect Information?" Mike asked, "Strange terminology. Why not Victim Information?"

"Who knows with student interns? They have their own way, that's for sure." Wes said as he got ready to push the video start button. He looked over his shoulder and added, "Here is our star student now. Why not ask her."

"Ask her what? Like maybe which kind of doughnut I want before you eat them all?" Eve was already reaching for a jelly-filled morsel while she dragged a chair behind her.

"We were wonderin' why your folder calls the Bad Boys 'suspects' instead of victims?" Billy Joe asked, waving the folder.

Eve was surprised that Billy Joe had her file. She had put it in her desk to work on later. 'So much for privacy in the Homicide offices,' she thought. 'Maybe I'll take my thesis home with me at night. I don't want everyone and his partner reading what I write.'

"I suppose I looked at it that they were only suspects to become victims. The victims are those already shot. They also are suspects, I believe, in what you're trying to find out about your Good Ol' Boys Club. What did those men do? Why are they so secretive?"

"OK, baby. You always have an answer. Wes, have you ever gotten ahead of Eve?" Billy Joe's smile was almost reaching from ear to ear.

Before Wes could respond, Eve said rather testily, "Of course he hasn't! I work very hard at keeping you both two paces behind like the ladies in the olden days! Survival means to stay ahead."

"Damn! Eve is on the feminist warpath and it's not even 9 AM. Truce. Let's watch the videos. We're probably going to see Temple Carrollton with his killer."

Surprise was registered on each face in the room. They all thought there were no solid clues. Now Wes was saying that there was a video of the guy. Even Eve put down her doughnut and was watching to see what was about to happen.

Just as Dino had reported, the person was never in full view. The hair was a real problem because it distorted the appearance of the face, neck and shoulders. The clinging clothes certainly suggested a woman but some of the dramatic gays could pass almost anywhere as female. The video ended. No one said a word as they thought about what they had seen; maybe something very big or nothing.

"What about digital enhancement? Everyone is talking about how, with technology, we can see anything." Mike Fisher was the first to speak.

"Yeah, like all that worthless stuff the CIA produced related to the Evil Axis," Billy Joe said cynically, "Our techies ought to be able to see right through that hair. Then our job is over. At least it's over as far as the Carrollton murder is concerned."

Wes turned and faced their intern, "Eve, you're our in-house techie. You love all this technology stuff. You also know that we don't know shit. So what do you say?"

"The video's interesting. It's so close to giving you the answer. So close but….no cigar, as they say. I don't know how you can just remove that pile of hair so you can see the face. Enhancement usually means that something is there that you can bring up to clear the image. If you had an idea of the murderer, you could measure or rearrange some lines etc. and see if they were close to matching up."

"You mean that, like, if you, Eve, were the person in the video and we wanted to match up stuff like height, approximate weight, maybe even size of your boobs…Well, you get the question," Golly was already laughing hard.

Wes was ready to tell Golly to get back on track, but Eve was too fast for him.

"Yep, you could do that. Just don't touch any of those body parts. Another scenario would be that the woman is a man, like, if you, Golly, were the person in the video," she paused to make the point of those repeated words, "They could check out that some of your body parts might not match your name, Mr. Goliath Grand."

Now they were all laughing except Golly.

Wes ended the fun,, "On a more serious note, what've we learned from this?"

"I think this is absolutely a woman. From the way she moves her body, she is young," Eve was the first to give her opinion. She then added a joke, "Oh, yes, and that isn't her real hair. She always wanted to be a blonde!"

Heads were nodding in agreement. Wes, Billy Joe and Mike were taking a few notes. Golly was deep in thought, "I'm wondering if it could be a man? I just can't get with the idea that a woman has killed four men this week in cold blood. What about the possibility of being a man and a woman? She reels him in. He kills him."

"Nothing should be beyond consideration, but we have nothing to suggest two people," Wes responded. "For each person added to the equation, there's a better chance of leaving clues, making mistakes. We have so little concrete evidence that I still believe it's one killer."

"I agree with Wes. One person," Eve interjected. "One person is eliminating the Bad Ol' Boys. The question is why? What did they do? Where do they cross over a line and all follow some common path?"

"And, who's next?" asked Wes, "We better figure that one before there's the fifth."

That sobered them all. They were not free of that responsibility. As police, how do they protect their citizens? Having gotten their collective attention, Wes added, "But, Dino, has created one more job for us before we split."

They all knew what Wes was reminding them: it probably was time to stop referring to the killer as a guy. It was time to give the suspect a new persona; perhaps a pretty face. They quite possibly are looking for a female, and even in a culture where every person under the age of thirty-five called both sexes 'guys,' their investigation now needs to center on women.

Wes reached for a legal-size pad of paper while Eve turned to the computer. Wes thought, "The generation gap. I'm still in the paper age when the rest of the world has entered the technology age."

"Eve, do you mind putting the list on the computer so we can each have a list?"

With her back to the group, she smiled and murmured sweetly, "No, boss. I'll do that."

"Great. Let's go. Throw out any name that we know is related to these cases."

Billy Joe was the first to speak up, "Related to Randy, we have Deanna, his wife, who probably hated the guy and we have her sister, Leanne, who Deanna admits was not one of Randy's fans."

"There's Augusta Martinez, who's still hiding something and her roommate, Annie."

Golly sat up straight, "Don't forget that there are at least three women who probably each thinks she should've been married to Temple Carrollton and her son the chosen heir. Shit, we don't have any idea how many other mistresses could be

226

listed for that motherfucker."

"Franklin Raub's wife, Iris."

"Don't forget, she has a sister, old what's her name?" Mike asked.

"Laurel Plitz."

There was a lull while the group thought about the cases.

"Janeen and Dani." Billy Joe suggested.

"Get serious, damn it," Wes blustered.

"Well, they've been around for every shootin'. Dani's been at every murder scene and receives suspicious calls. Janeen follows Wes' cases like she's really interested. I could be serious," Billy Joe said.

Eve turned around away from the computer, "If they're getting on the list, then put me there, too."

"CUT THE SHIT!" Wes bellowed. "Can't any of you stay serious for five minutes?"

"Relax, Wes," Billy Joe patted his partner on the shoulder, "You're really stressed. Too much Mayor Maxwell, me thinks. You know if we couldn't laugh it up as we do this job, we'd all be in padded cells. There ain't one of us in this room who's not nervous about this case. If somethin' happens to the mayor, how will that affect our jobs? And, now that the media beyond Atlanta is havin' a field day with these murders, we might be out of a job anyway before the mayor becomes a dead man."

"You're right, Billy Joe. I just don't want us to miss something. Each day that we haven't nailed this bastard, umm, I mean bitch, we just might see another Atlanta man shot!"

"Sorry, guys, this doesn't work," Eve broke in.

They all looked at her.

"Don't you read detective novels? You aren't supposed to have more than four or five good suspects. I guess it's because the reader can't handle more than that. We already have twelve named suspects, we have no women related to Irwin yet and we haven't completed the list of lady friends for the good reverend. Sorry, you can't sell this plot."

"OK, Eve, we know you're still kidding around, but you also have a point. We do have too many suspects. We also don't know if any of those suspects relate to all the victims. It seems unlikely, but we must find out. That's why we all better work harder, smarter, better and faster. We're running out of time. Since we can't get to all of these ladies today, we better start the other way and get to the men who we're sure are in the killer's sights. Our number one job is to get them to talk. They hold the key to why they're the ones, and it's fuckin' unbelievable that they're willing to let their old friends die. It just doesn't make sense. Let's take 'em on and try to get one to break their code of silence."

Chapter 39

Vance Bowman

It was decided that a question had to be asked of each of the victim's family: would considering a woman as the shooter create new avenues of possibilities? Wes pointed out that this line of questioning could have a variety of responses. Certainly it would be painful for the wives to have to dredge up thoughts of 'other women.' If one of the wives or other family member were the killer, she would be warned that the detectives were moving in her direction. If this new theory made sense, they would wonder what would be the tie that would make one woman kill the men they may not know well.

Billy Joe had started for the door when he added another thought, "Wes, maybe the video just documents that Carrollton was doin' his thing. You know, foolin' around with his li'l darlins. He spent some time with Ms. Big Hair. Then got popped by someone else."

"Anything is possible. Unfortunately, the possibilities seem to be endless. We just have to keep moving fast and trying to find the strongest thread between these men. I think I will go and try scaring the shit out of Vance Bowman. I'll try that before I have to face the mayor again. We might have to put more pressure on the other Bad Boys. Golly, why don't you try reaching them all again. Be sure you tell them that their friends are being killed off at the rate of one a day. If you get a whiff of nervousness or panic, go to Charlotte or Miami or wherever and knock on their doors. Mike, Billy Joe and I will cover the locals."

A list was made and divided among them. The families, friends and business colleagues were going to see different detective faces. Just in case they were becoming too comfortable seeing a familiar person. Approach would be to take a harder line. This call was not a 'hope you're doing OK' visit. They all knew the drill and were ready to go. The problem was that none of the four men believed that these interviews were going to be the answer. There still was the fact that it appeared that the tie among the dead men was from at least a decade ago.

• • • •

The telephone rang and rang. Vance Bowman was already sweating, wiping his forehead with a folded handkerchief, "Please, answer the damn phone," he whispered, "I have to talk to someone."

"Montrose."

"Houston, thank God. I thought you weren't there."

"Well, I am. Why are you calling?"

Houston Montrose sounded both aggravated and a little drunk. Vance was surprised. He had never seen his old friend take more than one or two glasses of wine. He remembered him hating beer even when they all would sit around with each having his own six pack.

"Houston, one of my reporters just called and said that Irwin was found shot. It happened last night at his new development site. What's happening? Who's next? Who's doing this?"

"Irwin shot? Is he dead?"

"Yes. Houston, that's four of us! What can we do? I think I must leave Atlanta. I can't sleep or concentrate. I'm afraid of everyone I see on the street." Bowman wiped his forehead and across the back of his neck. His collar was already soaked. He felt perspiration running down the middle of his back.

"Get hold of yourself, Vance! These killings have to be coincidence. How could they relate to our old group? Who would even remember that we had a group?" Houston asked shrilly.

"Just about anyone who knew us back then. Let's face it, Houston, we treated everyone like shit. We thought we were so superior to everyone. I'm sure there were lots of guys who hated our guts."

"Those jerks. They weren't smart enough then to be in our gang. They sure as hell aren't smart enough now to kill people all over Atlanta and get away with it. You're like you always were; a big worrier. You always thought we would be caught when we went through our missions, but you were wrong then and you're wrong now. Damn, Vance, stay cool and nothing will happen. Just don't go hanging out in deserted places. Look at each of the guys: Randy was outside of the Union Mission, Franklin was out in the middle of the night and now you say Irwin was at his development at night. And, where are you? At home where you belong or at places where there are other people. Stay cool, man."

"And Temple was in his hotel room. How about that?" Vance asked. He could not understand Houston's attitude. He didn't seem the least bit scared. Actually he also did not seem to care. Like Temple, Randy, Irwin and Franklin meant nothing to him.

"For God's sake, Vance. You knew Temple. He probably entertained every woman in town in his hotel room. He had illegitimate kids all over the south. Every one of those people had families who would love to see him dead. One of them just went ahead and did it. What a farce! He and his saintly façade."

Houston Montrose was pacing back and forth in his bedroom while talking. He passed by the wide, floor-length window and glanced outside. The wind was blowing gently. The bushes along his driveway swaying like dancers in a chorus line. He thought of Temple's conquests and wondered if his idea of who killed the preacher could be wrong. Was Vance right? Maybe someone was eliminating the Good Ol' Boys Club members. He reached up and pushed the control to close the drapes. He assured himself that he was not afraid. It was simply too bright in his bedroom.

"Vance, I have things to do. Rehashing all of this isn't going to help you to relax. Get over this crazy idea. Just don't panic. It's too bad about the guys, but they were at the wrong place at the wrong time. Got it?" Houston sat on his king sized bed and looked at the drapes that now covered the window. He gave a snorting laugh and added, "Stay away from the windows."

"This is not funny! Maybe you aren't smart enough to see a pattern. Serial killers don't just keep killing at random. This guy is looking for us," Vance Bowman was bordering on hysteria. He had called for support, but Houston Montrose was not the right man for that. Actually, he had always been cold. That's probably why he was always the first one to perform another stupid mission that meant prowling around town in areas that were scary.

"You do whatever you damn please. Worry or hide. I don't have time for your shit. Get real, Bowman." Houston slammed down the receiver and reached for the glass of vodka that had been sitting on his nightstand. He knew he was not as unconnected as he said but he sure as hell wasn't going to let that wimp know.

Vance heard the slamming of the receiver and said out loud to himself, "He hung up on me! That's great. Our lifelong pledges to each other did not last quite a lifetime. Good riddance. I never did like that dumb ass anyway."

As he replaced the receiver, the inner-com was buzzing. He wiped his sweating palms on his very damp handkerchief and pushed the button to connect.

"What is it, Angie?"

"There's another detective here, Mr. Bowman. He wants to see you now."

"I don't have the time to meet with him. Get his number. I'll call him later today. We have a newspaper to get out."

"I'll tell him," Angie said quietly, "I don't think he'll be deterred any more than Detective Wesley was." She lowered her voice even more and whispered, "Detective Wesley was polite and nice. This one is big and talks rough. He's kinda scary."

"Damn it, Angie. Your job is to keep people out of my office. Just do your job." It was his turn to slam down the receiver.

What next? Was there no place that he could find peace? Was his whole life being ruined because of his friends and their club? He wondered why he hadn't just joined a fraternity when he was a young man. He would have if he could have seen into his future. After all these years, why did the Good Ol' Boys gang have to be singled out?

Vance slumped in his chair and thought about getting out of town. He'd tell his wife that he had a surprise for her and they were taking a secret vacation. They could go to their ski lodge in Aspen. That was certainly far enough away to be safe. They could stay there until the killer was found and put behind bars. Then his life could get back to normal. Or could it? Would these terrible murders reach out and ruin all that he had worked for? He would worry about that after he came back from Aspen.

He was jolted again by a knock on the door. Angie opened it just a crack and poked her head in. Her voice quavered as she said, "Mr. Bowman, you need to talk to this Detective LaCrosse or then you tell him to leave. He's hovering over me like a vulture. Feeling threatened is not part of my job!"

Vance bolted out of his chair and strode quickly across the beautiful, silk Oriental rug. "Oh, get out of the way. I'll handle this. I don't know why these police are hounding us. We're good citizens and community leaders. I'm going to call the mayor. He's a good friend. He's been a good friend since I was in college."

He grabbed the door and swung it open. There stood Billy Joe directly in back of Angie Mason, "Right, Mr. Bowman, the mayor is a good friend of yours and of Mr. Phoenix Byrd. Let's talk."

Vance's eyes widened. He wanted to look cool as Houston had cautioned, but the name of Phoenix Byrd being said by this big, black detective was a shock. He did not know if he could take any more surprises.

The editor of the Atlanta Economic Review looked defeated. He motioned for Billy Joe to come in and told his secretary to not interrupt them. Like it or not, he knew he was going to have to talk with this man.

Chapter 40

Wes T. Wesley

Across town, Wes parked on the street in front of the Raub
house and walked up the driveway. He planned to talk with both
Franklin Raub's widow and her sister. It bothered him that there
could be so many female suspects, but that each of them seemed
to relate only to one victim. How could one woman be involved
with all four men? How could she want to kill them all? What
was the common thread?

The garage doors were open framimg two cars. He hoped
that would mean that Iris was home. He rang the doorbell. When
the door opened, it was not Iris who stood there looking quite
beautiful in a pale blue dress with a flowered scarf draped across
her shoulders. It was Laurel.

"I think we've already done this, Detective Wesley. You ring
the bell. I answer the door. What's next? We don't want to repeat
the first time we met, do we?"

"No, Ms. Plitz. There's no time for that. I'm glad to see you
here, because I want to talk with you as well as Mrs. Raub."

"You'll have to be satisfied with just me. Iris had an
appointment. I told her I could stay here until she returned. Look
at this place. Flowers everywhere, food sent from every neighbor
and enough mail to cover the dining room table. Come in. You'll
just add to the confusion."

"Your brother-in-law was known by every citizen in the city.
All of this seems to confirm that he was quite well-liked," Wes
did not want to start asking the hard questions before he even
was in the hallway. He could be gracious for maybe two minutes,
and then he would play bad cop.

Laurel suggested they sit in the family room. She said

the flowers had not yet spilled into that part of the house. Wes followed her and watched as she perched on the edge of the desk. Her pose was almost theatrical. She gave the appearance that she was in charge. The detective stood nearby and asked, "What was your opinion of your brother-in-law?"

Her eyes widened. She answered his question with a question, "What possible difference could my opinion make to this case? What are you suggesting?"

"I'm not suggesting anything. I'm looking for an answer. How did you get along with Franklin?"

"I don't like the tone of that question, Detective, but I have no problem answering. Franklin and I were relatives. We weren't close friends. I don't know that he was very close to anyone, mostly because he never had much time beyond his political life. He loved being the president of City Council. I think he would've run for mayor sometime and maybe later for governor. That was his life. Everything else came second. And that second was his family, Iris and Frankie."

"So his marriage was a good one. No secrets on his side or on Iris'?"

Laurel rose from her perch and exploded, "What's this all about? You're being very insulting. In two minutes you have made us all look tawdry. What are you trying to say?"

"Ms. Plitz, some new information has been found and, like it or not, it looks as if the murderer might be a woman. We're retracing our investigation with that possibility to find out what woman, or women, could have been the killer." Wes waited as Laurel thought about this idea. Her face was unreadable at the moment.

"I find this absolutely ridiculous. This wasn't a personal shooting. It couldn't have had anything to do with the family because the family had nothing to hide. And, if I believe what I read in the newspaper, the theory is that all four murders this week were related. You actually suspect Iris or me of running around Atlanta shooting Franklin and his friends? As I said,

Detective, it is ridiculous!"

"No, it may not be one of you, but it could be another woman who had a relationship with all four men. Stranger things have happened, even in Atlanta. I'm looking for a woman who knew them all and maybe just didn't like any of them. Now, can you think of any woman who bothered Franklin or simply pissed him off?"

"There may have been women who fantasized about Franklin. You know the political groupies. He used to laugh about those kinds of females. He would say that they were everywhere. Actually, he mentioned a couple times that Manuel's was a hangout for all kinds of folks. As you know there was politicians' night, media night and police night at Manuel's. He was there for politicians' night just before he was shot," Laurel stopped and took a deep breath, "Could that really be a possibility? Some crazed woman followed him home and shot him? How sick can that be?"

"Sick, yes. Possible, yes. Each man was shot in a rather secluded place, at night and each man was political in his own way. Community leaders are all political. Was it politics? Was it personal? Was it just a crazy? It could be any or all of those. We're still trying to fit all the pieces together."

Laurel continued to stand beside the desk. Her full, sensuous mouth that had always been quick to smile was stern and pinched. Wes wondered if it was all a reaction to his questions or more likely it was the reaction to the answers to the questions. Laurel would know if Iris had suspected that Franklin had been overly impressed with one of the political groupies. Wes was sure that the two sisters would talk about such things.

Laurel Plitz shifted her weight from one foot to the other. She appeared to be trying to find a comfortable position. "Detective Wesley, I think I know Iris and Franklin very well. I knew their relationship. We were family. We were neighbors. Easy to see and hear what's going on when you live so close," Laurel took a deep breath as if she needed extra energy, "I would have to say that I absolutely know of no problems between my sister and her husband. Actually, Franklin wasn't much of a ladies' man. As I said, his biggest love was his position and his politics. He never talked about anything else. At parties, at events you would always find him in a corner talking the same old line: politics. Great for votes, boring for those who had been around for years. That's how I see it. Even with your new evidence, whatever it is, I don't see some woman lurking around here waiting to attack Franklin."

"Laurel, how about years ago? Maybe when he was just getting involved with politics?"

"He was always involved even back to when he and Iris got married before he went to college. He was a returned vet and older than most of his class. They had Frankie before Franklin was a freshman. Iris used to go to campus political meetings with the baby on what should have been a Saturday night date. She knew that this was his life, but to be second to that was just fine with her. It was a good match."

"What do you know about a club that Franklin belonged to back in those days?" Wes decided to take advantage of Laurel talking about college days

"You have been doing your homework, Detective Wesley. That stupid gang. They thought they were really hot. They hung out together at least once or twice a week. Iris used to laugh and say, 'If I didn't know better, I'd say they were gay.' Only we didn't use the word 'gay' much back then. Then she would wink and say, "But, Laurel, honey, Franklin Raub is not a homo. He's too anxious to get in bed every night.

"No, it was our opinion - Iris and mine - the gang provided a support system that was stronger than any other that they had ever found. Franklin once said it was better than being in the military. Everyone supported everyone. I guess the support worked since the men I know from back then have all become successful and community leaders."

Laurel stopped and looked Wes directly in the eyes. She held that eye contact for a few moments before looking away, "I think

I just said something important. I don't even quite understand why I have this 'A-ha feeling.' You know what I mean. All of these men are community leaders, right?. Somehow that's tied into these killings. They aren't just random people. They have been friends for a long time, they have helped each other get where they are, they have stayed loyal and maybe it's because they were so tight when they were just beginning. Someone doesn't like them because they have been together or they have decided that they have had this relationship long enough. This is the end."

Wes remained silent, interested in what Laurel Plitz would say next. He heard outside noises: a car, a child's voice, a dog barking. He was reminded that he was in a regular, normal neighborhood. Why, then, were they talking about four murders?

"Detective Wesley, I don't see why this lead has to be a woman. It looks like it could lead to a man."

"It could, but there are signs that a woman is involved. I'm looking for that information to point us in the direction of that woman." He paused and watched. Laurel was in deep thought.

Wes continued, "Thinking back to those college years, Franklin was older, married, a father, a student. When he was a part of the club with Mr. Phoenix Byrd, what did he do with these other guys? Trade class notes or meet at the student union?"

Laurel smiled, "Of course not! Just hearing you say it sounds preposterous. The truth is, though Franklin was all you say, he was quite immature. He was still experiencing what he thought life should be.

"Those guys hung out together; they prowled the night spots. Often he would come in very late. Iris understood that he was carrying a big load with school and a family. She loved him, Detective Wesley. She was patient and gave him room to grow up, which is what he did. Her way was right because it built the life they had until this week. They were devoted. Franklin often said to her, 'You not only are my wife, you have been my salvation.'"

Wes decided not to question Laurel's observations. "Do you know where the boys hung out on those nights?"

"Hmmm, you're back to women again. I guess you want to consider a sex angle. Sex and money. Aren't they two main reasons for murder?"

It was Wes' turn to smile. This charming, lovely woman was also a thinker. She was doing quite well keeping up with him and his questions.

"That's what we often find. That and family problems. So, what about my question?"

"Funny thing occurs to me. One place the guys used to go was to Manuel's. Wouldn't it be prophetic if this began at Manuel's and ended after Franklin was at Manuel's? The other part of your interrogation, Detective Sir, you know, about additional people. I do remember that they would joke about if you wanted to meet anyone who was anyone, go to Manuel's. They thought it was big time to meet and talk with politicians and those who already were big deals in Atlanta. They would say with arrogance, "They're holding our places for us. We're on our way!""

"No special 'anyones'? No names?"

Laurel settled back on her desk perch, her eyes wide, "Damn, man. This was over ten years ago. I was still a young girl and looking for my own kind of fun. That was not hanging out at Manuel's. I really don't remember names mentioned. Since I was Iris' sister, why would Franklin mention anything that I could pass on to Iris?"

"Would you?"

She again looked Wes directly in the eyes, "No, I wouldn't. I love my sister. I always wanted her to be happy. I would do a lot to be sure my sister has a good life. She totally loved Franklin. I could live with that no matter if I didn't always think he was the greatest."

Chapter 41

Vance Bowman

Billy Joe closed the door behind Angie as she hustled out of the office. She looked as good going as coming. Vance Bowman definitely had an eye for good looking secretaries.

"Detective, I have just about had it with Atlanta Homicide! I suggest you hound someone else," Vance said with the emphasis on the 'else.'

"Who would that someone else be?"

"Maybe you should talk to Houston Montrose. He had the same relationship years ago as I did with our friends. You'll find that he won't take any shit. Why pick on me?" Bowman wanted to get rid of this man. He was willing to sacrifice Houston to do it.

"I might go to see him next. But I'm here now. In case you haven't noticed, Mr. Bowman, the detectives, three others and myself, are tryin' to save your life. I can always tell my partners that you'd rather be shot tonight or tomorrow than talk with us. You make the call to the mayor, sir. I really don't give a shit about your life. I'm just doin' my job." Billy Joe delivered his feelings with disgust. These men were just plain crazy---and just plain rude. It demonstrated the length they were willing to go to hide their past.

Vance was shocked. This crude, big, black civil servant had just talked to him like he was a 'nobody.' He paid him no respect.

"I don't like your attitude one bit. How dare you take that tone of voice with me? I help pay your salary!"

"Yes you do. And I can make that worthwhile if I keep you from endin' up on a cold metal table in the coroner's lab with your body split in half as she looks for the bullet in your heart. You can lie there with your sightless eyes starin' up at the ceilin' while your very alive picture appears on the front page of the Atlanta Economic Review with a banner, bordered in black that says, Publisher Vance Bowman Gunned Down. Today you may make me puke with your attitude, Mr. Publisher, but you'll still be dead tomorrow."

Bowman dropped into his desk chair and put his head in his hands. It was a position that he had assumed often during the past few days. He felt defeated. He felt lost. Yes, he already felt dead.

"I'm going to leave town, Detective. I'm getting out of this environment. I can't take it anymore. Just leave me alone!"

"Sure, go out of town. Don't help us catch this son-of-a-bitch and when you come back, there will be someone waitin' for you at the airport. It won't be me or Detective Wesley. We'll have given up, called the case unsolved and gone on to some drug dealer murder. I'll make you a promise, Mr. Publisher. I'll come to your fancy funeral, look at your casket and say, 'there lies the most stupid community leader in the city.'"

Billy Jo was now standing over Vance's huddled figure. He was leaning over him with his big, beefy hands on the armrests of the chair. His hot breath was being felt on the back of the man's head. Billy Jo did not retreat. He forced his presence on the little weasel. The Atlanta leadership should see him now.

Vance Bowman's shoulders began to shake. His head and shoulders sunk more deeply into his lap. He pressed the palms of his hands tightly into his eyes. He felt the warmth of snot running into his mouth. He didn't even reach to wipe it away.

"Leave me alone. Leave me alone," he begged. "Our only mistakes were when we were very young. It wasn't all that bad. We were proving how invincible we were. We were never caught. It was our secret. It was our pledge."

It became harder for Billy Joe to hear the words. The sobs became deeper, louder. The words were punctuated with gut-wrenching noises. Vance Bowman had told enough. Now Billy Joe needed the details.

"What were you provin'?" Gruffly, Billy Joe asked the questions not knowing if this would push the man over the edge. Where was his breaking point?

The reply was a hoarse whisper, "Proving? We were proving that we were above them all. We were even above the law."

"How did you do that?"

Silence. Then more snuffling and sobbing. Billy Joe could almost feel Vance Bowman's soul dissolving in the chair. He may have once thought he was invincible. Today he knew he was wrong.

"How did you do that?" Billy Joe raised his voice, but never changed his position. His words would be acid in the publishers' ears.

Again a whisper, hardly audible, "We did things that were criminal. We stole things and sold them for more beer money or to take jaunts to Florida. We always had money."

"What else?" Detective LaCrosse boomed.

An echo from the chair "What else? Yes, there was more. We beat up some guys we thought were queers. We knew they wouldn't tell. It was a different time in history. No one ever knew---until today," the sobbing began again.

"What else?" Billy Joe hissed.

"Aagh, oh, oh," Vance Bowman fell to his knees. He simply toppled off the chair.

"We each had sex with a little girl."

Chapter 42

Houston Montrose

"Where are you, Wes?" Billy Joe spoke into his cell phone. He preferred using it instead of the standard police radio.

"I'm just leaving Raub's home. I have had an interesting conversation with Laurel but never saw Iris. I can't imagine Iris is our perp, but I'll go back later."

"I think you should go check out Houston Montrose. Bowman never hesitated to finger him. I get the idea they don't like each other. But, that's not the big news, Wes. We've got ourselves some kind of child molestation thing."

"What? Holy shit. Do you mean the whole gang?" Wes was incredulous.

"I think so. I first thought maybe kiddie porn but it's probably worse than porn. Bowman was so hysterical that I may not have gotten it all straight but straight enough, pardner. The 'Bad Ol' Boys' are really bad boys. This ain't just a cutesy name."

Billy Joe continued to repeat the information that he had heard from Vance Bowman. Wes continued to be amazed.

"Billy Joe, what you're saying is that Raub, Lee, Carrollton, Bowman, etc. and our mayor have all committed serious crimes just for the hell of it. This is going to make not only our local media, but from coast to coast. It will take Atlanta years to overcome this publicity. The police department's going to be standing naked and alone when this breaks. Mayor Maxwell will cover up his part any way he can."

"Well, it's not gonna work, Wes. If Bowman's hysterical story is true, Maxwell is done. So are the others if all the names come out. And that's the way it should be. These guys are bad dudes man. They're scumbags. On top of that, they're pious, sanctimonious scumbags!"

Wes waited for Billy Joe's tirade to slow down. He knew that what his partner had learned broke every value that men who have set themselves up as leaders should follow. Petty theft, even breaking and entering, was nothing compared to child abuse and molestation. The whole premise was disgusting: prove you are special by being immoral.

"OK, Billy Joe, I'll call Mike Fisher and tell him I'm covering Montrose. I'll also tell him what we're probably dealing with. I'll give him the job of getting to Golly. We should all meet back at homicide as soon as we can. We need to talk and then get to the major. This is too hot for us to keep to ourselves.

• • • •

Wes entered Houston Montrose's corporate headquarters just 20 minutes later. The Montrose and Byrd Group was a fancy, high end investment and financial advisory firm located on Peachtree Street. It took three floors in one of the slick, high rise buildings and boasted having the best executive dining room in the city. Wes doubted that there really was a partner named Byrd. These men have created their own form of reality.

The reception area felt, looked and smelled like serious money. The pale pink Georgia marble floor, covered with pastel area Oriental rugs were surrounded by silvery gray walls embellished with soothing, pastel art work. Wes was sure that the environment was designed carefully to put clients in the mood to leave some of their money with Montrose and his associates. None of this seemed to fit with the reason Wes was there. He wondered what this 'Bad Ol' Boy' would add to the growing mess.

"Mr. Montrose, please," Wes said as he handed his card to the receptionist.

"DetectiveWesley? Atlanta Homicide?" the small gray-haired grandmotherly woman asked. Her matching gray eyes, filled with silent questions, looked at Wes.

"Yes ma'm. If you would tell Mr. Montrose that I need some time with him, I would appreciate it." He would leave the explanations up to Mr. Montrose.

Ms. Gray Eyes and Hair rang her boss and simply announced that Detective Wesley was requesting an immediate appointment. Wes detected a commanding tone in her voice as if she might have added, "You better see him!"

A door opened off to the right and a tall, slender man stood framed in the open doorway. He was dressed in the businessman's uniform; khaki pants, navy blazer with shiny gold buttons, a conservative blue and maroon tie over a blue oxford cloth shirt. His brown hair was professionally styled to look casual although every hair was carefully arranged. For a moment, Wes had the feeling that Houston Montrose was posing; perhaps giving an impression of his stature in life. Wes did not wait for him to speak. He strode purposely across the room.

"Mr. Montrose, Detective Wes Wesley, Atlanta Homicide. I have some things to discuss."

"Of course, Detective Weston, do come into my office."

"Wesley, Mr. Montrose. Detective Wesley."

"Yes, of course. Sorry."

The two men retreated into the office with Ms. Gray Eyes and Hair standing beside her desk. She waited until the door was closed, sat down and picked up her telephone.

"Sadie, you won't believe this but the detective that we saw on the news last evening just went into Mr. Montrose's office. I wonder what he wants here." She waited listening and then added, "I'll call again when I know more. This's really exciting." She waited again and then smiled, "Oh, yes he's as handsome as he was on TV."

As the call was being made, Houston Montrose was taking his seat behind his glass and chrome desk. He motioned for Wes to sit in the soft, gray leather-and-chrome sling chair facing him.

"Mr. Montrose, Vance Bowman suggested we speak. He said you could fill in some of the details about your old club that had as its patron Phoenix Byrd."

Wes watched Montrose and did not detect surprise or shock. A cool guy. Even if he had been warned by Bowman, he was unruffled. He had not had much time to be so composed. Yes, a cool character.

Houston Montrose was livid with Vance Bowman for sending this man in his direction. He would deal with him later. Right now, he had to be casual and unflustered.

"Phoenix bird? Oh, yes. When I was younger, I was so impressed with the imagery of Atlanta rising from the ashes like a phoenix bird. It was my heritage. My family was part of that wonderful time in history. The Montrose family was among the first colonists here in Georgia. You'll see our name in many places. You certainly know of Montrose, Georgia."

"I've heard of it, Mr. Montrose. Never been there. I'm an Atlanta boy. Also the Phoenix Byrd I'm speaking of has only a 10 or 15-year history. It was the one spelled B-Y-R-D who signed your little 'Good Ol' Boys Club' certificate. Since your memory for history is so good, you probably remember the rules and missions of the 'Good Ol' Boys' Club, right?" Wes watched. He saw no emotion in Montrose's face.

"Ah, yes, our little group. We studied together, ate together, hung out together. It was our time to be friends."

"Friends? You omitted accomplices in crime, Mr. Montrose." Wes spoke in a louder tone. He saw a slight twitch beneath Houston Montrose's left eye. A small break in his cool exterior, but a break none the less.

"Accomplices in crime, Detective Weston? Those are strong words. Do you think I should call my attorney?"

"That's up to you, Mr. Montrose. I'm here as part of the investigation of the murder of four of your 'Good Ol' Boys' group. I'm here with hope of finding a killer and preventing further shootings. I'm here to investigate if acts of yours and your friends many years ago have any bearing on this case. I believe they do. Now, do you want to call you attorney? I can wait."

Still with no emotion demonstrated, Houston Montrose quietly responded, "Yes, I'll call my attorney."

"Tell him my name is Detective Wesley, Mr. Montrose."

Chapter 43

Wes T. Wesley

Wes, Billy Joe and Mike Fisher were gathered around a desk littered with coffee containers, take-out bags and the remains of a fast food lunch. The smell was strongly of hamburgers with onions.

"What a can of worms!" Billy Joe announced. He had repeated most of what Vance Bowman had croaked out while pounding on his desk in desperation.

Wes had added his encounter with Montrose and his attorney, which resulted in the attorney suggesting his client make no statements until more was known about the case. He concluded the meeting with a typical pronouncement.

"If Mr. Montrose is a person of interest in these murders, proceed with your case. If not, this meeting is adjourned."

Mike Fisher had called on Mrs. Irwin Fitzgerald, who was the third. Mrs. Fitzgerald She was a twenty-three year old, blonde, trophy wife named Sugar dressed scantily in a mini skirt and low-cut hot pink knit top at least one size too small that stretched tightly over well-endowed breasts.

He told the others, "The gorgeous Mrs. Fitzgerald spent more time flirting with me than she did contemplating the serious questions I was asking. She did dab at her sparkling turquoise eyes now and then when I brought up her late husband's murder. With a sniffle she cooed, "Irwin was such a nice man. So successful. We only knew each other about six months so I wasn't really, really attached. You know, it's not like we were married a long time or something." They all laughed at Mike's falsetto voice that he used to repeat her words.

Then the detective reported that he didn't think this chippie

248

had the IQ to plan going out to lunch let alone four murders. She also barely recognized any of the names of the victims. When he said that these killings had all been in the paper and on TV this week, Sugar sweetly responded, "Oh, dear, Detective Mike, I don't pay attention to the news. I prefer reality shows!"

"Detective Mike!" Billy Joe exclaimed. "Now isn't that the cutest, little, ole name?"

"As a matter of fact, Bozo, it was said in such a way that I do believe it was an invitation to visit again without my badge. Just imagine, 'Detective Mike, Detective Mike. I'm coming, I'm coming.'"

"Oh, shit. You have such an imagination. Let's get back to the real reality show: Atlanta Homicide Strikes Out on Four Murders!" Billy Joe punctuated his exclamation by tossing one of the empty cups at Mike Fisher, saying softly, "Catch, Detective Mike."

"OK. Let's get our facts straight. I need to get to the major and let her know that we have some big problems here. We also need to let her know about our theory that it's a woman. We need to---------"

Eve came bouncing in the room tossing her backpack on the floor. As the bag hit with a bang, there was a clattering of small items. Eve looked at her backpack and gave it a push with her foot, "I guess I should have zipped up all the zippers." She smiled and went right on without taking a breath. "What's up? You guys look serious. Have you solved your case? Did I miss the big event?"

"Nope, Case is still open, but it's turned into a new case. Our focus is changing and maybe our unknown female perp does relate to all of the dead men," Wes responded as Eve pulled up a chair to join the circle.

"Related how?"

"As we've been theorizing, the motive for these murders has been hanging around for at least a decade. We now have information that the motive could be criminal activity of the whole gang," Wes explained.

Billy Joe interrupted, "Damn, Wes, we're not talkin' normal, everyday crime. We're talkin' child molestation, child rape. These guys deserve to lose their gonads!"

Eve was silent for a moment. Her lips silently pronounced WOW!. "When you guys finally find a motive, you surely do discover a sick one. Now we have opportunity and motive. We still need a murderer."

"Yep, all we've done is unearth more crimes. But, at least with these old crimes, we've got some suspects." Wes shook his head in despair, "I've got to talk to the major and the chief. We're all in deep shit. Before I go, Eve, let me help you pick up this mess from your backpack."

"Don't worry, Wes. I'll get it."

Ignoring her offer, Wes leaned down and picked up a pen, pack of tissues and several chocolate mints. Billy Joe joined in to retrieve several other small items, "Hey, Eve, what's this? You seem to have a very fat file here called 'Suspects? Yes/No.' It's fat enough to include everybody in the city of Atlanta. Why would you have one of our homicide files in your backpack?" Billy Joe turned to Eve with a quizzical expression on his face.

"Man, I can't believe I've been carrying around those files. But they aren't official files, Billy Joe. They're my thesis files. No big deal is it?" Eve looked blankly at the file folder in Billy Joe's hand.

"Yeah, little lady, it's a big deal. You may recognize them as non-official files but they're on our forms. Who would know? What if you spilled them out somewhere in public? You don't mess with this type of information. Why would your thesis be written on our forms?

"Because my thesis is presented as if it's a real case. I want it to be authentic." Eve sounded defensive and maybe a bit ticked off.

"The principle is OK," Billy Joe continued while he scanned the papers, "But what you have in these files is not. Look at this, Eve, you're documentin' information about women who

250

could all be victims yet placin' them in a folder you have titled 'Suspects.' You use that word suspect very liberally. Damn it, what if the media even had a glance at somethin' like this? Not only would you be out, we'd all be out too. We'd be out all over the six o'clock news. Even Dani would shoot us down."

Billy Joe silently handed the folder to Wes, pointing his finger at a certain sheet.

The silence was heavy as Wes took time to look at what Billy Joe had already perused. Everyone waited for him to speak.

"Eve, this is amazing. Not only are you carrying around confidential information about the women in this case, you have presumed to add your opinion as to who might be guilty. How do you explain that?" Wes was pointing at Eve with the handful of papers.

Eve looked perplexed, but she was not intimidated, "That's the way I read the evidence and people in this case. Isn't that what I'm supposed to be learning? Or am I just assigned to be your gofer?"

Wes' eyes narrowed. There was a flush on his face. He felt like he was facing his teenage son who had just been discovered driving Wes' car without a license. "Eve, are you or are you not a professional? If the answer is not, then it's time you find another internship. If the answer is that you are, then change your attitude, young lady. Tell us why you have documented your conclusions and then been careless with that information."

Eve looked Wes right in the eyes, "I've drawn my own conclusions because everyone else seems baffled about this case. As you can see, I don't think that most of the women you're looking at even rate to be called suspects." She waited for Wes' response but Billy Joe spoke up.

"Well, Eve, we'll study your research and your conclusions. We'll see if we can speed up this case. Just leave all of these files here. I'll go with you to your desk to check on what might be there that we don't want floatin' around Atlanta. Bein' an intern is a privilege and a responsibility. You've been around here long enough to know we take our business seriously." Billy Joe looked at Eve in the same way he would look at his own children.

"OK, but I haven't been careless. I really had these at home to work on them but brought them with me today. I'll give you whatever I have, if that's what you want," Eve said with a slight coolness in her voice. She added, "I feel like one of your kids, Billy Joe. It's nice to have a daddy looking out for me."

"I hope you don't mean that as a smart mouth remark. I know that you only have your mama. Maybe you do need some fatherly influence now and then, kiddo."

"My mom and you. Now that's a funny thought. She would think she was back in her hey days." Her head was down so they couldn't see the smirk on her face as she reached for her backpack. As she followed Billy Joe out of the office, Eve turned and said, "I get the message. I'm sorry I upset you, but my conclusions say these women aren't going to save you from more murders."

•   •   •   •

Wes approached Brassy's desk. The flunky of the Major was waiting for him. He immediately attacked in his usual irritating style, "Here comes our past wonder of Homicide. Can't live on your old successes, Wesley. The major is really pissed that she's getting the heat all the way from the mayor's office because you and your band of brothers can't find a very active murderer in Atlanta. How will you like patrolling in Zone One 'till you retire?"

Wes chose to ignore the obnoxious man, "I have an appointment with Major Dilbert. Please, tell her I'm here."

"I know you have an appointment. You made it with me. Without me, Wesley, you'd be cooling your ass until I decided to put you on the calendar."

Brassy announced Wes' presence with a sneer. The man then motioned for him to go into the inner office.

Even though the time between Wes' request to meet and when he arrived was less than twenty minutes, Major Dagmar

Dilbert was seated in her office with Chief Princeton. They both looked serious but were relaxing with freshly poured coffee. Brassy was such a thoughtful flunky.

"Detective Wesley, Major Dillbert asked me to join you two. It'll save someone having to repeat your findings. I think this will be helpful to us all."

"Yes, sir, time is always of the essence. We currently have too many avenues to investigate. We need all the time we can find."

"O.K., let's hear it. We're hoping for a fast conclusion, Wes. It's getting embarrassing. The mayor has been screaming at me to close the case under any conditions. He is so protective of his city," the Chief said.

"Of himself, sir."

"What does that mean? This is not a time for low, political blows."

"I wasn't being political, Chief. I was just providing thought provoking commentary."

Wes continued on for what seemed an eternity to the major and the chief. At first, they discounted the "Bad Ol' Boys Club" theory. As he added facts gathered by the team, disbelief turned to incredibility. Each person in the room had a different agenda. Each wrestling with how this sordid information could affect him or her personally. Wes wasn't making anyone's day.

The major looked stricken but said nothing. It was her style to say as little as possible in front of Chief Princeton. That way she couldn't be accused of saying the wrong thing. Her opinions would be formed when she heard what her boss had decided.

"Wes, you have found a real mess. If your discovery is as it looks, we have a tremendous problem for ourselves and our city. Mayor Maxwell cannot support looking for more proof. We cannot announce our mayor might be a criminal. And, you still need to find a murderer. The question is can you do this without media getting wind of this disaster?"

"Chief, I don't know. We'll continue to do our job. Finding a killer is what we're doing. The peripheral damage just isn't under our control."

Chief Princeton put his hands together like a church steeple. He put his head down, resting his forehead on his finger tips. Wes wondered if he was contemplating his career or simply praying. He looked up and said to Wes, "Do the best you can, Wes, but first comes finding the shooter. We must be above politics. It's just weird that we're talking about suspects and victims being the same people."

Chapter 44

Janeen Newman Carson

Wes looked at his watch on the way out of Major Dilbert's office. It was already almost seven o'clock. Since he had asked Billy Joe and Mike to place calls to each of the Bad Ol' Boys cautioning them to stay away from any place at night that they could be accosted, he felt fairly safe to spend the evening with Janeen. They had agreed earlier that he could just come by whenever he was ready to end his day. They could scrape together something to eat and forget all of Atlanta. That sounded like heaven to him. He was ready to leave hell.

It took less than ten minutes to get his car and be on Janeen's front porch. Wes took a deep breath, shook some of the tension from his shoulders and rang the doorbell. He leaned on the door frame for only a moment before the door burst open. There stood his 'heaven' in a pair of jeans and Georgia Tech sweatshirt. She was beautiful.

"I was thinking about heaven and you appeared. I must have come to the right place. Are the Pearly Gates open for a wayward detective?"

"Always, Goofy. You're welcome in this little Patch of Heaven anytime. Don't even need white wings. See, I don't have any either." Janeen reached out, put her arm around his waist, drew him into the foyer and closed the door behind him. She turned her face to his and kissed him on the lips, then the cheek and on the ear. She put her head against his shoulder and whispered, "Everyone here in heaven has been waiting for you. That everyone is me."

Wes said nothing. He just wanted to feel, hear and see the woman who was so important to his life. A person he believed was a big part of his peace and heaven. The ugliness of the day was shut out with the closing of the front door.

"Let's go up to the kitchen and get you something to eat. I know if you ate at all today, it started with doughnuts and ended with McDonald's. You need some real food before you expand into a huge caricature of the rural policeman. All you would need then would be a pair of mirrored sun glasses."

"Hey, that's my role model. We detectives always dream about our own motorcycle and menacing stare. Goes with the Ray Bans."

"Yeah, right! That'll be the day. I bet that's a threat you often hear if you do not do your job: Go back to traffic."

"You got that right. I was just joking. It's fun to be just talking dumb stuff. I get tired of life-threatening or worse conversations."

They walked into the kitchen. Wes took a chair at the table. What he had done had the feeling of being married. Janeen fussing with something at the range top and he sitting and watching. He could give her a hand, but he knew that she had it all under control. He would just be in the way.

"Since you gave me plenty of time, I made some chili and cornbread. Didn't matter when you got here, they would be ready to eat. I'm starving!"

Over the steaming bowls and hot cornbread slathered with butter, they talked about Janeen's day and what was new on the campus.

"I got a note from Laurie Lindholm. She's doing great. She's landed the job she wanted at Mills College in Oakland. She said she likes the Bay area, and she's still in the same state as her son, Lindy. She sounded so happy."

"She deserves to be. That scumbag of a husband of hers really made her life miserable. It's hard to believe that a president of a leading academic institution could have been so immoral and that that immorality caused the death of one of his own students." Wes hesitated, thinking about the case that had been on his docket only a few months ago.

"Ex-husband now. That, too, is behind her. She said she heard through the academic grapevine that he was still looking for a job. I guess his past is still affecting his present."

Wes was reminded of the Bad Ol' Boys. Their past was affecting their present and future. Actually, it was killing them. It seems that both former Georgia Tech President Lindholm and the Bad Ol' Boys let sex and power ruin their lives. The Bad Ol' Boys molested a child, and Lindholm was brought to his knees by a child-woman named Tiffany.

"Hey, where are you? Looks like you were way off in thought," Janeen broke into his musings.

"You're right. Those thoughts led me to how humans work so hard to ruin each other's lives. Which reminds me, does your up-to-date report on a past case include what happened to Miss Tiffany?"

"Oh, yes. As you know she left Georgia Tech to 'spend more time with her family,' the same as disgraced politicians. She's back in her hometown, learning to manage her dad's business. He told her she can learn on the job, because he's not paying for more college for her. I hear he is closely managing her social activities."

Wes then commented, "I was also thinking about how the murdered men in this present case have similar personalities to Lindholm. They're all successful in one way and complete failures in others. The guys who have been killed and Lindholm all seem to have some history in their pasts that have caught up with them. Now we have to find someone who's really mad at them to close this case."

"You'll do it. I'm sure of that. Let's take some coffee and brownies into the den. See what CNN has to say about the rest of the world."

"Sounds perfect if while watching I can hold you really close and maybe whisper in your ear that I'm glad that I met you." Wes was feeling very warm. Just the thought of Janeen beside him on the sofa, completely blanked out any thought of dessert or the news. Life was sweet, at least for this evening.

Chapter 45

Honeybun

Honeybun stared out the window. She saw nothing. She barely realized that she was staring beyond the room. She had been doing a lot of that lately as if her mind and the rest of her body were no longer connected. She had always followed the direction of know where you want to be in one year, two years or even five years. She thought of her plan and knew where she wanted to be. Always plan ahead for success.

She caressed the book My Friends that was kept in her purse. Honeybun could recite it by heart. It was the theme of the whole plan except these were not her friends. Soon she hoped they would be no one's friends. It was time that these "friends" of whomever were "outed." Their secret had ruined the lives of innocent children.

It was a long week. If luck lasted, it would soon close down with a story that would be told and retold in the city. It would be told in restaurants, offices and at dinner tables. People would ask, "How could this happen?"

She had a list of things to do. Because she was prepared, she would take no risky chances. Surprise is always the advantage. Arrogance is a disadvantage. She would not let her success so far make her get careless. She knew how it could be done. She had been planning her revenge and retribution for years.

She breathed deeply and closed her eyes. She was surprised that she saw exactly the same thing with her eyes closed. Nothing. She shook her head hard, her hair bouncing from the sharp, movement and opened her eyes. She could not afford to be acting crazy now. She looked at the little book and vowed again to follow her plan.

Chapter 46

Billy Joe LaCrosse

"Have we gotten through a night with no dead Bad Ol' Boys? Maybe somethin' good is comin' our way," Billy Joe said when Wes entered the office weighted down with his usual calorie-filled breakfast.

"Maybe our warning kept these guys at home. I think that's safe," Wes replied. "The shooter has not shown any evidence of daring or taking risk. She seems to choose her time and place carefully. Sometimes I think that she plans her hits just like we would plan our moves in a case. We know where we're going and go in that direction. If keeping those men at home last night changes her opportunities, she may have to change her plan. Hopefully, that will rattle her enough so that she might make a mistake, take an unplanned risk."

"We could change it around. Have the men go out, but we put surveillance on each one," Billy Joe suggested.

"The major and mayor would hate that idea, but it's not to be tossed out."

"The mayor could probably end this whole mystery. Can't we get him as scared as Vance Bowman?"

"Billy Joe, if you can think of a way to do that, you can have a day off with pay after this case is closed."

"Yeah, right! Gettin' the major to agree to that would be harder than gettin' the mayor to tell the truth. In fact, I'd rather work on the mayor than the major."

Both detectives had their mouths full of sugary donuts. They could always use a high spike of energy at the beginning of the day. Krispy Kreme had been keeping them running for more than twenty years.

"Well, Billy Joe, we're missing something critical in this case. It just proves the point that only hard work is not a way to success. We need some luck, some extra smarts or some of Eve's magic technology. Why doesn't that gal find the buried clue? She was chugging right along for a while, then she seemed to slow down. She became more interested in personalities." Wes hoped that in his collection of unimportant words, one for them would remind him of something.

"Actually, Wes, she found us the cigarette butt and sent it to be tested. We haven't paid much attention to that since she made the effort. Maybe she decided we weren't interested in what she did. I know things have been movin' fast, but could there be a clue in that butt? Should we consider again possible implications it could have?"

Wes sat forward and leaned his elbows on the messy desk top. Billy Joe noted that he was wearing his 'Ah, shit' expression, which meant he felt there were too many dead ends.

"Ah, yes, the cigarette butt. When were Templeton and Lee together? Does it matter? Why was it left when everything else was so thoroughly cleaned up? Could it relate to the Big Hair Lady? I regret that we don't yet have answers to any of those questions," Wes hesitated for a moment to take a big swallow of coffee, "Was there anything new from Mike after he interviewed Augusta Martinez or Deanna Lee?

"Nothin' that was suspicious enough to act on it. He did say that Deanna's sister had at one time been quite close to Irwin Fitzgerald. That they had dated for almost a year. He commented that it was rather weird hearin' that when he had just met the current trophy wife. Mike had asked to see a photo of Leeana. As expected, she was a knockout.

"Atlanta is still a small town in many ways. People's lives keep crossin' others and becomin' entangled. Obviously these Bad Ol' Boys ran in the right circles and also had plenty of sex appeal. Look at Carrollton and hints about Franklin Raub. Maybe we just haven't found the shit yet about the others. I definitely think our perp is a woman. Big question is still which woman?"

The question hung in the air like a piece of soot. Before either man could address it, their concentration was interrupted by the ringing of the telephone.

"Wesley, Homicide."

"Hey, Wes, how's it going?" It was Dani Swain.

"We're still employed. Trying to stay out of the major's sights. What's up with you? More mysterious telephone calls from genderless voices?" Wes smiled at what he thought was a joke.

"You're right on. I just hung up from our strange man/woman. The person said that you guys have got to stop fooling around because you're just going to have to pick up some more bodies. The person wanted me to pass on a message to you, 'Detective Wesley,' you got a night off last night, but don't think the plan has changed. Then added, 'He knows what they did. Even if he won't do anything about it, I will.' Then the phone went dead.

"Wes, I really think this is the real killer. Even if the voice is disguised, the voice and manner sounds sincere. I asked, 'Why do you call me?' and the response, 'I trust you. You'll take me seriously. Dani, you and every woman in Atlanta need to be saved from these predators.'"

"This person called you by name?"

"Yes. But that isn't strange. Thousands of people know my name," Dani Swain explained.

"That's true, but still he or she felt familiar enough to call you 'Dani.' I believe the statement is honest. The person trusts you and also feels comfortable with you." Wes was taking a few notes to add to the pages already in the records.

"That's interesting, Wes. When the person said my name, I was sure that it was a woman. It seemed to be the only time that her guard was down; like a conversation woman to woman. The rest of the message was disguised, but now I would definitely suggest that these calls are from a woman."

Wes nodded his head, "That supports what we believe too. What few clues we have all point to a female."

"And who is the woman? Want to give me that clue?"

"Would if I could. I was hoping you had an idea and I could ask you. Sounds like some kind of children's round robin game. You know: you tell me and I'll tell you."

"I'll do my best. If I get a flash of genius, I'll call again. Take care. Call me whenever you have a break." Dani said 'Bye' and was gone. Her life seemed to depend on perpetual motion. She wanted to be wherever news might happen.

Wes turned to Billy Joe, "Doesn't help much, but Dani got another call. She's almost one hundred percent sure that it's a woman. More ammunition for our theory. Now, who?"

"Maybe we should ask Eve to do some more research on the ladies we know. Even though she doesn't think they are guilty, she might find somethin' more that will be helpful," Billy Joe was looking around the room and out the door. He finally raised his voice, "Hey, anyone seen Eve?"

"She's not here. Hasn't called in," a voice yelled back.

"We can get her on this when she makes an appearance. I don't know why she thinks school comes before us. Or maybe she's still ticked off that we took her folder. We'll have to give her a little man to man talk. Homicide is no place for gettin' mad about differences of opinion," Billy Joe spread his hands as if to say, I give up.

Wes smiled, "Maybe that's our problem. She doesn't want to be one of the guys. What if we talked to her like we would our sister? Let's leave her a note about deeper research beyond what she's already done on our female cast of characters. The way she works, we'll have it by the end of the day. That's good. What's bad is that she carries it around.

"Let's face it, she's been an outstanding intern. There really are times when she seems to get the picture before we do. I just wish we didn't have to compete for her time."

"Just remember, you're goin' to be the big star in her thesis.

I'm sure that everythin' about this case is goin' to show up in her paper. Academics and students from all over the country are goin' to be standin' at your door beggin' you to solve another murder in their communities, right?" Billy Joe couldn't help kidding Wes about being all through Eve's thesis.

"She knows quality when she sees it. Now, 'pardner,' let's get moving on some more detective work."

Billy Joe was headed for the door when another detective called out, "Hey, we have a call for Eve. It's the lab. Who wants to take it?"

Wes reached for his phone, motioning Billy Joe to go on. "Wesley."

"Detective Wesley, it's Ray from the ABC Lab. I was calling Eve, but the decision is probably yours anyway. When we did the DNA on those three items, she forgot to tell us where to send the bill. She said something about bill separately, but I forgot to make a note. I assume they go to your department account, right?"

"Yeah, it's all the same case," Wes hesitated, then added, "Did you say three items?"

"Right, man. Cigarette butt and two other pieces. I ran 'em all at once. Two were the same person. The other was someone else."

"Oh, right. I got it. Charge them to Homicide. Thanks for calling. Wouldn't want another department to have to pay." Wes smiled to himself thinking, 'Why not?'

"OK, Detective. It's done. We love your business."

Wes replaced the receiver and thought about the call. He remembered the cigarette butt, but the other items did not ring a bell. He tapped his temple with his fingers and thought, 'I'm losing it. I'll just have to ask Eve.'

He thought, 'Damn, who needs these young, smart, ambitious Eves and Jasons reminding me I'm getting old? I think I'll consider myself highly experienced and sophisticated. I can live with that image rather than just plain old.'

Chapter 47

Wes T. Wesley

Where was the clue he was missing? Wes shuffled through his notes hoping to find it. He reviewed the list of women who had some relationship to the dead men. Those were the only names they had, but the killer could have been any of a hundred women who were still nameless. Eve's conviction that the murderer was not in this group preyed on his mind. Possible, but it just did not make sense. There had to be a tie among the men and the killer. His gut reaction was that they already were talking to the woman whom they would soon arrest.

He checked off several names that seemed more suspect, thought about them, nodded his head in affirmation and crossed out the check marks. "Shit, I just don't know. None of them seem right!"

The detective rested his hand on an unruly pile of papers. They were mostly white but several were pastels: pink, green and blue. Those were usually extra copies. He picked out the pale blue one that had 'ABC Laboratories, when time is important' printed across the top. Another invoice for tests. Since the GBI had gotten so busy, they had been using ABC. Sure it was more costly, but they weren't backed up for months.

Time was always important to Homicide, but even more important this week. They were lucky last night, but the silent, careful killer may be out again tonight. He hoped for a sighting of the Big-Haired Lady. She may not be a murderer, but he would bet that she knew something his team would like to know. He had a real strong feeling that she had some answers to their questions.

Wes jumped when he heard a voice right at his ear.

"It's me. Anyone home in there? You look like you're long gone. Is the space for rent?"

Wes turned and saw Eve's smiling face. Her eyes were laughing. She was enjoying that she had caught him with his guard down.

"You scared the crap out of me, young lady. You're lucky I didn't turn and knock you on your butt," Wes was laughing too. She really did bring youthful fun to the very serious office.

"Wes, I'm sorry that I upset you and Billy Joe. I've been trying to do everything: do what you want, finish my thesis, you know. To do that, I've been taking stuff home. I won't do it again."

"I believe you, Eve. We just can't take chances with people's lives and reputations. If you're serious and will do the work in this office, I have a question and a request. First, I got a call from the lab. They said you had them do three DNA tests. Refresh my memory. I only remember the cigarette butt."

"Oh, yeah, you're right. The cigarette butt is the one in Temple's room. The others were mine for my thesis. I'm sure I told him that they were to be billed separately. I'll get back to him."

"Well, that's a relief. I thought I was really losing it," Wes said, "I know you're using forensic technology for your research, but didn't know you were actually doing tests."

"Sure, Wes, how else could I prove my points? As I said, I'm doing the thesis just as if it's a case: filling out those pain-in-the-tail forms, keeping contact information, your kind of routine work. This is the real thing.

"Oh, yes, I'm paying for those other DNA tests. I told him that. This is my project. That's why you pay me, so I can have money to spend. I'll call the lab now. You also said you have a request."

"Right. Could you do some deeper research on a couple of women who are connected to our Good Ol' Boys? Mike just found that Randy Lee's sister-in-law once was close to Irwin

266

Fitzgerald. We're wondering what else might be lurking in the shadowy past." Wes handed her his list.

"Lots of stuff is lurking in the shadows. In case you haven't noticed, Detective Wesley, this is a very complicated case that seems to have years of guilt in the equation. Don't relax or you might miss something."

"OK, just say yes or no. I don't need editorial comment."

"For you, always yes. I don't want you mad at me," Eve gave him a sweet smile, "As you know; I already have a little research on some of your ladies. If that's the direction you want pursued, I'll do it. I guess one thing you're looking for is the mix between fact and fiction known as gossip. If that's it, sir, I'm on my way to find out who did what to whom."

Wes watched her bounce out of his office and was again reminded of youth and energy. Yep, he'd like some right now to overcome the lethargy that comes from not being able to solve a case. He felt he had to find this killer soon or he could predict who might be the next victim.

The very discouraged detective laid out several evidence items to review again. He handled each as if it were a precious stone. He knew he could not keep the potential victims hidden away in their homes. One night's reprieve was simply that, one night.

Billy Joe ambled into Wes' office, "You sure did get that little sister movin.' I saw her go directly to her computer with a determined look on her face. We'll get somethin' back soon; maybe yet today. Where're you now on siftin' clues and writin' plots?"

"I think the plot is long-term anger. The shootings are so methodical. There is no clue that looks spontaneous. Even the cigarette butt looks planted to me."

"Why?"

"Like the telephone calls. I think the killer is daring us to find her. I think she likes being just a few paces ahead of us. Think about Miss Big-Hair. We all had the impression that she knew about the security cameras. Yet she was willing to meet Temple Carrollton in the lobby and ride the elevator with him. She could have gone to his room another way. If she had, we might not have put them together until a lot more thought and time."

Billy Joe interrupted, "All gun shots have been similar. Same kind of nine mm bullet. It's always seemed that the victims were hit by a person they probably knew or had no fear of. We can identify a woman or two that each man would be used to, but identifying one that all would accept close up and personal is tough."

Wes picked up the thought, "They don't have to know her. She just has to be a non-threatening type. Being a woman, she can suggest having a drink and the guy would probably be a pushover. She gets his attention, he turns to face her, says something or simply looks at her. In that moment, she pops him and it's all over. She puts her gun in her purse, turns and walks away."

"Wes, it sounds so easy. She has it down to a practiced, repeat performance. So far that focused determination has made it easy to not get caught. The Bad Ol' Boys who are left should take our warnin' more seriously."

"If we proceed with this theory, all we have to do is find the right female who carries a gun with a silencer."

"Billy Joe, you remind me of another point. All our evidence and assumptions lead us to one woman, but the bullets haven't all been from the same gun," Wes pointed his finger at Billy Joe as if to say, "You're on."

"Not the same gun, old buddy, but it's always the same caliber. She is comfortable with her choice of weapons. It would surprise me if she changed to something else. It appears she also has had access to at least four guns. That is quite an arsenal for our suspect."

"Very interesting," Wes said, "We're getting a profile of our shooter. Now let's talk about the disgusting discovery from your publisher friend, Bowman. He said that the Bad Ol' Boys each had sex with a little girl. This little girl or girls are now grown up. Where is she or where are they? Is she still in Atlanta? Is she..."

"...Our Big-Hair Lady? Cool? Calm? Determined? And mad? Mad enough to kill those who hurt her as a child? Revenge for herself or maybe for someone close to her? Was she the rape victim or did she see it happen?" Billy Joe felt like they had made a quantum leap forward.

"Sounds good. And there are all these years in between, because she had to grow up."

"Does that eliminate the wives of these guys? Too old? What about the mothers of Matthew, Mark and Luke?

"Maybe so. Maybe not, Wes. We know Temple was already makin' babies when he was just a teenager. Augusta Martinez mentioned that the boys' mothers were good friends. They went out on the town together. So they too were quite young when this all started. We need to know exactly how old they are. I do think this theory eliminates some of the women."

Billy Joe threw up his hands like he was praying in church. "Hallelujah! Thank the Lord. We have had too many suspects and weren't gettin' anywhere. We still have a mixed bag, but we can pay more attention to the ones younger than Deanna Lee and Iris Raub. Irwin Fitzgerald's wife is probably close to the right age, but Mike's description of her sounds like she wouldn't be a serious suspect."

"Probably not but I bet we could get him to go back and continue his interview." Wes had a smile on his face as he remembered Mike's account of Sugar's fictional breathless words: Detective Mike, Detective Mike, I'm coming. I'm coming.

"Wes, I'll go tell Eve to not spend her time on our older women, but we do want her to do the research on the ones in their twenties. I will also go back to Bowman and get his definition of 'a little girl'."

Chapter 48

Billy Joe LaCrosse

Billy Joe went back to Vance Bowman's office, but found that the man had left town, which was no surprise. He probably took off for that vacation house in Aspen.

The detective pushed Bowman's pretty secretary - maybe he actually scared her - to call her boss. Once the publisher was on the line, Angie walked out of the room. Billy Joe was alone at the receptionist's desk, he asked, "How old was the little girl you mentioned?"

There was a long pause at the other end of the line. Billy Joe could hear breathing so he knew the man had not hung up. He let him think for maybe a minute. He repeated the question.

In a hoarse whisper, Vance Bowman asked his own question, "Why can't you leave me alone? Call Montrose or somebody."

"Look, Bowman, we don't have time to play games. We might save your miserable life or even Montrose's or perhaps the mayor's. Just answer the fuckin' question." Billy Joe was really angry. He wished he had this creep in front of him instead of on the phone. "Give me the answer and or maybe I won't see you again until your funeral."

He heard a sigh. Still in a hoarse whisper, Vance Bowman responded, "Maybe twelve. Something like that. It's not like she was a small child."

Billy Joe wanted to vomit. Twelve! He growled, "Tell me about your daughter when she was twelve."

A voice screamed, "Stop harassing me?" and the receiver was slammed down somewhere in Colorado.

Billy Joe replaced the receiver and stood looking out through the wide window. Much of the Atlanta skyline was framed like a beautiful modern graphic. He paid little attention to the fancy-topped buildings. He was thinking of his own little girl. He would strangle with his own hands any man who would do something so despicable to her. He even wanted to strangle Bowman and his friends, and he didn't even know who the poor child was.

His thoughts went to the mayor. If the clues coming from this investigation were completely true, he deserved to be caught and brought down. He could see Maxwell's politician's smile. He was conflicted between screaming and breaking the man's nose. How could all of this been kept a secret over more than a decade?

. . . .

Wes had asked the other detectives to call each of the possible victims to repeat last evening's warning: Stay out of questionable places. Stay at home with your families. He knew that this was the right thing to do, but he also wanted to take them to task for what they might have done years ago. He was thinking about the weird way this case was shaping up when he smelled strong coffee.

"Hey, Wes, you look like you could use a pop. Can't bring you anything harder than this, but the coffee is fresh and hot," Mike Fisher placed a heavy APD mug on top of the mess of papers on Wes' desk.

"You're a real detective, Mike. Maybe even a damn mind reader. I was about to head for that hole in the wall we call a break room. Thanks. This is going to save my life. I seem to have lost most of my energy and my concentration. The fucking unknowns are getting me down."

"Well, my news isn't going to make you any happier with this case. We made the calls again just as we did yesterday. The difference was that the men we actually talked to have become belligerent. One even said he didn't need some 'dumb-ass flatfoot' telling him what to do. Another one said he'd keep his own calendar, thank you. I ask you: Why do we even try? Let 'em get shot? It might be a favor to more people than we know."

Wes shook his head, rolled his eyes toward his friend and said, "We just do our job, Mike. We might not like it, but we do our best to be good protectors of the public. Billy Joe has said that he'd rather be on these guys' firing squad than trying to get them through another night. And, he added, 'I'd aim at the damn mayor first!'"

"Other than having thoughts of murder and mayhem, Wes, what's next? We seem to have hit a huge void. The killer is probably hiding just on the other side of our investigation, but we can't see her."

"That's what's so demoralizing. We aren't making any real progress. Billy Joe and I have the theory that these are revenge killings. That the shooter has been harboring the grudge for many years. I think she's been planning the killings that long too. This woman is more than lucky. She's well-rehearsed, intelligent and clever. We're sure that the calls Dani has been getting are the killer's way of telling us that she's all of those things and we aren't. Maybe we could get her to take over our training program."

"Speaking of Dani, I almost forgot to tell you that I saw her today at your favorite Krispy Kreme 'Number One' Emporium. She was scarfing down glazed doughnuts like she never heard of the 'no carbs campaign.' She said that when she gets a sugar attack, she heads for the KK.

"As long as we were talking, I ordered a couple of those sticky things and sat down. It worked out because she wanted to review what we knew and how any of it relates to her phone calls. She's positive now that it was a woman and in thinking about it, which she has done a lot, she thinks it's a young woman. She commented on the tone of the voice and even the choice of words. She said if she had to guess, she would say the woman was educated..."

Wes waited for more information but Mike was quiet. It wasn't great, but it did tighten the circle of possibilities. It also helped confirm the theory that they were working on.

"That's not a lot of new clues, but what Dani thinks does strengthen our own ideas. It's comforting to have support for our direction."

"She said one more thing that was far from scientific. It was more like weird. She said, 'You know, Mike, I think I would like this woman. I don't really want her to be caught.'"

"Even weirder, Mike, is that I feel the same way."

Chapter 49

Janeen Newman Carson

Hours later, surrounded by the late evening crowd, Wes and Janeen were sitting on the patio at Einstein's Restaurant. They were under the big tree that acted as a canopy over the tables huddled around its huge, dark trunk. A few heaters were casting just enough warmth that Janeen was perfectly comfortable in her bright red sweater set and trim jeans. The gold, loop earrings and chain around her neck sparkled in the flickering candlelight.

"Your jewelry is almost as bright as your eyes, Light of my Dull Life," Wes said reaching for her hand, "This was a great idea to come here for dessert and coffee. It's almost like taking a small vacation from Atlanta. I always feel like I'm away from the city when I sit under this tree."

"It's definitely one of my favorite places. I like it even better when you and I have walked here and didn't have to get into the car. Which reminds me, you must hear about my experience with my car and your police comrades."

"What? You weren't in an accident, were you?"

"No, no, this is entirely different. I thought I was going to be arrested. If necessary, I was ready to drop your name," Janeen hesitated as if for dramatic effect. "I think you know that my sister makes pottery. She's really quite good. Sells a lot of her things through a shop in Nashville. People here are always asking me about her things, so I suggested that she send me some pieces. I'd show them to friends. Well, tonight was the night. I was going to a meeting and took them all in my car trunk.

"After the meeting, several women who were there came out to the car in the back of the parking lot. It was kind of dark, but that's where I had parked because I was late to the meeting. We had the trunk open, using its dim light to see. We were looking at everything, wrapping and unwrapping newspapers, putting things aside, putting things back in the trunk. I'm sure you get the picture," Janeen was telling her story enthusiastically.

Wes was smiling, "I get the picture. You looked just like a drug dealer."

"Oh, my God, how did you know?" Janeen was amazed.

"Are you kidding me? I've been a policeman in Atlanta for most of my life. I've been on as many drug busts as you've been to meetings. The scene sounds suspicious to me. I'm sure in the dark you looked very suspicious. I'm going to have to be careful who sees me with you. They'll assume I'm part of your gang."

By now Wes was laughing. It felt good to see how worried Janeen was about selling pottery out of her car. This is as bad as it gets for some people. His life was exactly the opposite. At least for a few minutes he had stopped worrying about what might happen in the city tonight.

"So, what happened next? Did you get cuffed and read your rights?"

"No, of course not. The one officer went through everything in the trunk while the other one watched us, like we were going to start shooting or something. You know, Wes, you guys really are scary. After a lecture about being off in dark places, and behaving suspiciously, they left. For a minute, we were quiet. Then we started to giggle and couldn't stop. We decided we might be the strangest suspected drug dealers on Peachtree Street."

"Take their lecture to heart, Janeen. You were in a dangerous situation. If the police could walk right up on you, so could anyone else. Maybe the best thing that might have happened would be that they stole your sister's pottery to start their own shop. Pottery in the front and drugs in the back. It's the perfect setup." Wes had turned from serious to lighthearted. He did think it was funny that Janeen and her friends could look suspicious. What a catch: classy, professional women, dressed in their business attire with perfect makeup and hair styles. This would be a fun story for the metro section of the newspaper.

He thought about the whole conversation they had just had. The outcome was simply that in his opinion Janeen and her friends weren't even on the suspect radar screen. To the two policemen who came upon the scene of something unusual, they did look suspicious. Thinking of the women involved in the murders, he wondered who he was placing outside the suspect role. He wondered if his sympathy for what had happened many years ago could be clouding his professional vision. He was going to have to look at each of the women again. He would concentrate on each one without considering their pretty faces and engaging personalities.

"There you go again. Every now and then, Wes, you take off for outer space. I can see it in your eyes. Are you OK?" Janeen wanted to bring him back to the present.

"Sorry, you just reminded me of something that relates to this damn case that is driving us all crazy."

"Reminded you of it? What does that mean?"

"It means that I have to be careful about what seems OK to me but, in a different setting, it looks wrong. It's ridiculous to think that you and your friends could be questioned, but you did look suspicious to the other guys," Wes again took Janeen's hand while looking at the menu, "Let's forget my business and decide on something with high carbs, high cholesterol and lots of sugar."

"Sounds perfect to me. We did promise to try to keep your weird career at a distance."

"Let's do it. Instead I suggest dessert, coffee and hand holding. I'd rather have you curled up in my arms on your sofa but that won't work here. Wes moved his chair closer to Janeen. He took both her hands in his and kissed her fingers lightly.

Janeen looked at him and said softly, "I can't help but think of my nieces who always want their dessert before the meal. My point is, in case you missed it, is that our entrée is waiting for us back at my house."

Wes could feel his excitement overtaking his desire for dessert. Actually it was hard to keep his attention on cheesecake or chocolate cake when Janeen talked about later. Later was the topping for any dessert he could imagine.

Chapter 50

Houston Montrose

Another perfect evening with his most favorite person was now simply a sexy memory. Wes' Taurus shuddered to a stop. As he turned off the engine, he thought that it must be time for a brake job while he looked at his watch. He was surprised how late it was; almost two.

He yawned and thought about the past few hours. The crackling of his radio shattered his euphoria. He frowned and sighed. He felt that this call would relate to the Bad Ol' Boys. The timing was similar. The perpetrator working at her night job.

"White, male body found in the back of the parking lot of the Civic Center. Shot in the chest. Two cars dispatched."

Wes shuddered. He wasn't sure that his reaction was because of Janeen's parking lot experience or that he was sure this was going to raise the count on the case.

Wes pressed the button on the radio. "This is Detective Wesley, what's up? Just heard about a body at the Civic Center."

"Don't know yet except that tonight was a big, flashy concert. A few hours ago that parking lot was full of cars and people. The body is wearing a tuxedo. Pretty classy so I don't think it's a homeless guy or some petty crook."

"I'm on my way, if anyone asks. And that 'anyone' might just be our mayor. Shit, I wonder if the mayor was at this fancy event."

"Don't know, Detective. I have no details. I'll let everyone know that you'll be there, if they ask, that is."

Wes got out his blue lights, turned them on and slammed his car back into drive. He could be there in just a few minutes.

The Civic Center probably wasn't more than two miles from his home. He drove fast but carefully, which was easy since it was so late. The one-way streets made it even easier. The few cars he saw, he passed quickly and never slowed down until he was ready to turn into the parking lot. He stopped his car in back of several that had already arrived. He didn't know if he was glad or sad that the mayor's entourage wasn't already on the scene.

'It can't be the mayor. He's too well protected. It can't be Vance Bowman. He's in Colorado.' He thought of Houston Montrose. If this was a Bad Ol' Boy, Wes was sure it would be the disagreeable Montrose, who just didn't want to be bothered by the Atlanta Police Department. Maybe he should be feeling waves of sympathy for this leader in Atlanta's business world and society, but that was not one of his thoughts as he got out of his car.

As he approached the car that was surrounded by uniforms and suits, he noted that it was a silver Lexus. He tried to remember what cars they had listed for each of the men. He was sure there was at least one Lexus. This wouldn't be a surprise. Lexus was the car of choice of many who feel price was not a consideration.

"Detective Wesley, over here. Half the body is under the driver's side. He must've been getting into the car when he was shot." Wes recognized the officer from Zone Five. A young recruit who was originally from Romania. He had experience from his home country. Wes remembered that he had come to Atlanta because he had married a woman he met when she was on vacation in Romania visiting her grandparents.

"Igor, good to see you. Who would have thought we would have a homicide as the finale to a concert? Have you identified the victim?"

"Yes, sir, he is Houston…"

"… Montrose." Wes completed Igor's sentence.

"Yes, do you know him? Ach, does this relate to the case you are working on of what everyone calls The Nasty Guys?"

"Right on, Igor. It's another Bad Ol' Boy. Number five."

"Not good. You have mayor all over your suitcase."

Wes smiled broadly. He said to the officer, "All over 'my case.' That's correct. You're learning all of our slang as well as our language. You do better than any of us do in your native language."

"That's true, Detective. You guys only know English: Northern and Southern. Sometimes I don't get the Southern at all, but I try, sir."

"Let's look at Mr. Montrose. Was he dead when you arrived on the scene? Has anything been touched?"

"No, sir. EMs pronounced him dead. They are back at their vehicle getting what they need to transport him. No hurry for this man. Not going anywhere under his own smoke ever again."

"His own steam, Igor." Wes smiled again. "You're right. He's going nowhere. The shooter made sure of that."

Wes bent down, looked at Houston Montrose. He did not look mad at the police now. Except for the small hole in the middle of his ruffled formal shirt, he looked quite peaceful. It appeared at a quick glance he could have had a small flower stuck in his button hole. His head was lying on a program from the concert. The detective looked closely because there were a few words written on the cover. They were: 'Yes, it's me.' Incorrect grammar like Igor might use, but a huge announcement that this was part of the Boys case.

Wes looked more closely at the program. It had very little blood on it although there was quite a large spot reaching out from just below the shoulders of the body. It appeared that Houston Montrose fell where he had been shot. Almost like Franklin Raub: at the driver's side of the car with the door open. The difference was that Montrose was getting into his car after the concert and Raub was getting out as he came home from Manuel's. These facts seemed to indicate that the men were being watched and probably followed. Someone knew their habits or simply took the effort to find out what they were doing in their daily schedules.

"Hey, Wes, what do we have this time?" Billy Joe had just arrived.

"Houston Montrose."

"He didn't want any of us botherin' him. Well, he got his wish. We aren't goin' to bother him anymore. What's here for us to learn? I guess we all need to take a peek."

Wes, Igor and Billy Joe began looking around the site. They were still searching the area when the police photographer looked in their direction. He nodded and said, "Looks like the same person to me. Whoever it is has been staying one step ahead of us."

Wes sighed and thought, "We all feel frustrated. We can't even help each other."

As the man returned to his work, Wes motioned to Igor and Billy Joe. They walked over beside him and Wes took Igor's report clip board. He read the written words but felt that he could have recited them with no coaching. They read exactly like Franklin Raub, Randy Lee and Irwin Fitzgerald. They had similarities to the Temple Carrollton report. How did she know that Montrose would be here? Was she close enough to him that he might have told her? Did she know someone who was close to him who would tell her important information? Did she simply follow him?

"Who found him, Igor?"

"An Atlanta policeman doing moonlights for the Civic Center," Igor answered

Billy Joe smiled, "Moonlighting not moonlights, my friend." He then added, "He probably was checking out for any unclaimed cars so he could close up for the night."

"Yes, that is what he said. He added he has done this a hundred times Has never found a car or a problem. Most people do not hang up in parking lots after events."

Wes noticed the hang up rather than hang out. He thought to tell Igor the difference, but did not want him to feel that he was constantly corrected on his newly learned words, "Well, this discovery will keep him busy for a while. Because it's related to our case, it will require extra paper work and follow up. Maybe something he saw will be helpful to the case.

"Igor, you want to think of all the little details too. You just might have a clue that can break this case."

"I am already doing that, Detective Wesley. I look all around and do not see suspicions. Do you think the writing on the program means anything?"

"Oh, yes, it does. I believe we will find that it was written by the killer rather than by Mr. Montrose," Wes looked toward the corpse and shook his head. Someone was making him very angry. He believed that she was having a good time doing it.

The EMs were back with their gurney. They asked Wes if they could take the body away. Wes said to wait just a minute until he took another look at the crime scene. Maybe there was another message for him.

Wes walked away from Igor and Billy Joe. He hunkered down at the side of the car. Nothing much dropped on the ground. There were a few coins scattered by Montrose's hip, which he would assume came out of his pocket as he fell, and what looked like a silver charm. He carefully picked up the program again with his gloved hand hoping that there would be some fingerprints to lead them to the killer. As careful as this murderer has been, he doubted if it was going to be that easy. Nothing about this case was easy. Many criminals are not organized or strategic planners but Little Miss Somebody was both.

He scooped up the charm and held it toward some light. It seemed to be blank. He flipped the coin on the program and it landed on its other side. Wes bent closer and concentrated closely. He wasn't sure if he was surprised or had expected the image, but what he saw was a phoenix bird.

He didn't need confirmation about this killing, but there it was. He motioned for Igor and Billy Joe to come closer with their flashlights. Wes thought, 'We're not leaving here until we have all searched each inch of the car, in the car, on the car and maybe the whole damn parking lot. This little lady is driving me crazy."

Chapter 51

Wes T. Wesley

Wes and Billy Joe both yawned before lifting their cups of hot coffee. They had gone from the Civic Center parking lot to a Waffle House for a big, pre-dawn, heavy breakfast of steak, eggs and a huge pile of "scattered" potatoes, which were now all covered with ketchup.

"Billy Joe, we're going to be castrated today by the mayor and the major. Our only saving grace at this point is that it's so early. They're still postponing the beginning of their day. The Atlanta Journal and Constitution is going to be screaming for our heads, and the mayor will take that as an affront to his administration. It won't even occur to him that he's a part of this whole mess. I hope we can be there when he resigns. That will help justify all the grief he's giving us now."

"These guys are stupid bozos. Includin' our fearless mayor. They would rather see their whole gang picked off one by one than talk to us. I know the public is always suspect of police, but our own damn mayor doesn't trust us."

"Wrong, my friend. They have one humongous secret buried that they want kept in that proverbial place 'where the sun don't reach.' Except for the mayor, we're about out of Bad Ole Boys in Atlanta. Do you think our girl will take off for Charlotte or Miami? We better warn those men again. Anything can happen."

"Mike and Golly can do that while we take a thrashin' from the Terrible Twosome. I would be suspectin' that if they knew we were here, we'd see their cars in the parkin' lot. Wouldn't help Waffle House business any to be surrounded by flashin' blue lights. Sure fire way to drive your business to McDonald's."

"I'm outa here. See you back in the office. I need to do a lot of thinking before I get a call," Wes was gone before Billy Joe stood up.

They were both feeling the stress of this case. Billy Joe had seen the signs before when Wes was troubled about a homicide. His partner became quiet; almost distant. In that void, Wes' mind was speeding from clue to clue trying to see what was missed or what two possibilities added up to one solid fact. Billy Joe knew he reacted the opposite way. He wanted to talk it all out over and over again. So this morning he would give Wes some time to think. Then Billy Joe would go hunker down in Wes' office and start talking.

• • • •

Wes drove with extra care because he knew that he was upset. He was really pissed. He was good at his job, had many commendations, but right now he didn't see a clue that went anywhere. If he ever wanted to become a criminal, he would want to hire this woman to be his consultant. How has she been so good or so lucky to still have left no clues or made any mistakes?

"Left no clues?" he said out loud. "She has left clues. This morning she even left a note. She's not playing with us. She's helping us! She's helping us and we still don't know who she is. Next time, she'll stay there and wait for us to arrive."

Wes was weary. He wanted a good night's sleep. He wasn't brain dead but he felt completely drained. He was already bracing for the onslaught from the top. Before that happened, he was going back to the office, go through everything related to the case again and think about some angle that they hadn't yet considered.

• • • •

Billy Joe had gone from the Waffle House to Krispy Kreme. He knew they would need a sugar jolt if they were going to get through the morning. More black coffee with lots of caffeine was also on his mind. He could almost smell that strong aroma as he turned into the parking garage of City Hall East.

Each time he drove into the dark and dirty garage, he would think of the rumors that the city was selling this building. If true, Homicide would be moving again. It didn't much matter where they located their offices because homicide victims turned up anywhere. Billy Joe chuckled as he thought it would be really considerate of murderers if they would deliver the victim on the doorstep of 675 Ponce de Leon.

He parked the car and went directly to the Homicide offices. As he dumped their second breakfast on his desk, he started flipping through telephone messages. Nothing there of any interest. He was hoping there would be a call inviting him to come join the FBI or even the French Foreign Legion, if it still existed. This week he might even say yes to the FBI even though he would have to spend his first year's salary on a new suits, white shirts and get his hair cut. No, on second thought he decided he was not interested. Atlanta was his home and the APD was the place he wanted to be.

"OK, Wes, let's get primed. We have to look again at what we have and what we added this mornin'. How about the silver disc? Did it belong to Montrose or was it a gift from our mystery lady?"

"My guess is that it belonged to Houston Montrose but we'll find out. I think the gift to us was her note. I think she wants us to find her, but until we do, she's still on her vendetta to get these men. She's cool and she's methodical

"I can profile her feelings, her anger, her actions but I can't see her face. I can't give her a name. She is so fucking elusive. Yet she's standing right out in the open. I can feel her presence."

"Slow, down, man. You're scarin' me. You almost sound like a poet or a psycho. Don't lose your objectivity on me. Here, Wes, have a doughnut. You need some fortification.

"Let's not talk about feelin' a ghost or a goblin or somethin'. How about our facts? We have a lot. We just haven't found that common bond other than the Club. We need to look somewhere else."

"You're right, Billy Joe. We do have to keep looking but we have the bond. It is the Club. It's what they did. Who they did it to? Was it only one little girl? Was it more? Is our Big-Haired Lady setting us off in the wrong direction?"

The two men stopped and were lost in their own conclusions. The only two quiet people in the entire office area were Wes and Billy Joe. For all the other city employees, life was still moving right along. They did not even notice that the telephone had rung on Detective Wesley's desk until it rang several times.

"Wesley. Homicide."

"You won't be surprised to hear that the Major expects you to be in her office in less than two minutes." Brassy's voice was dripping with sarcasm.

"I'll be there." Wes said and hung up.

Chapter 52

Major Dagmar Dilbert

Brassy slammed the door shut to the major's office behind Wes. Wes was reminded of the reaction of first-time prisoners when they heard the metallic clank of the cell door shutting off the world of freedom. He was experiencing that same ripple of desperation. He knew the questions that would be asked, and he knew that he did not quite have the answers.

"The whole fucking world is watching Atlanta and our inept Homicide Department. You and your band of misfits are making our city look bad. Our mayor looks bad and I look bad. You will have a lot of fences to mend, when this is finally over. That is, if you're still around."

His boss continued, "The mayor has received calls from most of his colleagues heading up other major cities expressing their condolences. Condolences, Detective Wesley, because we have a Homicide Department that can't get it right. The damn killer has now given you five chances to get caught. I believe you still don't have a clue. Shall we go for six? Will that be the magic number?" Major Dagmar Dilbert's face was as red as a fire engine. Her eyes were scrunched into slits. She looked like if she opened her mouth wide enough, licks of fire would be sent spewing.

"You're right, Major. This is a tough one. We're working our butts off, but the shooter is still ahead of us. We've warned those who we're sure are on the perp's list to be cautious about where they go. The truth is that they think they're invincible, and we don't have any actual threats to be sure who the next man will be killed."

"Man? Are you sure that the next victim will be a man?" the major asked.

Wes was surprised at the question. They had already talked about the revenge theory related to the rape of a little girl years ago, "Yes, and we're almost one hundred percent sure that the killer is a woman. We are equally sure that the mayor knows exactly why this is happening but isn't talking."

"No wonder I forgot that suspicion. It's ridiculous. I do believe that you've been told the same by the mayor. He mentioned once that you're not much of a realist. You see a conspiracy in every case. I don't believe that the mayor holds you in very high esteem."

"The feeling is mutual," Wes responded.

Major Dilbert's face reddened again and she sputtered, "Do not impugn the mayor or any other person, detective, when you're the one on the carpet here. Your job is to find this brutal murderer and to protect the mayor at all times. Not speak out against him. Is that understood?"

"Major Dilbert, with all due respect, I will do my job and find this killer. I think we may be getting close. But a fact of this case is that the mayor, the one I am to protect, is mixed up in this situation. The whole sordid story will be known when the killer is apprehended. Mayor Maxwell's colleagues in other major cities are not going to be calling their condolences then. We'll do our best. We'll do what's right. Maybe, just, maybe, Dagmar, you might want to be on the winning side, so we can protect you."

Wes was as surprised as his major at what he said. He also realized for the first time in his career, he had called Major Dilbert by her first name.

Major Dagmar Dilbert's brown eyes widened and registered shock. Then Wes saw a change from shock to honest bewilderment. She did not sputter when she asked, "Detective, do you really believe that this history about the little girl could be true?"

"Yes, I do. We have to all be ready for the shit to fly when this comes out in the media. These men have kept this secret for years. But, it's going to be known. Our killer will see to it. That I guarantee you."

The woman had finally grasped the real situation. She was quickly getting used to the idea that however this case goes, heads would roll. She looked at Wes. In the most mellow voice he had ever heard from her mouth, she said, "We must find a way to protect ourselves. We're in an impossible situation. Wes, do the best you can. Let me know if you need more resources. Now, get going. I have to think."

He had been dismissed, but he hadn't been castrated.

Chapter 53

Wesley T. Wesley

The telephone rang, but Wes wanted to ignore it. He was not in the mood to bother with anyone's request, complaint or new assignment. He tried to will it to stop ringing. His mental power did not work, "Wesley, Homicide."

"Wes, it's me. Since this is my day off, I just wanted you to know I'll be late tomorrow." Hearing Eve's voice was a great relief. No new demands were going to be heaped on him.

"Ah, ha, Big date tonight? Can't get up for the old job?" Wes kidded his intern.

"You're right! I do have a big date tonight. But I also have a paper to hand in before I do anything else so look for me later."

"Will do. Have fun tonight."

"I sure will. See you in the morning, boss. Bye, bye."

Still holding the dead receiver in his hand, Wes sat engulfed in a cold, ominous silence. If there were others in the office, he was not aware of their presence. The feeling was overpowering and made him feel helpless. Just two words had changed his whole being. The words: It's me.

He shook his head, trying to drive out the thoughts that were troubling him. The thoughts that seemed to be holding him immobile in his chair as Eve's voice ran through his mind, "It's me." He frowned. As long as he could remember, she had always announced herself on the telephone and sometimes in person with a cheery "It's me."

He was shocked at the next question that hammered hard in his brain. Could Eve have something to do with these murders? The idea was ridiculous, wasn't it? After all, lots of people say it's me. In fact, most of the younger generation uses the word me where the word I should be used. How many times had he corrected his own son, Jason, when he would say, "Hey, Dad, me and Jordan are going to the game."

It's me.

Did the note on the concert program really mean something? Was it just a short taunt that could mean the police had still not arrested the serial killer? Or was it simply a signature to be sure the killer got the "credit" for another murder? Perhaps it was just a coincidence? If someone else had said those same words, would he have even given them a second thought?

Why would he consider Eve? Right age, right gender, knowledgeable about police procedures, knows how to shoot, busy during the day and available for the evenings and nights "moonlight job" of killing, and has been particularly interested in the female killer theory.

Wes reached for his notes that he always kept from meetings when cases are discussed as a team. He frantically flipped the pages. He knew what he was seeking. He could hear Eve's words again in his mind. They had been talking about the possible suspects: Deanna Lee, Augusta Martinez, Laurel Raub's sister, Iris, maybe one of Temple Carrollton's Li'l Darlins, or the mothers of his three sons. Pages continued to fly. Wes knew he had those notes.

Yes! There they were: "I don't think most of the women you're looking at even rate to be called suspects." But that statement did not prove anything. It certainly was not a confession.

He placed the receiver firmly into its cradle as if to end the suspicions. He turned to his box of evidence and tried to concentrate on something else. He had to have more than two words if he was seriously going to add Eve to their "Big-Haired Lady" list. As crazy as it seemed, the detective did not believe he should dismiss the idea. He also did not want to look for more reasons why it might be Eve. He felt his stomach churn. He tried to concentrate on the items in the box, but his thoughts were locked on this preposterous idea.

Chapter 53

Honeybun

It was time to organize her final murder. It was the killing to which all the others were the prelude.

Honeybun could go on. There were still a few Bad Ol' Boys left, but she was tired. No, she had made her point. She felt she had kept her promise. When the story broke with all the names she had gathered, the others will experience many days that they wish they were dead. The city will turn against them, their families will consider them depraved and their names that they wanted to go down in history as great leaders will turn dirty and disgusting.

She looked at the source of her carefully planned killing spree: The little book called My Friends. How stupid to keep such a record. How arrogant not to only keep the book, but to set up a situation that the story could be seen so clearly. She was still angered that the notes were written with a strong air of pride, but if the book had not been available, she would never have had her revenge.

Everything was in place. Today will be the end. Truly the end for what she's been doing. Also the end for the initiator of the filthy tale.

She had enough evidence that the police cannot ignore it. That was guaranteed by having in her plan that the media will receive the facts about the same time as the police. Once the facts are investigated, some were more than clues; the police will have to speak to the public. There were evil men loose. Predators. Men with no conscience.

Honeybun wanted to do one more thing before the end of the tale. She opened her cell phone and called the number of

WPTR. She was going to be sure Dani Swain was the lead on her story. She dialed the number and waited for the television anchor person to answer.

Chapter 54

Danielle Jarvis Swain

"This is Dani Swain."

"You'll get the story. It's yours as a gift from me."

Again the voice was disguised. Although she had thought it was a woman during the last call, Dani again questioned the gender of the caller. Her heart beat faster. Heat rushed to her face.

"Who is this? What story?"

"You know. You've been with me at every killing. As I kept my pledge, I was creating an opportunity for you to make national news. Dani Swain, you're the positive side of this story. You'll carry my voice to the public. We're a team."

Dani was scared. Was she being made part of this sinister plot? Was she somehow responsible for the men who had died? She looked at her small recorder that she always had close by. She picked it up, held it next to her ear, just touching the receiver and asked, "Will you tell me who you are? Do I know you?"

"You'll have all your answers before the sun comes up. I have a file that is addressed to you. It's an executive summary of the case. You may even know it all before the police. They don't get it. They never got it. Always thinking of the creeps that were killed as victims. Far from the truth. This is a sex crime, an abuse crime and a hate crime. The verdict is already decided by me. No one else ever cared. So you'll be the one to solve the executions for those police. You'll be one person who will care."

"Executions? Are we both thinking about the same murders of the Atlanta's leaders?"

There was a sound like a quick, hard laugh or a snort of derision, then silence before, "Murders! These killings are not that glamorous. These are executions done by a victim rather than by the courts."

Dani waited. Was this a confession? The person had not said 'I' at any time.

"I'm hanging up. You'll get all the file sometime tonight. Enjoy all the attention you'll get. Dani Swain will be commended for her investigative reporting rather than just delivering the message. I'll miss that grand finale. I know I would have enjoyed it."

"No, no, don't hang up. We need to talk. I know it's important to us both."

But Dani - looking lovely in her pastel pink suit, looking professional in the television surroundings, but looking terrified - was yelling into a phone that had no listener.

Dani placed the receiver back on the phone, checked her recorder and found she did get the conversation. Still with eyes wild and feeling short of breath, the television anchor dialed a number, took a deep breath and said in a controlled voice, "Wes, we must talk. I'm sure I have our killer's voice on my recorder."

"Dani, where are you? Wherever it is, I'll be there immediately."

"I'm at my office. The call came through the switchboard just before I called you. I'll be here. I think I'm having a panic attack, but I'm here. Hurry! I think something else is going to happen soon."

Wes grabbed a few things from his desk, caught the decrepit elevator and ran out of the building. He flew through the dirty, dark, parking garage; not even noticing his surroundings or that someone called out a greeting to him. He sped out of the area, put the flashing blue lights on his dashboard and only slowed down at each intersection.

He crossed Atlanta avoiding busy thoroughfares. The unmarked car made turns onto side streets that would take him to the large, impressive WPTR building perched overlooking the famous Peachtree Street. The detective's knowledge of the city enabled him to be there, parked and in the foyer with its high ceilings and tall windows in six minutes.

There was the beautiful anchorwoman waiting for him with a worried look on her face. He noted that he had never seen her perplexed before. Although it was a concern to him, he felt it gave her a more exotic appearance.

"Wes! I don't know why I'm in the middle of this sordid affair, but I am. I'm not even sure if this person doesn't think the two of us are connected. You know how often 'nuts' find and cling to a celebrity. I believe I'm being envisioned in this way."

"Slow down. Let's go where we can talk. You said you recorded a conversation. I want to hear it right away."

"There's a small office on this floor. It's private. We need privacy."

Dani was already walking quickly in front of Wes. He followed behind. He hoped that they looked calmer than either of them felt. Of course, this was his job. He faced surprises daily, but Dani's job was reporting disaster and mayhem after the fact not before. Unfortunately, her attitude was infectious and added to his anxiety about Eve. He hoped that the television celebrity's revelation would warrant all of her excitement.

Wes closed the office door quietly, looked expectantly at Dani as she took the small recorder from the pocket of her suit jacket.

"I called my manager to have him meet us, but he is still on his way back from Macon. Jimmy said he would come directly here when he arrived in Atlanta. He said to talk with you and plot our next move. If we were in agreement, he would be in our corner. Wes, the recording is ready to go. I rewound it so we could hear what I got. It's not complete because I didn't start it until I realized who was calling."

Wes pressed the rectangular-shaped switch and heard Dani's voice, "Will you tell me who you are? Do I know you?"

"You'll have your answers before the sun comes up. I have a file that is addressed to you. It's an executive summary of the case. You may even know it all before the police…"

Wes automatically moved closer to the recorder resting in Dani's hand. He concentrated on the tone, sound, accent and presentation of the voice that followed Dani's questions. He wanted desperately to not hear Eve. He was also being careful to not let his own personal friendship with Eve color his judgment. Was it Eve? Was it someone else?

Dani had told the truth. The voice was not natural. The speaker had made an effort to disguise it. It could be a man or a woman as Dani had told him, but his first reaction was that the voice was female. He hoped he wasn't being swayed because of the Big-Haired Lady theory. He didn't think so, but was it Eve?

The recording ended abruptly after Dani cried. "No, no, don't hang up. Why am I in the middle of this?"

The question was answered by her detective friend, "Because someone feels comfortable talking to you, honey. I'm sure, she wants you to have the breaking news story. Dani, this is going to be bigger national news when this shooter is identified."

"What? You suspect it is someone the public will know?"

"I'm not sure about that, but the motive and connection among the victims will be featured on the biggest evening news programs: CBS, CNN, ABC, MSNBC, FOX. For some reason, our mysterious caller has decided you'll have the lead. Who likes you that much, sweetheart?"

"I don't know. I can't even imagine that I know a serial killer. Do you have a suspect? Should I be worried?" Dani sounded alarmed, but not hysterical.

"No, you've nothing to worry about. I'm sure of that, Dani. Actually, it's just the opposite. This person is taking care of you. I know you've captured lots of hearts by just being yourself and perhaps fortunately for you, here is another heart you have touched. Now, I have a very important question. You said to me earlier that you felt an empathy with the owner of this voice. Do you have any thoughts who it might be?"

"I've thought of this a lot. I cannot imagine that I could know the person, but I do feel like I have heard the voice in another context."

"…..And, that context?"

"You're going to think I'm crazy, but I'm sure I have actually talked to her. And, yes, I no longer question gender. This is a woman, a young woman."

"Dani, quick, without any further contemplation. Who do you feel this person is that you have already met?"

"Oh, Wes, I hate to say this. It is so ridiculous. I keep thinking of Eve. It's just a feeling; like a song that makes you think of someone each time you hear it." Dani kept shaking her head back and forth. She wanted to clear her mind of this outrageous idea.

Here was another opinion that pointed to his attractive, talented, fun intern. Of course, he wasn't shocked. It was too late for shock. He had already been through that twice: Seeing and hearing "It's me" and again when he heard the recording. Now he had a very hard job. He had to find her before she killed someone else.

Chapter 55

Eve Zachary

Before she inserted it all into a large, white envelope, Eve was checking her thesis, reports and evidence. The case paperwork was completed. Contrary to most Homicide cases, the paperwork in the Bad Ol' Boys Club case was finished with every detail included before a killer had been arrested. She was sure her work would get an A. Wes will only have to write the end of the case. All the rest is done.

Major Dilbert won't have to threaten to get the paperwork this time. Her case study to complete her work for her degree will be sent by United States Mail. By sending it that way, it was guaranteed to arrive several days after Dani Swain will have an opportunity to announce the solving of the serial murders. Eve knew the thesis documentation was thorough. She knew who was truly guilty.

She regretted that she would not see Dani tomorrow on TV. The anchorwoman would probably use WPTR's instant news BreakIn! feature. Eve had always liked those special announcements that could happen at anytime. When she saw those flashing lights and heard the sounds of bells clanging with whistles in the background, she paid attention.

She regretted that she couldn't have her grade right now and receive her diploma today. She could envision her diploma and could hear the tune of Pomp and Circumstance in her mind. She was proud of the thesis she had created. Her project had turned out exactly how she knew it could. She felt like a victor.

Eve thought of her unhappy childhood with a mother who had no affection for her daughters. Her mother always ridiculed what she or her sisters wanted to do and assured them that they would not be successful. The calm young woman no longer regretted her life because she had made a promise to herself and had kept that promise.

Everyone should have a purpose to life and have an opportunity to fulfill that purpose. She had done that and she felt she had done it for her sisters too. When that happens, it is time to call it over. What greater victory than to have reached to the highest place in life by dedication to a mission for others you love. She needed nothing more. She will have had it all by tomorrow morning. She looked forward to whatever lay ahead.

Chapter 56

Walter

Walter was still not used to carrying a cell phone. In fact, at times he thought it was a serious intrusion of his personal time. Of course, he quickly learned how to handle that problem. He turned it off! Then switched it back on only when he wanted to bother with missed calls.

His time off began at the end of his shift at 7 AM. After taking a nap in the morning, Walter had had lunch with his wonderful Shana, who was the true light of his life. How trite, he thought, but that was how he felt. That was as poetic as he got. He thanked the good Lord and his wonderful friend, Andy Dren, daily for changing his worthless life to one full of satisfaction.

Walter's involvement in the Homicide case at Georgia Tech had earned him the reward money. The reward money gave him the means to go to computer school. The computer skills had gotten him a job and through his job, he had met the sweetest, little lady in the whole US of A. Although Andy's murder was a terrible tragedy, Walter was still proud that he had helped to find the murderer. His regret was that the shooting happened at all.

He laughed at this chain of consciousness because his next thought was that he definitely would not have a cell phone if he was still homeless and sleeping in a black, plastic garbage bag. He looked at the words: 'missed message' and pushed the button of his phone.

"Walter, when you get this message, I'll be planning to meet you at the Union Mission. I have some important news for you and Wes. Wesley. I want to tell you first so I'll be there at 10 o'clock. Don't stand me up. We need to talk."

Walter frowned. A crackling occurred, the voice faded. The telephone went dead.

"Damn. I lost the end. I don't even know who it was. Who says technology is great?"

Walter instinctively looked at his watch. It was just six o'clock. If he chose to follow the message, he had time to catch another short nap, get showered and dressed, stop at the Union Mission and be at work by eleven. That works. He wondered who the mystery person would be.

· · · ·

Feeling rested and squeaky clean from his hot shower, Walter pulled a green knit shirt over his head and ran his hand across his salt and pepper hair, clipped closely to his scalp. Glancing in the mirror above the dresser, he looked at the few lines extended from the corners of his eyes and frowned. Unfortunately, that caused more line above his eyes.

He said out loud to his image in the glass. "You're not perfect, but you look mighty good for an old guy. Anyway, Walter, my man, you're OK for being on the north side of fifty. You got it made. Didn't know life could be such fun."

He strapped his Timex on his right wrist and noticed it was already 9:30. He marveled at how fast time goes when you have the good things in life. With that thought in mind, he reached for his keys, picked up his used briefcase, bought for six dollars at the Junior League Next to New Shop. He took one last peak in the mirror and smiled at his reflection and his full life.

Walter drove directly to the Union Mission, which wasn't as busy as it was during the day, even though they had two shifts of sleepers: day workers and night workers. It should be easy to find the person who sent the message. He parked his car and got out.

"Walter, hey, man. Hey, good bro'. How ya' doin'? Ain't seen ya' for a few. Now, we has a date."

Walter turned and saw Ole Jasper coming toward him carrying a good-sized box.

"Jasper, what're you doin' hangin' here so late?"

"Meetin' yo, bro, and makin' money. My job tonight is to hand this box over to Walter and to absolutely no one else. I'm followin' my instructions. I is good at that, don't ya' think?"

Jasper was always full of motion as if he was attached to a generator. Walter immediately remembered the day he announced he wanted to be his dep-u-ty.

"Jasper, I guess you got to be my dep-u-ty ater all, because what you have there is to go to Detective Wesley. So you're right on the police team. You have an important job." Walter smiled at Jasper and received a huge grin in return. The former homeless man knew the importance of feeling recognized and having value. He knew most people looked right past the homeless on the street like they were as insignificant as dirt.

I knew this job was im-po-tent, man. I got twenty dollars for just sittin' here with this box waitin' for yo' to show. I knew my buddy, Walter, would come at ten and here yo' is."

Jasper handed Walter the box, which was sealed with wide, mailing tape. There was a note attached to the top: Walter, please, give this to Wes Wesley. He needs it tomorrow morning. Thanks for being the courier. I have something else I have to do. It was signed: Eve.

"Eve?" Walter questioned in amazement. He knew who she was but why was he asked to deliver this box? He turned directly to the man who was jiggling, as if he had to go to the bathroom, and asked, "Who gave you this, Jasper?"

"I guess Eve. She din't say who she is. She could have been an Eve or an Alice. I din't see much of her. All covered up with a scarf and a baseball hat way down to her eyes. But, man, she looked good in those jeans. Nice round ass there, my man." Jasper chuckled and did a little shuffle step.

"What else do you know about this woman?"

"Nuthin'. She was here 'bout three minutes. Maybe four, but I doubt it. I saw that twenty, heard what she wanted and I says, 'I is yo' man.' Walter, is somethin' wrong? Is ya' mad at

Ole Jasper?"

"No, Jasper, no. Just thought I'd be sure who gave this box to you. No problem, man, if it ain't tickin' like a bomb, I think we're OK. Detective Wesley will know why Eve didn't have time to deliver in person. Maybe she's off on a vacation."

Walter held the box in one arm and reached to shake Jasper's hand. He then reached into his pocket and gave a crumpled five dollar bill that he always kept handy in case he needed it in a hurry. Walter never wanted to be completely without money again.

"Wow, bro', you is the best. Yo' don't have to do that. I'm already paid. But I thanks yo'. I'm gonna go to McDonald's and buy me a Big Mac and fries. I can taste them now. They's good eatin'."

Ole Jasper was still hopping around like he could hear some music. Walter decided that at this moment his friend Jasper was as happy with life as he was. Even an extra five dollars can be important.

Walter was ready to go to work and would deliver the box to Wes on his way home in the morning.

Chapter 57

Eve Zachary

Eve was satisfied that Walter would get the box to Wes. She hoped that he did not feel it was urgent and deliver it right away. She knew Walter's job started at eleven. Her plan was to not give him enough time to go find Wes tonight.

She drove into the familiar lot and parked in the space that she had come to consider "hers."

There was a huge old oak tree at the edge of the black top paving, which always made her feel protected and secure. She knew that was a strange reaction when everything she had been doing was in opposition to being protected or secure. Fortunately, all of that was about completed. One more task: see her mother.

The young woman, dressed in everyday fashion of jeans, sandals and a yellow tee shirt that just reached her waist, tripped the lock on the entry door with her credit card. 'It's amazing how easy it is to break in. Maybe that was because there was no reason to want to break into a shabby home for senior citizens,' she thought.

A fat man was sitting straight up in a desk chair, his mouth open, snoring loudly. She quietly walked by him and looked down the hall where her mother's room was located. The nurse's station was empty, the linen closet door was ajar and Eve could smell cigarette smoke. She slowly pushed open the door of her mother's room. She noticed by the big, hall clock that it was 9:50. Walter did not yet have the box containing her class project. Wes was still uninformed. Dani was probably nervous and upset. That would soon change to being excited about being the reporter of this news story. A news story based on a serial murder case of which she was never the suspect, but was always the perpetrator.

The room was dim. The television blaring a reality show. Her mother saw them all. She could have written her own reality show and people would gasp, "Oh, no, that could never happen."

"Hi, Mom, it's me," Eve said brightly as she pushed the door back and walked toward her mother's raggedy chair. She was covered by an afghan that Eve had seen for years. Her mother was so proud that she had gotten it at a church bazaar; handmade, lovely soft wool and had paid only twenty dollars. Her mom always loved a bargain.

"Honeybun, what a surprise. You must have run out of things to do. Too bad you don't have some nice, young man taking you out on the town tonight. That's what I would have done at your age. Did I ever tell you how many men wanted to go out with me? Yeah, I guess I did. Didn't seem to have an effect on your social life though, did it?"

Eve sighed. Already her mother was repeating her favorite litany. Tonight it really didn't make a difference. She would have the last word about her mother and her "friends."

Before the young woman could respond, her mother continued, "What do you have in that bag? Something for me? You don't bring gifts very often."

"It's for us, Mom. I thought we could just talk and also celebrate that I've finished my term thesis. It's really good. I'm sure it will get a lot of attention."

"Humph! How could some paper get a lot of attention? You just want an A. You don't need any more than that."

Eve was opening the white paper bag while her mother spoke. She took out two, big, waxed cups and a small bag that held giant oatmeal cookies. She has brought maybe the only two things on which her mother and she agreed. They both loved lemonade and oatmeal cookies.

"Alright, girl, you sure did make the right choice tonight. I hope you didn't just open a can of frozen lemonade. You know I like the freshly squeezed kind."

"Oh, yes, I know that. I squeezed these lemons myself and added just the right amount of sugar. I do have to confess, mom. I bought the cookies. But they are just like home baked."

"Not surprised. You never were much of a baker. Not like me. I made fantastic pies and everything else that came out of an oven."

Eve took her time spreading a napkin on the bedside table, taking the lids off the cups, putting straws into the frosty liquid and arranging the cookies beside the cups.

"See, Mom, it's our party. Some time for us to just talk and relax. I'm so thrilled to have come to the end of my project and have the paper finished. What a humongous relief."

"There you go. Using those big academic words. But I can guess that you mean huge 'cause that big word sounds just like huge."

"Right on, Mom, it does sound like huge. Some words just have the sound of what they are. Like teeny or tiny…"

"Or slippery slope. I always liked the sound of that."

"Right! You almost feel like you are slipping when you say it. Friend is another word that sounds just like what it is," Eve said as she watched her mother take a long gulp from her cup to wash down her first bite of cookie. Her mother looked perplexed, but waited to respond until after she had more cookie and another drink of the lemonade.

"Friend? I don't get that one. Doesn't make an image at all for me."

"How about My Friends, Mom? That little book you used to keep," Eve said very quietly. She watched as her mother took another swallow of the refreshing liquid, looking a bit like she had seen a ghost.

"What book? I don't know what you're talking about. Honeybun, give me another cookie. This treat is nice. Now, tell me more about your paper."

"Oh, I will. Your precious book is part of my paper. In fact, it's the basis of the whole case study."

"What the hell are you talking about? How would you even know about a book called My Friends....ah, even if there was one?" The older woman was definitely agitated.

"The book was in with some of your old stuff that I cleaned out of your place when you moved in here. There were all kinds of mementos, Mom, but none quite as interesting as the My Friends reading."

"Don't know what you're talkin' about. It probably was somebody else's book. Maybe Sunshine's or Sweetie's. They always were little pack rats; saved everything."

"Hardly, Mom, the information in the book was exactly what all three of us wanted to forget. Forget, ha, as if we ever could. Sunshine and Sweetie escaped the horrible memories because they died. Did you ever think about how this information killed your two daughters?" Eve's eyes narrowed as tears sprang up behind her lids. She gritted her teeth and worked at not becoming too emotional. She wanted this conversation to be calculated. She looked directly at the pitiful wretch that she was forced to admit was her mother.

The old woman seemed to have aged another ten years in only a few minutes. She was not sure what was coming next, but she felt sure that her daughter knew more than she had ever thought she would know. She ate another piece of cookie and washed it down quickly with more of the tart, lemonade before making a response.

"There you go again. You always come out here to make me miserable. It ain't enough that you locked me away in this God-forsaken place. You have to torture me with your sharp tongue and wild imagination. Why don't you just leave me alone? I was the only person who ever took care of you and your sisters. Your bastard of a father never cared a damn about any of you."

"You didn't take care of us. You used us for your own benefit! You used us to make money. Used us to try to buy those big deal friends you list in the book. They must have thought you were a real creep knowing that you pimped for your own little girls!"

Evelyn Zachary had been drinking her lemonade while Eve hissed the words close to her mother's face. When she spoke, her voice rose. She became shrill, "Just leave, Honeybun! Get the hell out of here. I can't believe that I named you after me. That I thought you would be another me. A name you never wanted to use. Ha! I don't need an ungrateful pain-in-the-ass giving me a hard time." The woman caught her breath and felt almost faint. Honeybun, her daughter Eve, was driving her crazy!

"Let's read your precious book, Mother. All the wonderful memories that you brag about each time I come here. Memories of your filled dance card, your dates with politicians and even handsome young men who were barely legal age when you were already a mother of three girls. Ah, yes, Mother, how clear is your memory?"

Eve took the My Friends book out of her purse. Opened it at random. She knew it didn't matter what page. They all documented the price tags that her mother put on her three young daughters.

"Let's see. June 30, Sunshine, Randy Lee, $65, 2 hours; July 15, Sweetie, Silas Ocher, $50, 1 hour; July 27, Honeybun, Temple Carrollton, $25, 1 hour. Hmm, I wasn't worth much or he was a skinflint."

"He was a skin...." Honeybun's mother blurted out through her anger at her youngest child. "I didn't mean that, Honeybun, you just have me so damn mad that I can't even think." To have time to think, Evelyn reached for more to eat and drink. Food had always been her escape.

"Maybe I should read some more while you get your temper under control. Be like me, Mom, I couldn't be madder, but I've kept myself quite calm. Don't you agree?"

"Sure, you're under control because you're accusing me of all these terrible things. You have hurt me with your meanness. I haven't accused you of anything."

"Oh, and what would you accuse me of? Let's see, maybe not being old enough to be fondled, fucked and forgotten? Fondled and fucked by "Your Friends" and forgotten by you. You could also accuse me of keeping critical identification of one of Your Friends that has been used against him."

"What does that mean, used against him? I have no earthly idea what you think you're saying," Honeybun's mother slumped in her chair, but her eyes were blazing. She was beginning to comprehend that her daughter knew all about her formerly successful business. The business that fell apart when the word got around that fourteen year old Sweetie had died of AIDS. She could have made money for years with Sunshine and Honeybun but the rumors ruined that.

She repeated, "What does that mean?"

"It means, Mother dear, that even as a little girl too young to really know that what was happening to us was not how other people lived. I was smart enough to keep evidence that I later used to start tracking down these immoral, sick men that you thought were hot stuff. I didn't even know there was such a thing as DNA, but I kept a semen sample for all those years and finally matched it up with a pious son-of-a-bitch who after all this time was still taking advantage of young girls and women. This time in the Lord's name."

"Oh, my god. Oh, no," Evelyn Zachary gasped, turned pale, a small amount of spit trickled out of her mouth and landed on her flabby bosom. "You know something about Temple Carrollton's death. You told someone."

"No, I wanted to tell you first. I wanted you to know what I knew before the public knew, and while I still had a chance to tell you. I've been investigating many of these men, specifically the ones who called themselves the Good Ol' Boys Club. I have evidence and I have educated suspicions. What I learned and discovered was enough to avenge the deaths of my two sisters and for the ruination of all our lives. All for your ego and profit. Now I've written up the whole sordid tale. It will be on the news tomorrow. All of the documentation is in the hands of the police and Dani Swain, the TV woman."

"Dani Swain. Why would she have the information?"

"Because I sent it to her."

"How could you do this? She and everyone will think you're involved with the murder of Temple Carrollton. Then they will learn that you were a prostitute."

"Prostitute? You crazy old woman! Prostitute? At age of twelve and thirteen with my mother making the deals and keeping the money. That was child abuse child, trafficking and molestation, Mother, in case you never admitted to yourself that was what you were doing. Emotional and physical child abuse," Eve was shocked that her mother still saw no problem with what she had done. She didn't know right from wrong. She was responsible for the early deaths of her daughters just as if she had shot them in the heads.

"No way, girl. Havin' sex with a couple men wasn't going to hurt you at all. Girls are built for sex. It weren't no problem. Still wouldn't be if you would keep your mouth shut, but, no, you have to go to the biggest TV person in Atlanta and tell tales out of school. You sure aren't very smart. They're going to come and get you. And, don't expect me to take up for you. Not me!"

Evelyn Zachary felt a headache thumping between her eyes and her mouth was dry. She picked up the cup and swallowed the rest of the lemonade.

"Humph, you thought you could bribe me with a treat. Forget that. When I'm asked, I'm gonna tell them you were always bad. I could never keep you from men. You were born a slut, Eve Zachary. You liked it when I dressed you up pretty at night. You thought you looked like a Barbie doll. Too dumb to know why I dressed you pretty. How about that …?"

Chapter 58

Wes T. Wesley

Dani and Wes were still standing by the desk in the private office. He looked at the small, leather clock that matched the desk set and saw that it was going on eleven o'clock. He knew that he had to find Eve. He was sure she was going to do something else.

Wes sat down in the desk chair and looked at Dani, "OK if I use the telephone?"

"Of course. What can I do? Since I'm in this drama, I want to help. Right now, I feel helpless." Dani pulled up the side chair closer to the desk.

Wes dialed a number and raised a finger toward Dani as if to say: wait a minute. He waited, then said, "Eve, this is Wes. I need to see you right away. If you come in soon and get this message, give me a call no matter what time it is. Don't wait until morning. I'll be waiting up for you." Then he looked at Dani and said, "Answering machine, damn."

"Now what, Wes?" Can we find her some place? Where does she hang out?"

"On campus, at our office, some little restaurant on Highland. Yeah, she has a friend there. What was the name of that place?" He closed his eyes trying to see the sign, "Yes! It's Roman Lily."

Dani opened a telephone directory from the shelves behind her. She felt better to be doing something.

"Here it is. Call. Quick. I know we have to find her."

Wes again dialed and waited. Even sitting on the other side of the desk, Dani could hear noise from the receiver. Wes sat up taller and spoke louder, "Is Eve Zachary there?"

He waited again hearing the person call out, "Have you seen Eve?"

Another short wait. "Nope, she's not here. Can I tell her who called?"

"Yes, ask her to call Wes. Tell her I need her help right away on some research on a case."

"Oh, yeah, Detective. I'll do that. She'll be anxious to help. She loves working with you guys. Come have dinner soon again. Gotta run."

"Strike two. If I knew where she was, my next try would be her mother," Wes said to Dani. "I know she mentioned the place to me. I didn't think I'd ever need it so I didn't write it down." He looked quizzically at the pretty anchorwoman.

"Don't look at me. I didn't even know she had a mother. You said 'the place.' What were you referring to?"

"Her mother is in one of those assisted living places. I guess we can start by trying the telephone book again. I know it was a silly name. It will come to me. Just let me look."

"Here we go: Nursing Homes; seems to be lots of them." Dani turned the pages toward Wes.

The detective scanned the listings and the ads. He brightened quickly when he got to the Ts.

"Yes! Tara Plantation Assisted Living. Told you it was a silly name. Let's give them a try."

Wes soon got a night supervisor on the phone and asked if they had a guest named Evelyn Zachary. The person answering the phone hesitated and said that they do not give out that kind of information. Wes identified himself as an Atlanta police detective and the person responded, "Yeah and I'm Rhett Butler. That's why I answer the phone at Tara." He then hung up.

"No help there but I'm going to go down there anyway. There's a bigger chance that her mom will know where she might be than anyone else I know. I know it's the right place. Eve even laughed about the name one time. Can you stay here and wait until the package is delivered? Then call me right away. I'll have someone pick it up. You also should be here when your boss returns so he knows you're safe and that a big story is coming his way."

"Are you sure of that, Wes?"

"Absolutely. For some reason we're coming to the end of these killings. You want to look gorgeous to be ready to tell the world. We're always glad to have you on our team, Dani." He put his arm around her shoulders in a reassuring way, handed her a slip of paper with a number on it and continued, "Here's the fastest way to get me. Call the minute you have any more news: another call, the package arrives, an unannounced visitor appears, whatever. I'll come as fast as I can or will send someone."

Wes was gone as fast as he arrived. He headed south keeping the address of the Tara Plantation in his mind. He had never been there but he knew almost exactly where it was located. The area did not warrant such a fancy name. The best that could be said for the neighborhood is that it was in transition and still had some beautiful old trees and lovely azaleas in the springtime.

The detective dialed a number on his cell phone. "Hey, Billy Joe, wake up and listen to me. We have a big problem. I think you ought to meet me at the Tara Plantation Assisted Living as soon as you can get there. I'm still in Midtown headed in that direction so since you're already farther south, we might arrive there about the same time."

"Hey, man, what's happened? Do we have another shootin'? What about the mayor?"

"Don't know about the mayor at this moment, but I do know who the killer is."

Wes hated to tell Billy Joe what he suspected. He probably liked Eve even more than Wes did. She had been Billy Joe's and Cleo's babysitter from time to time. Eve had taken the LaCrosse children to the zoo. Gave them panda bear stuffed animals to remember the wonderful day. This was going to hit him hard.

"Who?"

"Eve."

Chapter 59

Eve Zachary

Eve watched her mother's face transform into an evil mask. She could hear the sound of triumph in her statement of what she would tell. Tell who? No one will ever ask her. Eve would be sure of that because she did not plan to leave her mother alive.

"I doubt if anyone will be very interested in your opinion, Mom, when they learn what you did to your girls. You killed all three of us. You killed your own babies for money. Actually, maybe somebody would listen. They would listen in horror of how low one woman could be. Everyone is so afraid of terrorists these days. You were a terrorist to your own flesh and blood."

"That was my decision. You were mine. Yes, my flesh and blood. No one else took a lick of interest in you. I was stuck with you. So I saw where I could win instead of lose having to support you for years and years. It worked, too. For a while, I had money, clothes, fancy men and hardly had to do anything for any of it. Then that Silas Ocher brought AIDS to Sweetie. Sure, he paid by dying, but he killed my business too. Too bad he had such a big mouth and had to tell everyone."

Evelyn Zachary reached up to her head again and drove her fists into her eyes like she was fighting off sleep. Her hands then fluttered back to the arms of her chair and her head sagged. To Eve, her mother looked like she was going to take a nap but she knew better. The Valium that she had added to her lemonade was beginning to take effect.

"You omitted that it was Silas Ocher who also killed your daughter."

"Oh, yeah, that too. That's why my business failed, because

people knew that Sweetie had AIDS. Assumed that you and Sunshine did, too."

"You know, Mom, here is another way that you and I are alike. Not only do we both like lemonade and have the same name, but we have no regrets for our decisions. You still don't care what you did to the three of us, and I have no apologies for executing Randy Lee, Temple Carrollton, Houston Montrose, Franklin Raub or Irwin Fitzgerald. I could have continued until all the names in the book belonged to dead men, but I'm tired and also satisfied that I paid them back for my sisters. I have just one more execution on my list. Then I follow you all into hell."

"You all? What does that mean?" Her mother seemed to perk up, but her speech was slurred. She lifted her head and looked through half-closed eyes at her youngest and only surviving daughter. "What do you mean, you all?"

"I mean, Mother dear, that you're the last on the list. I will follow you all. This is the last conversation you'll have with anyone about your past glorious life financed by your pitiful children."

Appearing much like a sloth, every movement so slow and labored, Evelyn Zachary widened her eyes and reached out to her pretty daughter, "Don't hurt me, Honeybun. I'm your mother. I'm all you have."

"Too late for the maternal act, Mom. We know who we are. You know what I have done and I know what you have done. We're going to hell together and I couldn't be happier. I'm ready. I can't remember a day of my life that had hope or happiness. You stole our childhood and you stole our adulthood. I'm ready to die happy. I don't need another day to feel that my life is complete. This is truly my birthday."

Eve took a small pistol from her purse. It was a 9 mm Loren. She had chosen to drug her mother so that there was no chance that she would call out and alarm the staff. The heavy dose of Valium might have been strong enough to kill her, but she didn't want to take the chance that it might not act in time.

Her mother gurgled something that sounded like 'NO' just before her eyes rolled upward as if asking for heavenly help. The shot ended any hope of help for Evelyn Zachary.

The second shot followed immediately. The sound was in the opposite direction. Eve, the grown-up Honeybun, slumped back and all that remained of the last execution was a small red hole between her beautiful, brown and peaceful eyes.

Chapter 60

Wes T. Wesley

Two cars raced into the Tara parking lot within seconds of one another. Wes didn't have to look at who was right behind him. Who else but Billy Joe would be hightailing it to the nursing home in the middle of the night?

They had both jumped out of their cars when they heard the first shot. They turned toward the front entrance and were reaching for the door when they heard the second shot. The door was locked. Wes pounded on the door and rang the bell at the same time.

"Shit, it sounds like we're too late," Wes said.

A face covered with stubble of beard and a body wearing a huge, dirty sweat shirt appeared at the glass window in the door. By the look of the man's face, he was somewhere between sleeping and shock. Wes raised his badge and yelled, "Open the damn door!"

The door opened immediately, and the man stood back to let them in.

"Rhett Butler, I presume. OK, creep, where did that gun shot come from?"

The man now looked embarrassed. He realized he really had been talking to a detective on the phone. Now something awful was happening. He knew he was in deep-shit-trouble.

"From back, in the hallway where the bedrooms are. It sounded fairly close. I'll show you."

The three men raced across the foyer, past the darkened dining room and made a sharp right turn. "Rhett" slipped and banged into the wall, but stayed on his feet. He was still moving ahead as he tried to regain his balance. He saw that the nurse's station was empty and a door was open just past the desk. They had just reached that door when a woman came out screaming. They had found the nurse who would have been at the station if she had not needed a cigarette.

"They're both shot. They look like they're dead. This is awful. We must call the police. Clyde, call 911!"

"These guys are the police. Who's in there? Did one of the men try to make out with Mrs. Zachary?"

"There are no men in there. Just the guest and another woman."

"Damn, it's not going to be good. Get out of the way and go call 911. Tell them what has happened," Billy Joe took the nurse by the arm and pointed her in the direction of her station. He then followed Wes into the room.

Each checked out one of the women. Billy Joe was the first to make an announcement, "This lady's gone. How about Eve, Wes?"

"She's gone, too. It's obviously a murder-suicide. I don't think there's any reason to suspect that there's someone else involved, but we'd better look around. You take the building, and I'll go check out the grounds."

There was the sound of feet shuffling and voices in the hall. Some voices had already reached an hysterical pitch. They saw a man appear at the door wearing red and white striped pajamas. He asked, "What's up? Who's in there?"

"Hey, 'Rhett,' do your job and get these people back to their rooms." Wes yelled over his shoulder. "Help them to get calmed down. They don't need to see this or you're going to have a bunch of heart attacks on your hands. Now get moving. Try earning your pay." Wes was still angry with the man called Clyde. His earlier action may have prevented this. He may have become the hero; instead he was going to lose his job. He won't try to be funny very soon again.

Wes turned to leave the room. He passed Clyde who was still standing around with his mouth hanging open. As the detective started down the hallway, he said, "Nobody enters that room. Everyone back to your rooms. Don't touch anything out here. This is a police investigation. Clyde, you get moving!"

Wes was out of sight in a few seconds. He was sure there was nothing to be seen outside but he had to be check. Eve could have had help but he didn't think so. He saw her car and went over to it. It was not locked. He opened the door, the light went on and he saw that it was what he expected; messy with her papers and other personal items. He pulled the lever to open her trunk and looked inside; nothing obvious there. He would have the lab guys do a thorough search, but he was going to walk the grounds and see if there was anyone hanging around.

He was returning to the building with no results from his search when the ambulance arrived. He followed the EMTs into the building.

Wes knew that he had to cover this murder-suicide in the usual way. He didn't want to do any of that. He wanted to have a chance to go back and start again before Ramblin' Randy was shot. Could he have anticipated any of this? Were there early clues that the murderer sat in his office, helped him read evidence, ate meals with him and was his friend? Should he have spent more time getting to know about Eve's childhood? Would he have learned that Eve was the little girl who the Bad Ol' Boys were molesting? What about Eve's sisters? Were they molested too? He had so many questions.

Chapter 61

Danielle Jarvis Swain

It was already after 2:00 AM. Dani was experiencing mixed feelings. She was high with anticipation of the package arriving, but she was getting so tired that she was constantly yawning. No way would she go to sleep.

Her boss, Jimmy London, was back in the office. She had told him all that had transpired during his absence. Then he had gone searching for coffee for them both. He too thought his day was going to close when he returned to Atlanta, but sensing an important breaking story, he was ready to wait with Dani.

"OK, Dani, this will help a bit but it won't shorten the night. We're going to wait for that package. Let's hope that it's as newsworthy as we all think it will be," Jimmy said as he walked back into the office carrying two mugs of coffee and a box of Girl Scout cookies. "I found these in my drawer. I never opened them so they should be OK."

They heard a knock. Behind them the door quietly opened a few inches. The night security man said almost in a whisper, "Dani, there's a courier for you. Do you want to sign for a big envelope?"

Dani looked at the beefy man dressed in a gray uniform. The collar stretched around a thick, muscular neck. If she didn't know better, she would think that he was the brother of the daytime security man, Tony Jones. She was sure that the men were chosen for the job of security, because they looked like heavy weight boxers.

"Lex, you don't have to whisper. No one is asleep in here even though it sounds like a good idea," the general manager quipped. Jimmy looked at Dani as she started for the door. He nodded his head. "I'm coming along. So is Lex. This whole situation could be a problem. You're not meeting some stranger alone in the middle of the night."

"Come on then. We need to see what we have and call Wes right away. I really feel nervous. Isn't that weird?"

Lex Andrews led the threesome to the foyer where a middle aged, heavy set man with red-rimmed eyes was waiting with an envelope held in one hand. He did not look threatening to anyone.

"This is addressed to Dani Swain. That's you, right? All you have to do is sign here. Must be important for you to be here now. Will this package be in the news tomorrow?"

"It's a possibility. Now, I'll sign this so you can go back home to bed."

"Nope. I have more deliveries. One is out in Dunwoody. Might as well be going to Chattanooga," the courier said as he handed his clip board to Dani.

Jimmy laughed briefly, "Not quite, but it isn't just around the corner either. There you are. Thanks." Jimmy London shook the man's hand as he handed him a ten-dollar bill.

"Thank you, sir. Just doing my job. I'm going to watch all your news tomorrow and see if I can guess what I just delivered."

Jimmy and Dani waved to the security man, then retreated back into the small office. Jimmy handed her a small pocket knife from his pants pocket. The envelope was slit in a moment. Dani hesitated. She looked at Jimmy. She wasn't sure she wanted to know what was inside. Would it help solve the murders, or might it make things worse? Who sent these to her? Was it because she somehow had a role in this case?

"Dani, are you going to look at the contents? That's why we're still here."

"Right, Jimmy. It's that I feel somewhat responsible. I don't even know why."

"Well, you aren't. You're simply a well known person who

is being used to deliver a message. Happens all the time. This whole situation has nothing to do with you, but I believe you're going to be the one who solves the case. So, solve it now. Let's look at the stuff!"

Dani had a sheaf of papers in her hand with a hand written letter on top, "Dear Dani," she began reading, "You have here the executive summary of my thesis. The completed work is being delivered to Wes soon, but what you need for BreakIn! is here. It was my pleasure to know you and be able to add you to the conclusion of this case.

"You may not believe it yet, but this city is better now that many evil men are no longer with us. The story of why I have executed these men is included here. They're responsible for the deaths of my two sisters and perhaps others as they satisfied their own egos and self gratification. These despicable men banded together to keep their actions secret for over a decade. They never felt a pang of remorse nor tried to atone for their behavior. I have taken care of this for them."

Dani stopped reading as her eyes scanned the next words of the letter. She put her hand up to her mouth and whispered, "Oh, no. This can't be."

"What is it, Dani?"

"Jimmy, the next sentence is unbelievable. We must call Wes right away."

Jimmy snatched the letter. Dani didn't want to hold the paper. She wanted to go back to being innocent.

"The writer is Wes Wesley's intern, Eve Zachary. She claims to have killed all of these men. She is a lovely, sweet student who has become part of the Homicide team. This is going to be so difficult for Wes and for Billy Joe. They're all buddies, really good friends."

Dani immediately dialed the number Wes had given her. He answered on the first ring, "Wesley."

"Wes, I have the package. Mr. London and I are here in the office."

"What's in it, Dani?" Wes asked the question because he had to, but he already knew the answer.

Dani felt her face getting hot. Her eyes became teary, "It's awful, Wes. The packet is from Eve. She says that she killed these men in Atlanta."

Hearing the concern in her voice, Wes said simply, "Yeah, I'm not surprised, but I need to see what you have. I'll be heading your way in just a few minutes."

"We're here as long as you need us."

Wes pressed his phone off button and sighed. He really did not need to look at the package except to get some details. That was Eve's way. She never skimped on her research. He wished he could feel good about the excellent work that he was sure he would see.

Chapter 62

Walter

The night shift was closing down and the day shift would begin to arrive. Walter was ready to go home, but knew he would be delivering the package to Wes first. Of course, he knew where his friend lived since he had lived with him for several months.

Walter parked his car and took the package from the seat. He bounded up to front door of Wes Wesley's darkened house. He noticed that the same things, plastic chair, bicycle and some fertilizer, were still on the porch that were there when he stayed here. That was one of the traits he liked about Wes. He was not all hung up on appearances. He was perfectly happy being relaxed and unfazed with what might the neighbors think.

He rang the bell several times and then knocked. He hadn't remembered that the detective was a particularly sound sleeper.

He smiled to himself. Probably Wes had stayed over at Janeen's place. He knew they were a really hot twosome. Too bad he was going to have to bother him, but he needed to get this delivery made and head for his own bed. He took out his cell phone and dialed.

"Wesley."

"Wes, it's Walter. I'm at your house. If you're here, you aren't hearin' me."

"Walter, I'm not there. I've been on this Bad Boys case all night. What's up? Are you OK?"

"I'm fine. Just tryin' to do my job. Got a package for you. I was told to get it to you this mornin' and I'm tryin' to do that."

Wes was surprised to hear from Walter but not surprised about the message. This is what he was waiting to see. "Who gave you the package?"

"Ole Jasper."

"Ole Jasper? Are you kidding me?"

"Nope. He got it from some skirt with a nice ass. That's accordin' to Ole Jasper. He's the one who actually saw her. He was told to get it to me and I would get it to you. That's where we are now. I have it and I'm tryin'."

"Walter, my friend, I've been waiting for this. Since you're at my house and your place is close to Krispy Kreme, how 'bout meeting me there and I'll buy you your first doughnuts and coffee of the day? I need a pick-me-up" Wes experienced the first feeling of relief from the past miserable hours. Walter was always good for his soul, and a few hot doughnuts were good for his stomach.

"That's a plan, old buddy. I'll be there in just a few minutes. You can order if you get there first."

Walter thought about this being the end of his work day. He would be heading for some sleep after meeting Wes. Then he thought about Wes who obviously already had a full workday yesterday that never ended. The days when he might think it would be good to be an Atlanta policeman, he'd better think twice.

Wes had arrived first. "Hey, Walter, we have doughnuts on the way. They're hot and sweet. Coffee is hotter and almost as sweet by the time you finish adding all that sugar."

"Hey, man, I'm Southern. I like sweet tea and sweeter coffee. Keeps me virile. Don't need no Viagra or Cialus. Just give me a big 'cuppa' coffee," Walter was smiling broadly and his eyes were twinkling. He liked kidding around with Wes.

"Spare me the details. Let's just enjoy our breakfast."

"OK. This is the package that I got from Ole Jasper. Am I carryin' somethin' dangerous? Is it goin' to blow up any moment? Is it something for Homeland Security?"

"Nah, Walter, if you have what I think you have, it is going to cause some political explosions here in the city. Let's see it."

"I thought I had somethin' related to those murders. I've

been thinkin' about it all night. Maybe someone knows who the killer is and they're tellin' you this way." Walter frowned as he took a big gulp of his coffee before continuing, "I thought about callin' you sooner, but Ole Jasper said that there was no big hurry so deliver it in the mornin'."

"It's important, Walter, but I'm sure the die was cast by the time you got it. I think the whole plan was timed carefully. Our perpetrator was smart, trained, educated and aware. No taking chances. I bet she knew exactly what time you went to work and when you got off."

"You said 'was' and 'she.' You know most of the answers before you even open this, right?"

"I do. What I don't know are all the details, but I'm sure they're all there on the table. Once again, Walter, you're part of the history of Atlanta. You just hang out with the wrong people," Wes' little joke was weak, but his words were true. Walter knew that he was referring to the murder of the Georgia Tech student who brought them together the first time.

"No way, my man, I hang out with the best. You're one special dude It's OK. I understand your job and your position. I also know that you're the best ever Atlanta po-lice detective and I'm your best ever dep-u-ty."

Wes laughed. Walter really was good for his soul.

"Hey, Dep-u-ty, you're the best, all right. No question about that, but now it's time for us each to get going. I'll be in touch soon and bring you up to date about what you've been carrying. Now go home and get some sleep. Hey, get some for me too. I'm going back to the office."

Wes waved at Walter and drove away. Although he did not like the ending of this case, he would be glad that the Bad Boys case was solved. He headed back to his office, pulled ito the dingy parking lotand soon was sitting at his desk.

He reached for the package and the big white envelope, went through security and up to his office. He sat at his desk for a few minutes with his head in his hands. He knew he could not delay longer. He needed to review it all, then start making telephone calls. This was going to be a bad day for the Atlanta Police Department, the mayor's office and the city. It wasn't going to be great for him either.

Chapter 63

Wes T. Wesley

Dear Wes,

*First, I must apologize for leaving you in a
difficult situation. You will be commended for solving
the case and for the executions ending, but I fear that you
will also be given blame for not knowing what was going
on right in your own office.*

*The department and the city must accept that there was
no way you could have known. I had planned this carefully,
every detail, for years. Long before you ever met me. When
I was interviewed for an internship, I appeared to be
just another, average student. Actually, I was just another
student, but a student with a mission and a painful and
destructive past.*

*I planned to avenge my sisters' deaths when I was still
a young teenager. I had years to perfect how it could be
done and how I could keep my identity unknown until I
was ready.*

*Wes, you know by now that I am ready for it all to end.
I have killed enough. I have rid the city of evil and
unrepentant people.*

This day has been one of the happiest in my life.

*My last killing was my mother who started all of this,
because she was willing to sacrifice her three little girls
so she could have money. How did she ever get that
way? I still don't know, but I also no longer care.
She's where she should be—on her way to hell. I'm
sure she will meet the others that she kept in a
journal titled 'My Friends.'*

*This box is for you. You will not have to write one
report. Every thought and every act that I had working
this case on both sides are here. You're going to
take a lot of flack. Of course, you deserve better, but this
is the best I can do.*

*Thank you and Billy Joe for letting me be a part of your
team. Also, tell Dani, thank you for being a role model
that I could never live up to.*

*But mostly, thank you for giving me the first respect
and caring that I ever had. Because you made me feel like
I had a family for even a short time, I hope I will remain
in your thoughts. You always treated me like I could
have been your daughter. If I had had a dad like you,
I would still be with you giving you my affection for
many more years.*

Always, Me

. . . .

Wes felt tears well up in his eyes. One trickled down his
cheek, and he wiped it away. He looked at the damp spot on his
hand. He wished that he could have helped her with whatever
problems she had had. It was too late. He took the next letter out
of the box.

. . . .

Dear Chief Princeton,

*I take full responsibility for my acts that are
documented in this report and apologize for any
embarrassment to the Atlanta Police Department in
general and to you and your outstanding Homicide
detectives in particular. I did what I had to do. It was
time for the guilty to pay for their own actions, as today, I
have paid for mine.*

*Please do not fault the intern program or the
police with whom I worked. I planned these
executions before I ever enrolled in the program
and already knew the course I was going to take.*

*I began my mission when my two sisters died because
of these men and their willingness to accept my
mother's offer to pay for sex with her three young
daughters. The men and my mother started out
happy and died miserable. I started out miserable and
died happy.*

*I am sorry if I have hurt you and the department.
I have no other regrets. Sincerely, Eve Zachary*

. . . .

Wes took a deep breath, closed his eyes and sat with his
thoughts. Eve, of course, was there, but so were his son and his
own, supportive father. He saw Eve's mother, whose own selfish
desires affected so many people. His thoughts went back to Eve
and the wonderful team member she had been as their intern.
That is how he would remember her.

He did not usually buy into the 'victim' excuse for behavior,
but from what was known, Eve truly was a victim.

The Homicide detective opened his eyes and reached for the
next item in the box. He knew when he had seen it all; he had to
call Major Dilbert and Chief Princeton. Their day was going to
be a hard one, too.

Chapter 64

Chief Alan Princeton

The killer was known, but the story was not ended.

Entering the offices of the chief always had a bit of awe. Within these walls, was a man who had an exemplary history in police work, had all the qualities of a professional and he looked like he had just come from central casting. He was built like a runner He moved with a loose elegance that made even a simple police uniform look like a CEO's best Armani suit.

Before he was completely in the waiting area, Wes was assaulted by a harsh voice, "Well, Wesley, looks like you have brought us another sticky situation; maybe the worst in your history. How could this all happen under your watch?"

Major Dagmar Dilbert was standing in her carefully tailored uniform, with every hair sprayed into place and a scow on her face that could scare the most hardened criminal. Wes responded simply, "Good morning, Major."

"I hardly think this is a good morning, and it obviously isn't going to get any better. I want you to know, Detective, you're on your own on this one. I'm not going to defend your situation nor defend your choice of intern who you allowed to run loose.'

"Yes, m'am, I'm used to being responsible and on my own, as you say," Wes said looking the major directly in her eyes.

"Don't get uppity with me, Wesley. It's possible you just made a mistake that could change your whole career in the department. The chief is going to have some decisions to make related to your future."

"Yes, m'am, he has a huge responsibility."

"I feel that you are laughing at me. We will discuss..." Major Dilbert began.

A door opened on the opposite side of the room and a small Latino woman appeared. She was wearing a uniform that indicated that she was a sergeant. "Chief Princeton will see you now. Would either of you like coffee?"

"Yes! I want coffee with cream and one sugar," Major Dilbert responded first.

"Nothing for me, Sergeant, thank you," Wes replied knowing that nothing about this meeting was social.

While the sergeant stood aside at the door, Major Dilbert and Detective Wesley entered the chief's office. Alan Princeton walked around his desk and offered his hand, "Dagmar, thank you for coming. It seems we have a problem here that may have serious media attention. We need to stick together on this."

The man turned slightly and clapped Wes on the shoulder, "Wes, I'd rather be meeting you at Manuel's, but let's get down to this case. Have a seat and let's get started. Gloria will bring your coffee, but we won't wait.

"Wes, tell us everything from the beginning to the happenings of last night.

"Sir, I'm going to report the sequential actions of this case and the important reasons why it all happened. I'll leave you this packet of details that's done in official and proper department form. If we could put aside what has happened, I could present this box as the best researched and documented Homicide case report ever completed."

"Your intern might have had all the wrong motives, but it sounds like you did teach her that it is critical to document even the worst information," the chief commented.

"Eve Zachary was a fine intern. It was the rest of her life that had been on the wrong course for more than fifteen years."

"Fifteen years? That would have meant that this all began when she was a child," Princeton exclaimed.

"That's true, sir. It does begin when she was a young girl."
Wes continued, "Chief, this story includes meanness, greed, sadness, violence, frustration, revenge, dishonesty, love, and

regret. It will captivate all who hear it. Today's report is simply the beginning of what must be done to truly close this case."

The chief asked a few questions about details as Wes progressed, but Eve had such a precise account of her acts that there was very little not to understand. All three of them knew that there was still an epilogue to this account. What would the police department do now about the men who were involved with the rapes of three little girls years ago? The crimes allegedly had been committed, but the only evidence close to proof was the DNA match of Temple Carrollton. Even that might not have stood up in court. Actually, it made no difference. He was dead. It had been proof enough for Eve.

"Wes and Dagmar, we have more than six murders here. We have an explosive political situation. We have what looks like written evidence that some very important men in Atlanta and other cities in the south have been involved in child molestation. Why these men, even if they were young and obviously foolish, would sign that 'My Friends' book is beyond my comprehension, but they did. Of course, if they were willing to rape little girls to prove they were 'men,' why would they hesitate signing their names beside their payments?

"I suppose it was because they were at an age and of the opinion that nothing could ever touch them. They felt invincible. What they did was OK, because they were bigger than the law or the law of averages. They made their own rules. Now what do we do about it?" The chief's eyes went from Dagmar to Wes and back again. Wes decided to wait for the major to make the first statement.

A long silence followed and finally Major Dilbert said, "I've not been on the front line with this case. I would like to hear what Wesley has to say. I barely knew Eve."

Pass the buck time.

The chief turned and looked at the major, "Maybe you should have, Major. She still was under your authority. But this is no longer about Eve. It's about a citywide crisis. Wes, have you an opinion?"

"I have opinions but, they're not based on the law. They're based on what I think is best for our city. They're based on my kind of common sense."

"Let's hear it. I have never been opposed to common sense."

"I believe we should go to the media with only what we know is fact: we have had six murders, we have a confessed murderer, the murderer has committed suicide and her motive was that she believed that these victims molested her sisters and her years ago. We should not mention the others or their Good Ol' Boys Club. At the present time, the complete story is known only by the three of us. My partners, Dani Swain and Jimmy London know much of it but not everything.

"We speak privately and confidentially to the others whose identity we have. Tell them we will do our best to keep their involvement in this case confidential and out of the news. They would have to know that we have their signatures because we possess the book. They in turn will resign from any position of prominence and decision making. Therefore they're no longer in situations where they can continue to profit by their flagrant actions to beat the law, ignore basic ethical behavior and hold evidence to protect each other.

"I've come to the opinion that a case could never be made on those who remain. It would all become a slimy tabloid circus. Even if not convicted, the story will drag through all media, the public will argue each side, the mayor will still have to resign, Vance Bowman will have to leave the paper, and the others will be outcasts from their families and communities.

"Chief, as we know, child molesters aren't even safe in prison. What we suggest to these disgusting men is a chance to stay out of court and out of prison. Obviously, we can't guarantee that the story will not come out. We do know that Dani and her boss have a brief version of the murders from Eve.

"We don't know if Eve has shared this packet of information with others, but we can tell the men that they have been spared being the next victims of Eve's campaign to eliminate the world of men who should have been locked up long ago."

Alan Princeton responded, "This is a very important decision. The child molestation crimes of these men began so long ago that putting together a case will be difficult. Yes, we have the book and the signatures, notes written by a very evil woman who is now dead, the tape that Eve made during her last conversation with her mother and information put together by your intern as she completed what she called her thesis. All of these develop a story from her point of view. Defense lawyers of today would have a field day shooting holes in most of that. And, do not miss the point that these men have the finances to hire the best legal representation in the whole country.

"Sure, with your suggestions, they might get off but they won't escape. Their lives will change. They will be constantly reminded why their lives went sour at this time. We can't be sure now, but the story might play in the news for months. It would be a wild media circus. It's better for Atlanta and other cities for us to fold this case as quietly as possible."

Chief Princeton sat back in his chair, appearing to relax for the first time since the conversation began. Wes took advantage of the lull and said, "Sir, if we want to try and keep the lid on this, you must immediately get to the decision makers at WPTR. You know they have similar information that we have and news is their business."

The chief reached for his intercom and said flatly, "Gloria, please get the manager of WPTR on the telephone. Find him wherever he is. This is critical."

While he waited, the head of the Atlanta Police Department turned to Wes, "I suggest I'm the person to talk to the mayor after we talk to Jimmy London. If they are going to agree to our plan, we want to contact the remaining men immediately. How many need to be seen here?"

"In addition to the mayor, we still have three in Atlanta, two in Miami and two in Charlotte. Oh, yes, one of our local boys, Vance Bowman, currently is in Aspen hiding out."

"And you have how many detectives already on the case?"

Wes answered quickly, "There are three: Billy Joe LaCrosse, Golly Grand, and Mike Fisher. We're each familiar with someone on that list. We have been in touch with them all."

"Good, with six of us of us covering the meetings, we should be able to have this done in a day." The chief was talking as he was making notes.

"Six, Chief Princeton? Wesley said he only had three detectives working with him." Major Dilbert looked perplexed.

"You're forgetting to count yourself, Dagmar. You'll join the men for the Atlanta contacts." He smiled. His major did not return a smile. She looked stricken.

"But, I'm not involved. Detective Wesley has been in charge of this case."

"You're involved, Major, and you will make the calls that Detective Wesley assigns to you. We all work for the city and this is for the city." Dagmar Dilbert's boss' smile was gone.

The conversation ended as the intercom buzzed.

"Jimmy, Alan Princeton here…. Yes, that's why I'm calling…. Yes, I know what Dani received. I appreciate that you've honored our request to hold the story for a few hours…. Yes, I know how important it is. We've said nothing to anyone. As soon as we talk, you're free to break it."

The chief continued talking to the WPTR manager. Wes could sense that he was getting resistance, but Chief Princeton never backed down. He stopped talking, listened and made a few short comments.

He took charge again, "Jimmy, I understand your points, but this is imperative for our city. We have to stick together. Please, don't do anything. Detective Wesley and I are coming to your office right now… Fine. You can expect us within 30 minutes. Thank you, sir."

Without another word, the chief pressed the intercom button.

"Gloria, get me the mayor. Tell him it is very important."

Chapter 65

Mayor Erich Regis Maxwell

Atlanta's City Hall is an impressive building. As Chief Princeton cleared security and walked into the large foyer, he looked up to the open area that was surrounded by a balcony ending at graceful white stairs leading to the mayor's offices.

He was angry that his visit was to talk with the mayor about this repulsive topic. Mayor Maxwell had hired him. He had been elated when he had received the call from him saying, "Alan, you are Atlanta's choice. We await your affirmative response. Together we will make this city better than ever."

The Chief of the Atlanta Police Department felt sick and depressed. He knew that this was going to be one of the hardest encounters that he had had since taking the job. The mayor had not been a close friend, but he had been a respected colleague. It was still difficult to think about the words he was going to have to say. It was stressful to imagine the mayor's reaction. He could not even guess how the man would react to the deal that he was bringing to him.

Lost in his thoughts, the chief had arrived in the reception area of the mayor's office. "Chief Princeton, it's good to see you. The mayor is looking forward to your visit," the handsome and well dressed receptionist said to him as he approached his desk.

The chief smiled. He knew the young man was simply doing his job. He had no idea how wrong his comment had been.

Immediately, a gray-haired woman had joined them at the desk. "Chief Princeton, how good to see you. The mayor is just finishing a telephone call with the governor. He said to bring you in at once. He's hoping you have news that this terrible killer has been found."

The chief nodded to the receptionist and turned to follow the mayor's secretary. Maggie took him directly through her office space and into the mayor's office. Erich Maxwell was replacing the telephone receiver as they entered.

"Chief, it's good to see you. Having you call gave me great hope that you have closed the serial killer case. Please, tell me that's why you're here." The mayor had risen from his chair and walked around his desk to meet this chief of police as he entered the room. He was wearing a dark charcoal gray suit contrasted by a bright red tie. He looked like what he was, mayor of a major city. He did not look like what he once was, a molester of children.

"Maggie, get us some of that special French roast coffee. The chief and I both like lots of sugar. We may be celebrating this morning," Erich Maxwell said with an air of buoyancy in his voice.

'Oh, shit!' thought the chief.

"What's the news, Alan? I was overjoyed this morning to come into the office and not find another message about another of our fine Atlanta leaders gone. Do you think we have turned the corner? Is this terror over?"

"I'm quite sure that we'll have no more shootings, Erich. Our problem hasn't related to Homeland Security but everyone in Atlanta has been on high alert."

"Apparently, the alert wasn't high enough to stop five shootings. It's not been a good week for your department."

"Unfortunately, the men involved wouldn't heed our warnings. They didn't even try to keep themselves out of harm's way. Houston Montrose should never have been alone in an empty, dark, parking lot." The chief was not going to allow anyone, not even the mayor, to accuse the department of not doing its job.

The mayor looked toward the door, "Hey, here's our coffee. Thanks so much, Maggie," He turned to his colleague, "You're going to know this is special. Our girl really knows how to brew coffee." The mayor still thought he was going to hear good news.

The mayor's secretary gave each man a steaming cup and placed a tray with sugar and small frosted, cinnamon rolls on the table between them. She smiled broadly and was gone as quickly as she has appeared.

Both men ladled a heaping teaspoon of sugar into their cups and stirred the dark liquid. The chief placed his cup back on the table and said, "Erich, let me bring you up to date on the murders. We are quite sure we have our killer and that killer has committed suicide."

Chief Princeton told the story from the beginning and ended with the meeting with Wes. He held back nothing that he knew. He watched his boss's face as the facts unraveled and saw very little reaction. He came to the end of his tale. He waited for the mayor to speak.

"Well, Chief, that's quite a story. Of course, there are parts that are complete fabrications. The young woman obviously had a mental problem. And on top of that, she was a liar. Now, how are we going to keep this from the media?"

"We will have to make a deal with the survivors of your gang, Erich."

"Then do it. I don't want this to be made public, Alan. Go make a deal."

"I'm happy to hear you agree with us. We must protect the city and its reputation," the chief was choosing his words carefully.

"The city's reputation? Dammit, you're supposed to protect my reputation. I'm the mayor!"

"Erich, you're going to have to be a part of this deal related to the media. If you won't, this case is going to be all over the United States. Not only as news but every talk show host will be ranting about three small girls who had been molested as initiation to a club."

"I don't like your words nor the tone of your voice, Princeton. I'm not the one who has to deal with the media; you are. These men who have been killed have nothing to do with me."

"Yes, sir, I'll deal with them. But before I do that, you and I need to talk about the other members of the Good Ol' Boys Club who are still around. We want to be sure we contact them all."

The mayor's face went chalk white. He looked away from the chief of police. His hands clasped the arms of the chair.

"How would I know that? I can't help you there. You have detectives. I guess they could find them, but what difference does it make? The stupid girl is dead."

"The difference is that the members of the Good Ol' Boys Club committed serious crimes trying to prove their manhood or trying to prove something. Erich, you do know who the other surviving members are. We have heard that there were thirteen, but was that a steady number of thirteen members or the same group of thirteen? You can tell me now just as you could have told Detective Wesley. The question is: Should these men be arrested for their previous crimes?" Chief Princeton did not care that he was making his mayor nervous.

The mayor shifted several times in his seat. He continued to clutch the arms of his chair. He did not look up but said, "Arrested? Are you crazy? Arrested? Even if these assumptions are correct, these men were young when this happened. Just kids. I'm sure they felt it was no big deal."

"Raping little girls is no big deal, Erich? I'm sure I misunderstood what you said."

"That's not exactly what I meant. It doesn't sound like rape to me. You admit that the mother was agreeable. Perhaps she even encouraged it. Except that she's already dead, she might be the one to arrest," Mayor Maxwell was talking fast. His eyes looked wild.

"Selling children is neither acceptable nor legal in our country; shouldn't be in any country. The mother was morally and legally wrong, but the men who did this and paid money to commit the crime are equally wrong. The remaining members of the group can all become the target of general conversation, media shows and perhaps the court system. Is that what you want to happen?"

"Why ask me? Each can decide for himself. I don't want to continue this discussion. Just go talk to the media and tell them that the case is closed. They don't need to have the details. Just get it over with!"

"Mayor, the deal to keep your name out of this sordid...."

"My name? You bet your ass, you will keep my name out of this. I assume you like your job, Princeton?" the mayor was speaking with such fury that the chief thought he might have a heart attack.

"Mayor Maxwell, let's stop kidding ourselves. We both know that you were one of the Good Ol' Boys and that you participated in these relations with little girls to be accepted into the group."

The mayor rose from his seat and growled, "Get out of here. Get out. You're finished; not only with this meeting, but with your position. Get out!"

"No, sir, I'm not getting out. Sit down and we're going to come to an agreement. If I leave this office now without resolution, your name and your complicity in this case will be from here to San Francisco within two hours. Now, sit down and let's decide what is going to be done that best serves the city we have been asked to honor."

"You can't make this up and expect me to support your trumped up story. I'm not going to agree to anything. You cannot relate me to what you say happened. There wouldn't be proof after all these years. The ones who were guilty are dead. That little intern slut took care of that. That's the end of the story." The mayor was almost out of control. His arms were flailing as he emphasized every word. He had raised his voice but was careful that he would not be heard outside of the room.

"I'm sorry, Erich. We do have proof enough that this could become headline news. You and your friends were dumb enough to sign the woman's book that describes who you molested, how much you paid, when you did it, and even how long you lasted.

Your name and signature are in the book more than once. I guess it wasn't just a silly juvenile mistake. You appeared to be a regular customer."

Chief Princeton ended his statement and watched Mayor Maxwell as he sat down.

"This is outrageous. Why would I sign my name? That would be like admitting guilt. Surely, you can't believe that I'm that dumb."

"Not now, perhaps, but over a decade ago, you were that dumb. We have the book. We have your signatures and those of the other members. We have copies of the same Phoenix Byrd certificate that you hang here in your office. We have some DNA reports. We have a confession of one of the members. Erich, you have got to do the right thing and close this case without all the ugliness getting out and making Atlanta and the mayor's office look tawdry."

"I cannot believe that any of my friends would confess to this. It could be my word against his. Of course, I would do what needs to be done to save my reputation, but I shouldn't be condemned because of a boyish indiscretion. Unfortunately, there just is nothing I can do. You say you have all the proof. We can talk about this some more, but I can't do anything."

"You can resign."

Chapter 66

Danielle Jarvis Swain

Dani was poised to announce the closing of the serial killer case in the city of Atlanta. She already was looking at and hearing the familiar words: BreakIn! She counted the seven seconds that the bright colors and sirens announced that the time had arrived.

"The serial killer case that has had Atlanta terrorized for the past week has been closed by the Atlanta Police Department. Chief Alan Princeton met with this reporter today."

A cut was made to Princeton and Dani standing in front of the police department.

Chief Princeton's terse remark followed, "The killer has been identified as Eve Zachary, a student at Georgia State University. The case ended with a final murder and the suicide of the perpetrator."

The camera switched to Dani's face, "Five of the murders were of Atlanta civic leaders and the final shooting was of the murderer's mother. WPTR has been working closely with the police on this case. We will cover the details at six and eleven. Stay tuned for the Evening News."

Once she was sure they were no longer on the air, Dani turned away from the camera and looked at another sheet of paper on her desk. She saw that she was going to have another BreakIn! feature before the six o'clock news. It would be when she announced the resignation of Mayor Ehrich Regis Maxwell. He said his reason was "to spend more time with his family."

Epilogue

Eve's bittersweet story is paradox personified; contrary to the truth, but in reality, could be quite true. Her pleasure in committing murders and her suicide may appear to readers as a tragic waste. Unfortunately, thousands of young lives are being wasted because of adults' actions. Children are being used for sexual gratification and for profit in rampant proportions.

Georgia's Juvenile Justice Fund and its A Future, Not a Past have been tracking the commercial sexual exploitation of children for several years. Sadly, the numbers are getting worse. More children are victims of this despicable industry. The second year of a multi-year tracking study of adolescent girls prostituted in Georgia revealed many noteworthy findings:

On the average, 250 to 350 adolescent girls are prostituted each month in Georgia, a 14% increase over the previous study year. The more than 300 girls each month breakdown in the following categories:

▶ An average of 28 adolescent girls prostituted each month in major hotels
▶ An average of 63 adolescent girls prostituted each month through escort services
▶ An average of 67 adolescent girls prostituted on the street each month along four known prostitution corridors
▶ An average of 137 adolescent girls prostituted online each month through the website Craigslist.com

University of Pennsylvania professor of social work and president of the International Society of Quality of Life Studies, Richard J. Estes, PhD, states, "It is the nation's least recognized epidemic."

Estes and Neil Allan Weiner, PhD, Senior Research Associate, Center for the Study of Youth Policy in the School of Social Work, University of Pennsylvania, are the primary investigators and authors of the study The Commercial Sexual Exploitation of Children in the U.S., Canada and Mexico. This study, published in 2002, was conducted over 27 months. They collected data and true stories from 17 American cities as well as cities in Canada and Mexico. These locations were chosen for size, known problems, history of attempting to reduce commercial sexual exploitation of children in their communities, and a presence of a network of child- and youth-serving organizations.

A few of the major findings were:

- ▶ Major groups of sexual exploiters of children include parents, older siblings, boyfriends, strangers and "opportunistic" exploiters.
- ▶ Sexually exploited children are quite heterogeneous. These include those living in their own homes as well as those who are runaways and throwaways;
- ▶ Criminal networks are actively involved in the sexual exploitation of children, a financially lucrative enterprise.

In Atlanta, Georgia, supported by Mayor Shirley Franklin, another study was commissioned in 2005. The Atlanta Women's Agenda, the mayor's initiative to highlight issues affecting women and bring together new energy for change, conducted the study entitled Hidden in Plain View: The Commercial Sexual Exploitation of Girls in Atlanta. Mayor Franklin pledged funding and her time to bring these facts to the public and help to the girls.

The report of this study initially explains:

"The prostitution of children is usually thought of as a third world country problem, along with poor water and endemic disease, but this abomination takes place all over the United States. In 2001, the groundbreaking study by Estes and Weiner revealed that between 200,000 and 300,000 children are believed to be at-risk for sexual exploitation in the United States. The sexual exploitation of children has become the third-largest moneymaker for organized crime, right behind guns and drugs.

Atlanta is not exempt; in fact it has been identified as a hub for this appalling trade."

A Future, Not a Past has partnered with WellSpring, another dedicated group, on projects that can help exploited children, convict adults who participate in this criminal business and bring the horrible truth to the public. Much of their efforts are based on the results of the four-year on-going research study commissioned by A Future, Not a Past. The growth in the numbers of adolescent girls being sexually exploited is frightening. To put those numbers in context, there are more girls harmed by prostitution in one month in Georgia than are killed in car accidents in an entire year.

Executive Director John Croyle, of Big Oak Ranch, Springville, Alabama, states, "Many of the 160 children living at the facility have been sexually abused or exploited by their own family members."

In 2007, Alesia Adams, Youth Development and Sexual Trafficking Prevention Coordinator/Trainer with The Salvation Army in Atlanta was named full-time director rather than part-time; a sad commentary on the extent of this problem. Ms. Adams has compiled a fact sheet with appalling information. Some of the facts included are:
? The chances of a runaway child being recruited into the sex industry are better than 50%
? The average age of the sexually exploited child is 13, and the market is increasing for
  younger and younger children
? Many children stand minimal chance of identification or rescue since they are imprisoned in houses, hotels or even on business premises, with threats of violence to themselves or their families should they try to escape.

Ms. Adams also talks about our society's acceptance of – or indifference to – the problem. She makes this point abundantly clear when she states, "In March 2006, I watched the Oscar Award for Best Achievement in Music Written for Motion Pictures go to a musician who sang the song called *"It's Hard Out Here for a Pimp."* Here are some of the lyrics:

'You know it is hard out here for a pimp,
When he's trying to get his money for the rent,
For the Cadillac and the gas money spent.

That's the way the game goes, gotta keep it strictly pimpin'
Gotta have my hustle tight, makin' change off these women, yeah.'

It's harder out there for the children and women who are being sexually exploited and abused. Even if pimps are brought into the justice system, rarely will charges be made against them or the "John." Therefore, child exploitation continues to flourish and grow.

An April 2007, Detroit Metro News and The Associated Press reported that a mother in the Detroit area was arrested for trying to sell her seven-year-old daughter for sexual purposes. The mother has since been charged with other crimes such as child abuse.

Deborah Richardson, former Executive Director of the Atlanta Women's Foundation, said in an interview with this author that several reasons for the epidemic proportions of this problem are the watering down of family values and less quality time spent with children. Even more important is that female children are not valued as highly as male children. "If we valued our girls as our boys, there would be little trafficking because men would not participate." She added, "Sadly, many of the men involved in sexual exploitation of children are fathers themselves!"

Ms. Richardson is proud that Atlanta has established Angela's House, a safe haven where children can also get help toward rehabilitation. She says, "We are hoping that this concept will soon be set up in other cities. These children need help now."

Although these reports and statements are recent, this is not a modern-day phenomenon. Thirty years ago in Toronto, Canada, a mother began selling her seven children to her friends. The victims, who have not been named to protect their identity, were assaulted from age three. These small children were raped, forced to perform oral sex, strangled, drugged and beaten with objects. The mother served only six months house arrest. Her children are serving life sentences of emotional and physical problems culminating from their childhood exploitation.

Crimes against children, too often with their own families being the perpetrators, also are becoming more public because of the use of the Internet. Pornographic photos of youngsters may haunt them for years if not for the rest of their lives. Parents also have found their children's Internet activities are increasingly more difficult to monitor. In many neighborhoods, children are on their own after school until parents return from work. These risks that threaten today' children must be understood and acted upon by individuals, child protection agencies and public efforts. We cannot continue to be ignorant of this problem. It will waste more young lives and cost society tremendous losses in future talent, future leaders and public dollars for rehabilitation and care of the damaged children.

To get more information or to get help call: The National Center for Missing and Exploited Children 1-800-843-5678 or go to www.ncmec.org